Mr TOM

The True Story of Tom Simpson

CHRIS SIDWELLS

Foreword by Phil Liggett

For Kath

First published in Great Britain in 2000 by
Mousehold Press
Victoria Cottage
Constitution Opening
Norwich, NR3 4BD

in association with

Sport & Publicity
75 Fitzjohns Avenue
Hampstead
London NW3 6PD

Reprinted 2002
Reprinted 2006
Reprinted 2010

ISBN 978 1 874739 14 2

The Author

Chris Sidwells is Tom Simpson's nephew. A former police officer, he is now a successful writer, journalist and photographer. Mr Tom was the first of seven books he has written so far, which include best sellers in their genre, and his work has been translated into 24 languages. He contributes words and pictures to numerous cycling and lifestyle magazines both in the UK and abroad.

Author's Acknowledgements

I would like to thank all of those people who have given so freely of their time to share with me their memories of Tom Simpson. Many of them I have quoted in this book and my debt to them will become obvious. I would particularly like to thank Dave Marsh and Alf Baxter for all the assistance and encouragement they gave me; Ray Pascoe for helping to keep the Simpson story alive; and Richard Allchin for helping to bring this book to fruition.

Tom Simpson
(photograph courtesy of Helen Hoban)

CONTENTS

Publishers' Acknowledgements

For their invaluable help in the preparation of Tom Simpson's *Palmarès*, the publishers would like to thank Dick Yates; Jim Lowton; the author, Chris Sidwells; and, most especially, Chas Messenger. The publishers would also like to thank Luke Evans for helping us with the selection of photographs, and *Cycling Weekly* for permission to use a number of their photographs, and Harry Maylin for permission to use one of his.

FOREWORD

For almost a century youngsters in continental Europe have dreamt of winning the Tour de France. In Britain, slightly more than 30 years ago, one young Englishman had the same driving ambition. It was an ambition so lemming-like that, in the end, it took him to his death, but Tom Simpson left behind an indelible mark on our sport as we wait, at the beginning of the twenty-first century, for a rider of his qualities to appear again.

In 1967, I had been a journalist for only three months and was still an active racing cyclist. Because I could do both, the London magazine *Cycling and Mopeds*, for whom I worked, had asked me to interview Mr Tom, as he was affectionately known, during the New Brighton Cycling Club's famous races on the Wirral.

It was to be the last interview he gave on mainland Britain, and in less than a month our former World Champion and Classic winner would be dead – his body flown off a mountainside in Provence by helicopter, his dream of winning the Tour de France for Great Britain shattered, paying the price of his ambition in full.

As I write this, I can see his full smile, his cocked racing hat, his set jaw and his Yorkshire grit as he turns from a friendly, amiable person into a winner-at-all-costs. He was everything a young rider should want to be, and there has never been a rider emanating from British roads to match him since.

Tom was born in Durham, brought up in Nottinghamshire, but always thought of himself as a Yorkshireman as it was in this county that he learnt his craft. In any case, he was a northerner where they bred 'em tough, and there was no finer example than Simpson.

I began racing in 1961, and a year later my best friend sent me a card from Luchon, in the Pyrenees, which said: 'Some British guy is leading the Tour down here.' It was, of course, Tom, and although he lost the *maillot jaune* on the climb to Superbagneres on the very next day, he had done enough to make us all believe that he could become the first British rider to win the toughest sporting event of all.

Tom would have laughed at the present-day rider who slows down when his heart-rate monitor on his handlebars is not in tune with his calculations. For him, his legs did the talking, his strength lay in his determination, and if the pace hurt he would go even harder to prove his point. He never looked a strong man and perhaps his mind was too much for his body, and maybe, just maybe, this is why he died on Mont Ventoux.

It was a day which all who lived through this period will remember, just as others do the death of American President John Kennedy. For me it was particularly poignant.

My form was good, and I had had a string of results in local races around north London. On the night Simpson died, I was finishing second in a race less than a mile from my home, so I rode across the line and went to shower in my own flat. I turned the television on at precisely 9 p.m., just in time to hear the news-reader on the BBC say: 'The British cyclist, Tom Simpson, died today in the Tour de France...'

I never took the shower; I just sat down and cried.

This is a beautiful book of our Tom, but, try as we would, it would always have a sad ending.

Phil Liggett
May 2000

Picture reproduced by kind permission of Jeremy Mallard,
from his limited edition print 'Simpson on Ventoux'.
© Jeremy Mallard

GETTING IT OVER WITH

When Tom Simpson died on Mont Ventoux whilst competing in the 1967 Tour de France traces of drugs from the amphetamine group were found in his body. Similar drugs were allegedly found in his clothing. There, I've said it, got it out of the way right at the beginning of the book.

Because of this, notwithstanding that the official cause of his death, arrived at after investigation by the French authorities, was heart failure due to dehydration and heat exhaustion, to which it was said that the drugs could have been a contributory factor, Tom Simpson has been portrayed as anything from a straightforward cheat, responsible single-handedly for subverting the ethics of sport, to a hapless victim whose wings got burned flying too close to his dream of winning the Tour de France.

Neither of these theories are true and both do him, and come to that the people who propound them, a disservice. Tom was neither of these. He was a talented, driven professional who paid the ultimate price for pushing a bad situation too far. He was no cheat. To my mind a cheat does something his competitors do not and thereby gains an advantage. This is clearly not the case. Stimulants such as amphetamines were widely used in cycling in the sixties and today the sport is still beset by a drugs problem – the events of the 1998 Tour de France highlight that. Indeed, a drug culture has existed in professional cycling almost since the first race was run. As for being a victim, forget it! Tom knew what he was doing. It was not something he did lightly, too often or without professional advice.

The truth is that Tom knew nothing of the dark side of professional bike racing when he went to live in France in the spring of 1959, but he quickly realised that sometimes he was beaten in races that he just had to win by riders of lesser ability who had taken drugs. What was he going to do? Forget about it all and take the next boat home? Not Tom; he could never have done that, it wasn't in his nature. So, he turned to the people he'd met over there – people he respected – and, like many before him, and since, he began to use drugs – stimulants, because that's what they used then. Not often, but use them he did, and I can't change that. It wasn't something he was particularly proud of, and I know that it worried him. He would have liked not to have done it; indeed, as we shall see from one particular incident later in the book, he was one of the few top riders who supported what meagre efforts cycling authorities were making at the time to rid the sport of this problem.

Unfortunately, the part that drugs played in Tom's death has been picked over to such an extent that it has overshadowed everything he achieved in his remarkable career, a career that more than 30 years after his death has yet to be equalled by any of his countrymen. I hope that this book will go some way towards restoring that balance. It won't be a whitewash. I won't try to present him as a saint. I won't be making excuses for him; he doesn't need them. I will just tell you the story of his amazing life, and I hope, at the end of it all, that you will understand Tom Simpson and why I felt that this book needed to be written for his sake. Why I could no longer bear to see a man who had already lost his life, also lose his reputation.

1

A BOY AND HIS BIKE

On a cold northern winter's afternoon in 1950 Harry Sidwells was making his way home from the day shift at Harworth Colliery when he saw, lying in the middle of the road, the tangled wreckage of a delivery boy and a butcher's bike. The delivery boy was 13-year-old Tom Simpson; he'd skidded on the icy road, fallen and broken his arm. Harry scraped the injured lad up off the floor and took him to the first-aid post at the pit before walking him home, all bandaged up, to his anxiously waiting mother. There they parted: Harry went home to his dinner and Tom got a telling off from his mum for racing on his bike. Little did they know that their paths would soon cross again and that they would play an important part in each other's lives.

Tom Simpson was the last of six children born to Tom senior (it was a family name, shared with his grandfather and great-grandfather) and his wife Alice. Tom's dad was a big, strong man. He was a miner who, as a young man, had competed in semi-professional athletics meetings when he was capable of running the 100 yards in a shade under 11 seconds. He was a very warm, likeable and well-respected man who enjoyed the company of others and a good story (and a good pint), but he was very cautious, a worrier, and surprisingly sensitive. Alice was different. She was small, frail even, but tough and sharp, almost ruthless in her way. Tom may have inherited his natural speed from his father, but it was his mother's hardness and determination that made him a champion.

Although always regarded as a Yorkshireman, Tom was actually born in the village of Haswell in County Durham on 30th November 1937. He shared his birthday with Winston Churchill, a fact that was to fascinate the continental press during the sixties when they were just about the two most famous Englishmen in Europe.

When Tom was born the family lived in a tiny terraced house in Station Street. It's not there now and the space it occupied is someone's lawn. There wasn't much money about and even less space, but things started to look up when, in 1943, Tom's parents took over the running of the working men's club. This meant a move to much bigger premises over the club and a whole new world opening up for Tom. Times still weren't easy, though: the war was on and Tom's father continued working down the pit because it was essential war work, leaving Alice to run the club herself.

In those days, working men's clubs were the focal point of mining village life, providing entertainment, company and beer – the latter being very necessary for taking the taste of the pit out of your mouth, and sometimes that needed quite a bit. It was certainly a colourful environment for a young lad to grow up in, and one particular aspect of it had a profound and lasting effect on Tom.

The north-east has always been a hotbed for aspiring comedians. In the days when Tom and Alice had the club, hundreds of them travelled the district appearing at a different venue each night. Of course, Tom and Harry, his older brother by a couple of years, were sent to bed long before these exotic characters arrived, but nothing could be done to stop them hanging out of their bedroom windows on long summer evenings listening to the likes of little Bobby Thompson. From their lofty perch they were captivated by these men and the response they heard from their audiences. It's easy to see that the entertainer in Tom was born on these northern nights. The entertainer who was to thrill and excite audiences of his own in the coming years, and bring him thousands of supporters. The entertainer who would often dictate his tactics and his life. The entertainer for whom the spectacular show would sometimes seem even more important than the result.

Aside from this exposure to a world beyond Haswell, Tom's life was pretty normal. The youngest in the family, he had four sisters to look after him and an older brother to look out for him. All nice and safe you might think, but being an adventurous kid he managed to get into more scrapes than the rest of them put together.

One particular incident occurred soon after the end of the war. Haswell is only a few miles from the coast; however, during the war, the beach was strictly out of bounds. So, naturally, when this restriction was lifted it was a great attraction to the young lad. Unfortunately, there were one or two items left behind after the clean-up operations that were much more interesting, and dangerous, than crabs and jellyfish. So, innocently playing on the sands one day, Tom picked up what turned out to be a detonator.

Of course, he didn't know that at the time – all it was to him was an interesting find – so he put it in his pocket and for a while it became his prized possession.

About a week later Tom and his mum were visiting her brother, Dick, in Seaton Delaval. By now, Tom had grown bored with his find – it didn't do anything after all – and unfortunately, he chose to dispose of it by simply throwing it on the fire. To add insult to injury, Uncle Dick hadn't had the chimney swept for some considerable time, and, when the resultant rubble and dust had cleared, there he was, sat in his armchair, pipe still firmly clenched between his teeth, but covered from head to foot in thick, black soot.

It was a good place to grow up in, but the time came to move on. Coal reserves in the North-East were becoming exhausted, and consequently the new colliery villages of South Yorkshire and North Nottinghamshire began to attract thousands of northern miners in search of a new, and more prosperous life. So with the hope of ensuring a bright future for their two youngest children, who by then were the only ones left at home, Tom and Alice moved to Harworth on the Nottinghamshire-Yorkshire border.

Ironically, Tom's dad found that after years of working crouched in the thin, wet seams of the Durham coalfield he could not adapt to the conditions underground at Harworth, where the seams of coal are thick and the miners had to stand to hew it from the face. Eventually, he injured his back. Fortunately, after a brief period working on a road gang improving the Great North Road just south of Doncaster, he found a steady job at the Glass Bulbs factory (now known as Demaglass) and the family settled down, looking forward to life in their new home.

Tom quickly adapted to his new school. His reports reflect a hardworking, interested pupil with no particular flare for sport. Like so many cyclists, Tom couldn't do any sport that required skill with a ball. In fact, years later in a Belgian TV interview he was asked why he took up cycling, and not football or cricket like the rest of his compatriots. He graphically demonstrated his problem when, with a wry smile, he replied, 'I was useless. I couldn't even catch a ball in football.' I think that says it all really. Still, he made a good enough impression and eventually gained a scholarship to the Technical College in nearby Worksop.

Not long after his move from the north Tom began racing on a bike, and what a bike it was, too. A real old battleship with big rubber pedals and fat, heavy balloon tyres. He even had to share it with his older brother and two cousins. The four of them, plus a gaggle of other kids, would race this thing in hell-for-leather round-the-block time trials, each one taking his turn while the others timed him using an old wrist-watch. Timing was up to broad interpretation, though: the watch did not have a secondhand, never mind tenths or hundredths.

Harry decided to make his cycling a little more official and joined the local club, the Harworth and District, only to be followed, like little brothers do, by Tom. Harry did show a flair for sports on his school report, having already gained county selection at cricket and football. He was immediately successful on the bike as well, winning and setting records in the club's junior championships before returning to football and playing for the legendary Blackpool United for a short time.

For Tom there was only ever the bike. Right from those first round-the-street races it had captivated him. Unfortunately, in those early days his guts and enthusiasm exceeded his physique, but then they probably always did. In his first official race, a five-mile time trial, he was bitterly disappointed with his time of 17 minutes 50 seconds. On the face of it an inauspicious start indeed – that is until you realise that he was still 13 years old and had raced on the very same butcher's bike that had dumped him on the floor the previous winter, although he had removed the bike's wicker delivery basket to improve its aerodynamics.

The first thing Tom decided he had to do if he was to stand any chance against the others was get a proper racing bike. This was going to cost money, and though he was saving like mad from his delivery round it was going to take for ever to get enough for a real racer. So what did he do? He spent all his savings on red paint, did up his old butcher's bike and literally pestered a local miner he'd seen riding a dropped-handlebar sports bike to the pit, into swapping it for his. So now he owned a bike that looked the part at least, even though it still needed racing wheels and lots of other go-faster bits.

Whether his next step was a stroke of calculating genius way beyond his years we'll never know, but by now Tom's unmarried sister Renee had also moved down from Durham to join the family and at mealtimes Tom never stopped talking to her about Harry Sidwells, the man who had taken care of him when he'd broken his arm, and who was, coincidentally, the secretary of the Harworth cycling club. Tom really laid it on thick, though: to hear him talk you would have thought Harry was a cross between a saint and a Hollywood movie star.

Harry happened to be the owner of a Carlton Flyer race bike, just about the best money could buy in those days and way beyond anything Tom could afford. Now, it's probably just a coincidence that Harry and Renee started going out together, and eventually married, but shortly after they met bits from Harry's bike started to appear on Tom's. One way or another Tom had got himself properly equipped and was ready to take on the world, but as he put it himself years later, 'even with the right tools I couldn't do the job properly because I was so small'.

It didn't stop him trying though. Racing was just part of the British cycling scene in those days; just as much importance was attached to the weekly Sunday club run. These were usually marathon rides with a race-like burn-up at the end and no favours done for hopeful youngsters.

One of the more popular runs undertaken by the Harworth club was to Cleethorpes on the Lincolnshire coast and back, a round trip of about 120 miles. The stiff climbs of the Wolds would soon see Tom left behind by his older mates. No one waited, and Tom would arrive in Cleethorpes, red-faced and out of breath, just in time to meet the rest of the club coming the other way, refreshed by a rest and a cup of tea on the seafront. The return journey would be a repeat of the outward leg, with Tom arriving back in Harworth exhausted and a good many minutes behind the others.

All this may seem harsh to anyone not involved with the sport in those days, and while it is true that it must have put thousands of youngsters off cycling for good, at least the ones that got through were tough; and it is a tough game – a very tough game.

This happened week in and week out, but Tom kept coming back for more. Some of the older riders started to notice him and, appreciating his fighting spirit, they took him under their collective wing. They nicknamed him 'Four-Stone Coppi' after the legendary Italian cyclist, Fausto Coppi, and because he looked as though he only weighed four stones.

He was so proud of his nickname because Coppi (along with the Swiss, Ferdi Kubler) was his number-one hero. The walls of his bedroom were covered with pictures of the Italian who is one of cycling's all-time greats, and probably the most charismatic rider the sport has ever seen. Once, when his mother was chastising him about the state of his room he pointed up at Coppi's picture and said to her, 'I'm going to be like him before I'm finished.' He was 13 years old and got left behind by his mates every Sunday. Only he believed it, but that was enough.

Although his eyes were always set on the dizzy heights that Coppi reached he really got stuck into his local racing. Right at the start of the 1952 season, in March, he took part in the Harworth and District junior five-mile time trial. Riding his new bike Tom gave it everything and improved his time to 14 minutes 31 seconds, just two minutes behind the winner, his brother Harry. An encouraging improvement, though nothing remarkable for the Harworth club of the fifties which was stuffed full of talent. For example, Tom was beaten in that race by a 12 year old called Lenny Jones who went on to win some big races in the following years and eventually raced successfully in France.

Another young rider who beat Tom that day, Bill Womack from nearby Bawtry, still vividly remembers him from those early days: 'My first memory of Tom was as a scrawny kid on the club runs and what stood out was that, even then, when he hadn't done anything on the bike, he had his own views and he wasn't afraid of voicing them. Cycling was split then between the fixed-gear time triallists and the continental roadmen on gears, Fausto Coppi, and the like. It was the continentals who were Tom's heroes and he wasn't afraid of telling the good time triallists in the club which of the two he thought was the best. It wasn't a view they all shared either.'

Bill and Tom became close friends, even buying a car together for £25 to take them over to Manchester when they started racing on the track there. 'It was an old Ford Ten, and it hardly had any brakes or clutch. The lights were hopeless as well, but it never let us down, and took us over to Fallowfield track every Tuesday to race. Later Tom bought my share back off me and got a fibreglass body for it; he was going to race it, but I don't think he ever got it finished.'

Lenny Jones also became close. He was two years younger and very talented – a fact not lost on the ultra-competitive Tom who, to a certain extent, used Lenny as a target to beat and a training partner to draw him out. Their early friendship, however, was forged on those long Sunday club runs that they endured together, encouraging each other after they'd been left behind by the rest. They trained together during the week and together they lived the dream of becoming great cyclists. Lenny remembers those days as if they were yesterday. Days like the time when they were lost on the moors behind Sheffield in a snowstorm and were wandering off the road, lost until they saw some lights which luckily turned out to be the Langsett café, and safety. Days when they went for long rides with just bits of bread they'd scrounged from home and a few pennies in their pockets for emergencies. And days when they adapted the training methods they'd read about in magazines, sprinting after lorries and sharing the pace in short, all-out efforts to build speed, things that no one else did in their time trial dominated club.

The friendship developed. Lenny followed Tom to France and raced there successfully in the early sixties, but wouldn't take the risk of becoming a professional. What he saw there scared him – good riders burned-out by racing. Lenny came home. Tom would visit him, though, every winter. One day he said something Lenny will never forget: 'If I win the Tour, then I'll stop.' Tom was only 27 at the time so this puzzled Lenny and he asked him why. Tom became guarded and said 'I'll tell you when I stop.' Two years later Tom was dead.

In those early days, though, they were rivals as much as friends, and sometimes it created a bit of friction, though it was only one way. Lenny recalls, 'If Tom beat me in a race then that was fine. We'd ride home together and arrange to meet in the week and go training. But if I'd beaten him then he wouldn't speak to me and he'd go home on his own. Once I even saw him push his bike along the inside of the hedge in a ploughed field and get out on to the road 200 yards away just to avoid speaking to me. Then in the week he would train like mad on his own. If he beat me the next weekend it was as though nothing had happened: we were friends again. I think that it was what spurred him on. He just had to win.'

It's true: as a kid, if he was playing a game at home with his family, Tom just had to win. He hated losing. This ruthless, selfish streak contrasted vividly with his outgoing nature and could make him difficult to handle. He would exasperate and upset several people over the coming years, but I have never found anyone who could stay upset with him for long. Why? Because the root of this apparently unsportsmanlike streak was always anger at himself for losing, for not trying as hard as the person who had beaten him. He never accepted that anyone was physically better than him, just that they'd tried harder or been more tactically astute. He believed this when he was 14 and would die believing it when he was 29.

In March 1952, all this was a long way off. Tom may well have believed in his talent, but no one else did. Perhaps this was a good thing, as it allowed him to develop at his own pace, and he applied himself to racing and riding his bike as much as possible in 1952 and '53. The great change began towards the end of that year when Tom finally started to grow. In 1954 they were going to see a very different Tom Simpson.

And they did. In March of that year he was beaten into second place by only one second in his club's medium-gear 10-mile time trial. He was second again in May. The big day just had to come and in September he won his first race, setting a club record of 23 minutes 41 seconds for ten miles. A week later he won again, recording a time of 1 hour and 34 seconds for 25 miles, this at a time when under-the-hour times for that distance were still fairly rare, and very rare for 16 year olds.

Next came Tom's first title when he won the North Midlands Junior Hill-Climb Championships promoted by the British League of Racing Cyclists in Derbyshire. It was finally happening for him, and, boy, did he enjoy it. Never a believer in false modesty his rapid rise over the preceding few months, and more particularly his delight in talking about it to anybody who would listen, was starting to upset some of his older Harworth club-mates.

The 1955 racing season couldn't come quickly enough for him. As soon as March came round he was off into battle. He won his club's 5-mile time trial in a terrible snowstorm, beating all of the older riders in the process. This was just too much for some of them. Later, Tom recalled, 'I don't think it was my winning that they minded, but my bragging about it.' The upshot of his victory celebrations was that one of them said to Tom, 'Think on. Little stars don't shine for very long.' A bit unfair, perhaps, after all it was just youthful enthusiasm on Tom's part which made him boast, that and the struggle he'd had to do well. Still, Tom knew things would never be the same at Harworth.

Adding fuel to this particular fire, there was a power struggle going on in British cycling (when isn't there?) and Tom's position regarding this was only helping to widen the rift between himself and the older club members. Tom had so far only ridden time trials, which are events where individuals start off at minute intervals and ride a set distance – out and back along a route or round a circuit – and the rider with the fastest time wins. This was the mainstay of the sport in this country. In Europe, where the sport has always been much bigger, racing on the roads was predominantly what in Britain was called massed-start, where all the riders start together and the winner is the one who crosses the line first. There, did you follow that? Anyway, the English racing on open roads was called time trialling and the European, massed-start – or, as it is known now, road racing. Tom wanted to be like Fausto Coppi and ride the classics and the Tour de France; they are road races, so, naturally, Tom wanted to be a road racer.

Luckily, to accommodate his ambitions and those of thousands of others, a band of heroes had got themselves together and formed the British League of Racing Cyclists, the B.L.R.C., whose sole aim was to promote the cause of road racing on the open road. The older members at Harworth were dyed-in-the-wool time triallists, not that there's anything wrong with that I hasten to add, but they were dead-set against the B.L.R.C.

So the cat was really thrown amongst the pigeons when, at the annual club meeting, Tom proposed that the Harworth and District join the B.L.R.C., the proposal being seconded by Lenny Jones. Things got a bit heated, and one or two more hurtful things were said. It was time to move on.

The motion to join was defeated. Tom would have to leave the club to pursue his road-racing ambitions, anyway, but he was hurt by what he saw as rejection by people he had looked up to. Also, he couldn't understand why they wouldn't encourage his racing ambitions. So he started to look for a new club, though he never forgot Harworth and the warm welcome they gave him when he was a scrawny 13 year old.

The biggest club in the area at the time was the Scala Wheelers, based in Rotherham. They had a real race pedigree and the club was full of established stars; with them Tom would be starting at the bottom again, but that was the challenge he wanted now, and he joined as quickly as possible, taking Bill Womack with him. Lenny Jones wanted to join the Scala Wheelers as well, but was still too young to ride road races, so Tom advised him not to make waves and stay put with Harworth. Perhaps in the back of his mind he also thought that Lenny was a bit too talented a fish to take with him and benefit from the competition in the bigger pond he'd found for himself. Ruthless? Yes, but you have to be.

If you had asked Tom at that time, or indeed any time after the first day he'd ridden a bike in anger, what he wanted to be when he grew up, he would have replied, 'A professional cyclist.' It was all he thought about, all he talked about, and it wasn't just a dream, either. Those close to him at the time, like Lenny Jones, and later on George Shaw from Sheffield, said it was the big difference between Tom and them. Tom was going to do it. They wanted to do it, but only wanted; Tom *had* to do it.

This was all well and good, but even though they had arguments about this, Tom's dad very sensibly insisted that his schoolwork came first, and that he gained a trade qualification to fall back on before he could even think about giving his full attention to the bike. In fact, Tom worked full time almost until the day he left for France in 1959, despite a racing and training schedule that in later years demanded riding as much as 400 or 500 miles in a week.

In order to qualify as a draughtsman – a nice, steady job in those days, and incidentally the job his daughter Joanne now does in Belgium – Tom started work as a 16-year-old apprentice at a factory in Retford, doing the 20-mile round trip to work on his bike as extra training. Just as important was the extra money available from his earnings, after contributing to the family purse, to spend on cycling – which, as any young, ambitious rider will tell you, isn't a cheap sport if you want to keep a tip-top race bike on the road.

Even though Tom did as his dad wished and worked hard enough to get his qualification, it's fair to say that he never once put school or work in front of the bike. For example, whenever there was a big race like the Tour of Britain going through the area he would play truant from school and ride miles to stand by the roadside and watch his British heroes, Brian Robinson, Bob Maitland, and 'Tiny' Thomas race by. Later on, when he'd started work, there was more than one occasion when his drawing-office colleagues had to cover for him because, on a fine afternoon, he would nip off early to get in some extra training.

One of the places Tom used to ride to and watch his favourites race was the Forest Recreation Ground in Nottingham. Many cyclists started their road-racing careers there, although more than a few will have mixed feelings about the steep climb which had to be negotiated each lap. Even more people will remember the great international stars brought over to race there, in more recent years, by local cycle giants Raleigh, including a Tour de France winner, Lucien Van Impe, and the multi-classics winner, Jan Raas.

So it was natural that our budding road racer should make his debut in the branch of the sport at which he was to become world champion, in the Easter 1955 junior 25-mile massed-start race at the Forest. On that same day he also slipped into the tactics that he would use for his entire career.

These were very straightforward: when the starting flag dropped Tom went for it. He attacked from the start and led the race on his own until the final lap. Then something happened which was also going to be repeated throughout his career: he ran out of steam and was joined by someone on the very last lap who had been biding his time in the chasing group, and was outsprinted for the line.

It didn't matter, though: he had made his mark. A few weeks later he returned to the Forest for another junior race and repeated the same exploit, only this time he stayed clear of the others and won the race. He was three weeks stronger and his conviction that this was the way to race was set in stone.

A few days later Tom put up another remarkable performance by finishing fourth to the fifties time-trial idol, Ray Booty, in the Sheffield Mercury Mountain Time Trial. Booty really was the hero of the British club scene at that time. He was the first rider to break the four-hour barrier in a 100-miles time trial, a feat comparable to Roger Bannister breaking the four-minute mile barrier in athletics. He was also an accomplished road racer, winner of a Commonwealth Games gold medal and the Isle of Man International.

Booty was very much the established star, yet here we had a junior getting very close to him in his own backyard of time trialling. Even then Tom wouldn't allow himself to be in awe of anyone. This thread ran throughout his career; it was central to his whole racing philosophy. While he would never underestimate his rivals, he refused to make them out in his own mind to be better than they were. It was something he felt very strongly about and in later years saw it as the only reason why there weren't more British cyclists as successful as he was. It was a frustration he carried to his grave.

He had made a good start to his road-racing career and went on to win 16 more junior races in 1955, all in the same go-from-the-gun style. However, before all this, he had his first go at a form of racing that was to bring him to world notice long before his exploits on the road.

Track racing in the fifties couldn't have been more different from the road: British riders were a real force on the international scene. The great Reg Harris was World Professional Sprint Champion in 1949, '50, '51 and '54, after winning the Amateur Championship in 1947, and huge crowds flocked to any meetings he appeared at. Our pursuit racers weren't far behind, either. The individual pursuit over 4,000 metres was introduced to the World Championships in 1947, and Manchester's Cyril Cartwright took our first medal, a silver, in 1949. This was followed by a gold medal in 1955 for Norman Sheil from Liverpool, who was to win again in 1958. All of these riders would be a big influence on Tom over the next few years.

Just behind these champions were a number of very good riders, notably Mike Gambrill, John Geddes and Pete Brotherton in the pursuit, and Lloyd Binch and Cyril Peacock in the sprint events. On top of this there was a very active track-racing scene throughout the country to keep them sharp, for as well as permanent hard tracks in big cities, every town and village had either a cinder or grass track around its sports field, or cricket pitch.

These tracks were used to stage annual meetings held in conjunction with colliery sports days and agricultural shows. The locals loved their bike races because in some of them the competitors were handicapped according to ability, a system which ensured that everyone had something to race for. The result was very fast and aggressive racing as the stars tried to make up their deficits and the front markers fought desperately to stay ahead – and if that front marker was a local lad, then so much the better.

There would very often be as many as seven of these short handicap and scratch races in one afternoon, with good prizes. This resulted in a band of tough 'trackies' travelling from meeting to meeting in search of prizes to augment their incomes. For although the prizes were 'in kind' – canteens of cutlery and the like – they could readily be converted to cash by selling them to the spectators. Very often track meetings ended up looking more like car-boot sales. Sadly, most of these tracks and meetings have gone today, and it's a shame because they were a good shop window for cycling.

One of the biggest grass-track meetings in the country was held at Blyth, just a few miles south of Harworth. Wanting to try his hand at everything, Tom entered without the slightest idea of what was required in the way of tactics or equipment, and because of this he nearly came unstuck before he started. He just turned up on the bike he used for time trials, which had tyres that were totally unsuitable for grass-track racing. The organisers weren't going to let him start, but another competitor, Eric Gordon from Birmingham, took pity on him and lent him his spare wheels for the meeting. That problem over, Tom took to the racing like a duck to water and got through the heats to the final of every event, ending the day with a third place in the half-mile race. A good debut against some of the best riders in the country.

The story of his track début and his lack of knowledge about equipment may surprise many people today, when young riders have access to all the information they need about specialist areas of the sport. Many things have changed today: successful riders have coaches and physiotherapists, and the like, to guide them as soon as they show any promise. Also, nearly everyone has access to a car, so very few cyclists ride to events. Though, with the state of the roads, who can blame them?

It was quite the opposite in the fifties: riders either rode as a club or individually to races, and often hung around afterwards so that they could ride home with their mates. A race was, therefore, a great social occasion as well as a competitive one. By doing this the riders clocked up a lot of extra training miles, too. To get an idea of just how many we can take a look at one particular Sunday in Tom's 1955 season. The date was 15th May.

His weekend actually started on the Saturday when he rode the 50 or so miles from Harworth to Collingham in Yorkshire with a friend, the Barnsley rider Eric Clayton. Eric remembers that journey for one reason: 'Tom went on for the whole ride about how he was going to win the race we were riding the next day, and that I would come second.' The race was the Holbeck Junior 25-Mile Time Trial.

Tom and Eric spent the night together in a youth hostel, with Tom still banging on about how the event would turn out the next day. He did this to such good effect that by the time they rode Clayton says, 'He'd completely psyched me out; Tom won and I came second.' You see, it's not all in the legs.

This was just the start of their day's racing. After receiving their prizes the pair rode off to Brodsworth, just north of Doncaster, some 30 miles away, to take part in two rounds of the North Midlands Pursuit Championships being held on the cinder track there that afternoon.

Tom got through both rounds, beating his old friend and rival Lenny Jones in the semi-final. Eric was due to ride in the pursuit, but withdrew due to his efforts in the time trial, though he thinks it might have been as much due to the mental effects of Tom's nagging the night before. The day was rounded off with a quick 15-mile dash home to Harworth. Not a bad days training, was it? Later that same week Tom beat Alan Collings from Doncaster in the final to become the first junior to win the pursuit title.

The year continued in very much the same way: Tom competed whenever he could, riding to and from events and begging lifts to those that were too far away. He won every junior race he rode, with the result that he was refused entry to some of them and made to ride the senior race instead.

These senior races were no joke. Distance and toughness seemed to be the objective of every organiser, whose usual course selection method was to find the biggest hill in the area then route the race over it about ten times. This led to some long, stretched-out races with the field spread over several minutes by the end. You might think this a bit boring now, but these were still the days of super-long classics like the 365-mile Bordeaux–Paris, and distance riding was much more appreciated by the cycling fan, both here and on the continent.

By now the 1955 season was drawing to a close, but Tom still had one racing date left in his diary that was to bring him to national notice for the first time. This was the B.L.R.C. National Hill-Climb Championships, held on the Snake Pass, near Glossop.

It is a peculiarity of British cycling that the season ends with a flurry of hill races. These are held as time trials from the bottom to the top of a notable local hill. The hills are typically British: short, straight and hellishly steep. British road builders never have cottoned on to 'nancy-boy' European ideas like hairpin bends and using the natural contours of a hill to gain altitude, especially in the north of England where most of these events are held.

Having said all that the Snake Pass climb isn't a particularly steep one, rising 600 feet in just under four miles. Tom competed in the junior event and, starting at number 9 on the card, recorded a time of 16 minutes and 2 seconds to win that title by 30 seconds.

Given the successful year he had just completed, an easy win in the junior section was not unexpected. What was a surprise, though, was that only four of the professional and senior amateurs, riding their championships on the same day, beat the new junior champion. These included a star of the Tour of Britain, Brian Haskell, who won the pro event with the day's fastest time, 15 minutes and 28 seconds.

One week later Tom rode the Circuit des Grimpeurs, a road race for independents (semi-pro riders) and senior amateurs, held on the tough Crich circuit in Derbyshire. The organiser of this race was a man who over the years has done as much as anybody to further the cause of road racing in this country, Dave Orford.

Dave remembers the letter that accompanied Tom's entry which read, 'Can I please enter your event? I know that I am a junior, but I am 18 in two weeks.' Well, it was more like four weeks, actually, but Dave didn't know this and the letter had impressed him. He told me, 'I thought his three shillings and threepence entry was as good as anyone's, and I've never taken much notice of rules.' So Tom got in the race, his first one against men, the independents, who actually earned money from cycling.

Towards the end of the race Dave was beginning to wish he hadn't let the young lad ride, for although he won he only got rid of the 17 year old on the last climb of the day. Years later, in 1963, at the start of a race on the Isle of Man which Tom won, Dave reminded Tom, who by then was ranked number one in the world by virtue of leading the Prestige Pernod competition at that stage of the season, of how he'd actually beaten him in his first ride against paid riders. Dave will never forget the deadpan look Tom gave him when he replied, 'Well, let's see how you go today, then.'

Tom's first big season had come to an end. He was a national and area champion, he'd won almost every junior race he'd entered, and, more importantly for a future pro, had won in every discipline of the sport, from sprints on the track to long road races. Next year was to be his first as a senior rider, and he was certain now that he could go as far in cycling as he had dreamt he could when he was a young kid with the Harworth and District. It was time to take stock and plan. If he was going to achieve his ambitions then he would need to know everything he could about race preparation, position on the bike, training and diet. It was time to get serious.

2

SUPER PURSUITER

That Autumn he began a trawl for information that would continue throughout his career. Always seeking to get more out of himself, Tom was to become one of the first riders to prepare scientifically and with intelligence. He questioned established methods and could see the logic in some of the new ideas that were going round at the time. Every book, magazine or scrap of information was devoured in his quest for improvement. He wrote to current and ex-champions seeking their advice. He even told Lenny Jones that he had written to Coppi and had a reply, though I've never been able to find it.

One of the letters which did survive actually resurfaced in 1965 when the much-revered cycling journalist (and I mean cycling journalist literally because he actually used to cover many events by bike) Jock Wadley was writing in his *Sporting Cyclist* magazine about Tom's win in the world championships. Jock started his article by remembering a letter written by the 16-year-old Tom to the great champion and trainer Francis Pélissier, asking for advice. In 1955 Pélissier had shown the letter to Wadley who, for some reason, kept it. He never knew why, but it provided a remarkable introduction to his article ten years later. It's a funny thing, but lots of people I've met whilst writing this book kept the letters they'd received from Tom, long before he was famous and long after they'd thrown away letters from other friends. Did they know that they'd be precious to them one day?

One man who did reply to Tom's letters was an Austrian-born naturalised Englishman, George Berger. George had raced in France for a number of years with the Vélo Club Lavallois. There, he was trained by the famous coach Paul Rouinart, a giant figure in French cycling, who absolutely insisted on a professional attitude from all the riders under his control. George, a very intelligent man, was a huge influence on the young Tom. He was able to give him the benefits of years of experience and discipline in just a few months, and provide him with information that simply wasn't available in Britain. A linguist, he translated articles for Tom and even translated the whole of Jean Bobet's book, *En Selle*. Jean was, of course, the brother of three-times Tour de France winner Louison Bobet and his book was considered a training bible in France.

Influenced by Rouinart, George instilled in Tom the need for correct mental, as well as physical preparation. He stressed that at this early stage of his career Tom must not be satisfied with his performances, but at the same time he should not worry about them as they were just the foundations on which he was building his future. Why did this man take such an interest in Tom? Simple: because after years of involvement in the sport he was in a position to recognise that he, George Berger, had discovered a huge talent. A talent he later said, 'the like of which had never been seen in this country.'

Soon after their correspondence started George visited Harworth, and the first thing he asked Tom to do was show him the bike he'd been racing on. George remembers that the bike Tom showed him was more suitable for a 12 year old, and that he had to alter the saddle height and handlebar reach by inches, not just the few millimetres he'd expected. Remember, this was the bike Tom had already won many races on, including a national championship. Physically, George's first impression was that Tom was 'bristling with talent, though lanky and somewhat ungainly in physique.' George made up his mind there and then he'd do everything he could to help the lad reach the potential which he could see, 'just oozed out of him'.

A lot had happened in 1955. Tom's raw ability and thirst for hard work had taken him from being a promising club junior to a national champion. On top of this he had found himself a coach and, typical of Tom, he was not a local ex-bike rider keen to pass on his knowledge to the lads – indispensable as such chaps are – but someone with a deep understanding of training techniques who had studied under an expert in the very heartland of cycle racing.

Tom looked set for great things in 1956. However, even though he would end the year with an Olympic Bronze Medal, there was a big cloud hanging over the start. I've already alluded to the war that was going on in British cycling at this time, and to continue the story I need to tell you a little bit more about it.

The official governing body of cycling was called the National Cycling Union, known as the N.C.U. They were responsible for track and massed-start racing, but would not allow the latter to take place on the open road except, once a year, on the Isle of Man. They allowed it on closed circuits like the Forest in Nottingham, or around airfields and motor-racing circuits, which was all well and good, but some riders were determined to do this kind of racing on the open road, just like they did over the Channel. Unlike the N.C.U., they thought that staging races on the open road, preferably multi-day races on the lines of the Tour de France or one-day events between large centres of population, was the only way they could raise the profile of their sport in the consciousness of the average man in the street. They could also see that limiting our racing to closed venues was severely handicapping British riders when they competed in the World Championships, and the like. So they formed the breakaway body I have already told you about, the B.L.R.C.

On 7th June 1942 their founder, Percy Stallard, organised the first road race on the open road to be held in mainland Britain, between Llangollen and Wolverhampton. Stallard was immediately suspended for life by the N.C.U. – an act of arrogance that made him a martyr in a lot of people's eyes and did more to increase the membership of the B.L.R.C. than anything they could have done themselves.

The struggle between the two bodies was long and bitter, resulting in many people turning their backs on the sport in disgust because of the entrenched views and lack of freedom they encountered. The problems Tom had experienced at Harworth were just a small example of what was going on, and it was many years before the warring factions found common ground and joined together to form the British Cycling Federation which runs the sport today.

One of the many things the two bodies couldn't agree on was the question of suspension when a rider in a race committed an offence under the Road Traffic Act, and because of this Tom received a very stiff six-month suspension for an infringement which occurred in a B.L.R.C. road race.

In those days, when riders in a road race came up to a stop sign, irrespective of whether there was a marshal there, they were expected to do just that: stop and place one foot firmly on the floor in order to comply with the letter of the law, which said that this was how a cyclist was to behave at a stop sign. Anyone not complying with this committed an offence, and some promotion-mad policemen, instead of ensuring the safe passage of riders at such a junction, used to just hide behind bushes and pounce on any unwary offender. So, in a race towards the end of 1955, Tom fell foul of this situation when, alone in the lead and trying desperately to put as much daylight between himself and the bunch, he shot through a stop sign and was duly collared by a guardian of the law, reported, and disqualified from the race.

The result was a hefty six-month suspension from racing and, given all the effort he had put in, he took it very badly, nearly turning his back on cycling altogether. Much of the ban was served in the winter, but when you are 18 and every minute seems so important, six months is a long time, and you react like that.

Like a lot of teenagers Tom was into motorbikes. He owned an old one and fancied himself as a bit of a trials rider on it. He hammered that old bike wherever he went – so much so that one day, when he was turning into the car-park at a trials event he'd gone to watch, the sidecar parted company with the rest of it and carried on alone into a neighbouring field, scattering his fellow spectators as it went.

If he was going to take up this new sport Tom knew that he would have to get a proper trials bike. The one he wanted cost £100, but he only had £75, so he put his beloved pedal bike up for sale at £25. Thankfully, the best offer he got for it was only £20, and he'd spent so long trying to raise the money that the six-month suspension had nearly passed. There was nothing for it but to get back on his bike and prepare for the 1956 season, an Olympic year.

The games weren't until November, and anyway they were the last thing on Tom's mind at the beginning of March. All he wanted was a good start in his local road races, and he did just that, winning his first race, the Sheffield Atlas Kermesse. This was followed by victory at the Circuit of Swannick, after suffering a puncture.

I recently met one of the riders in that race, Archie Reeves, now a successful businessman, but then a young hopeful and mad keen Coppi fan with the Mansfield Aces Club. He recalls that towards the end of the race, with the field well spread out, he came across Tom changing his tyre by the side of the road. There was about ten miles left to the finish and Archie thought, 'Good, I'll get a tow to the finish at least, and maybe we'll catch the bunch.' So he continued riding and waited for Tom to catch him up, whereupon he planned to tuck in behind him and get his tow to the finish. The memory is still fresh: 'Get tucked in behind him! He went by so fast I nearly got blown off by the draft,' Archie told me. He goes on, 'I carried on, and at the finish I asked somebody who'd won. "Simpson," he said. It seems he'd not only caught all the other riders, but left them for dead and gone on to win the race alone. And all this happened in the last ten miles, remember.' Archie smiled ruefully and shook his head, still amazed after all these years.

Although now officially a member of the Scala Wheelers, Tom had ridden these events for an offshoot of the club which he had formed and christened the Scala Road Club. This self-styled group consisted of Tom plus three similarly ambitious youngsters: Mick Bingham, Maurice Hart and a man who was to become a lifelong friend, George Shaw.

George told me, 'I don't think the other members even knew about it. Tom banded us together and got hold of some Italian National Champion's red, white and green jerseys for us to ride in, just like the ones his hero Coppi used to wear. God knows how he got them because you couldn't get that kind of thing in this country then. I think George Berger must have helped him to get them.'

It was all very unofficial – the Scala Wheelers' colours were blue and gold – but Tom wanted to look like a continental road rider and have his little team all well turned out, and looking the same. It wasn't a daft idea, either, because things like that can have a demoralising effect on the opposition – something that Tom learnt early in his career.

This wasn't the first time he'd ridden in an unofficial jersey either. I have seen a picture of Tom riding a time trial in 1956 wearing a St Raphaël team jersey. This was one of the biggest pro teams in France in those days and would eventually be the first professional team Tom rode for. These two stories might not seem very significant today when any cyclist can buy all the kit his or her hero wears, but it was very hard to get hold of this stuff in the mid-1950s, not to mention expensive. But Tom showed that it was worth it. If you live the dream and want it enough you really can make it happen.

He was also making progress at the time-trial side of the sport with a number of under-the-hour rides for the 25-mile distance, including a local record of 58 minutes 53 seconds done in the spring of 1956 and fourth place in the very prestigious Solihull invitation 25-mile race. Local rivalry with Lenny Jones pushed both of them to new achievements at this 25-mile distance: when Lenny beat Tom's record with a time of 58 minutes 33 seconds, Tom replied by going under 58 minutes for the first time to beat Lenny in the Scala Wheelers event. Tom was so nervous about beating Lenny that he couldn't sleep the night before that race. Nervous energy as much as class took him to that victory; nervous energy that he would come to rely on many times in the future when the chips were down and he just had to win.

Everything then looked set for him to progress to international level as a road rider, but George Berger had other ideas. Ever with his eye on the bigger picture, he felt that to achieve his true potential on the road, Tom would benefit at this stage of his career by concentrating for a short time on one particular event on the track, the 4,000m individual pursuit.

His thinking went something like this. The key weapon in the armoury of a pro road racer is sustained speed. And what is a pursuit race? A long, drawn-out sprint. To succeed at the pursuit a rider has to develop pure speed, transfer that speed with a smooth and efficient pedalling style, and have huge physical capacities of oxygen utilisation. Basically, just the things you need to win a professional road race.

And Tom listened to what George said. Sure, he wanted to be a road racer, but hadn't his great hero Coppi first come to light as a pursuiter before going on to his great exploits on the road? It made sense, so he decided to concentrate on the pursuit and ride the 1956 British National Championships; but first there was a hurdle to clear.

Good pursuiters were falling out of the trees in 1956 and when it came to assembling the field for the National Championships the organisers would have a huge array of proven talent to choose from. Tom was the Division Champion at this event, but he'd won that on the very slow cinder track at Brodsworth, a far cry from the Harris Stadium at Fallowfield in Manchester where the championships were to be held. Tom needed a qualifying time and he needed to do it in front of the Manchester promoters, but time was running out before the championships. How was he going to get a ride in a prestigious enough meeting to catch their eye?

To the rescue came Sheffield's Doug Bond. Doug was the established local pursuit specialist and had been invited to compete in a pursuit race at Fallowfield about three weeks before the championships. Tom had already spoken to Doug during the winter when Berger suggested he take up pursuiting, trying to find out how to train for the event and what tyres to use. Doug, who would admit himself that he was never one for an overcomplicated approach to racing, had then just told him to train hard and if he was any good someone would sort out tyres for him. Now he was able to help him in a more practical way by giving up his place in the pre-championship pursuit to Tom. Doug was sure Tom would do well, but the organisers took a bit of pursuading to let the novice into their prestigious meeting. He ended up having to give his word that Tom would not let them down, and thankfully Doug's word was good enough. Tom was in.

The organisers soon saw that their misgivings were totally unfounded: Tom actually won the event in a time of 5 minutes 16 seconds, not only fast enough to qualify him for the championships, but one of the fastest times recorded in the country so far that year, and fast enough to make him one of the favourites for championship victory. Plus he did it all on his old time-trial bike, the one that George Berger said was more suitable for a 12 year old.

The Manchester officials and regulars at the track were really impressed. Albert Hawes, an official at the track that day and, incidentally, still officiating down the road at the new Manchester Velodrome, remembers the day Tom stood them all on their heads: 'He impressed the big promoter at Manchester, Norman Grattage, and I remember that Cyril Cartwright took him under his wing.'

This was the same Cyril Cartwright who had won Britain's first medal in the World Pursuit Championships, and by then a bit of a talent scout in the Manchester area, but he'd never seen anything quite like Tom. 'My first impression was that he had a natural turn of speed and was very fast for about two and a half laps, but he didn't know how to use it.' Cyril recalls. He didn't mess about though and told Tom there and then that he could win the National Pursuit, and that he, Cyril Cartwright, could show him how. 'But I also remember that at first I made no impression on him at all, and that he went away without listening to a word I had said.'

What was this? Did the young novice think he knew more than a World silver medallist or was he, just like all teenagers, difficult to give advice to? No, the truth was that he just wanted to go away and evaluate what he'd been told, and check it out with people he knew and trusted. The response he got was that Cyril certainly knew what he was on about and that Tom had better start listening to him. So he accepted the advice Cyril proffered at their first meeting and took his annual holidays in order to stay with Cyril in Manchester for the two weeks leading up to the championships. When Tom returned to Manchester, Cyril noticed the difference straight away: 'Somebody must have talked to him because he hung on every word I said, and took it all in.' Cyril was also very right about Tom's natural speed because just before the championships he won an 800-metre event on the Brodsworth cinder track in a record 57 seconds. Now that is fast for a cinder track.

The story of Cyril Cartwright's silver medal is a remarkable one in itself. He had been a national time-trial champion and record holder when in 1948 he fell victim to the terrible wasting disease, rheumatic fever. He lost a tremendous amount of weight, all of it muscle, and could hardly walk. The traditional doctors could do nothing for him and his situation looked hopeless until he met someone who I suppose, nowadays, would be said to be into alternative medicine. He treated Cyril with nature cures and got him to eat only fruit, vegetables, and nuts from natural sources. Slowly but surely Cyril began to regain his health. So much so that he began to ride his bike again and was soon able to compete, resulting in that tremendous silver medal in 1949.

Not unnaturally Cyril's belief in the diet that brought about his amazing recovery was absolute. He argued that by eating as much raw fresh food as possible, toxins could be limited and the body's energy requirements in dealing with these much reduced. He advocated taking meat in fairly normal amounts, but the emphasis was on salads and liquidised concoctions of fruit, vegetables, and nuts.

Bill Womack remembers meals at the Cartwright's house: 'I was staying there once with Tom, and Cyril's wife prepared all this beautiful wholesome food; everything was fresh and the best quality. Cyril put our plates down in front of us and told us that this was how you got good, by eating only the best.'

All this knowledge about nutrition was imparted to Tom over the two weeks he spent with Cyril, and he stuck with some of the principles throughout his career, although true to his northern roots he never could go the whole way and give up chips. Cyril reckons that at the end of two weeks the teenager had assimilated the knowledge of diet and race preparation that it had taken him 28 years to gain.

Cyril lent Tom his medal-winning bike, a chrome-plated Carlton, and even more importantly introduced him to the best training partner a young hopeful could wish for, Reg Harris. The man the Fallowfield track was named after was still very strong in 1956. He spent as much time as he could with Tom, who soaked up information from him like a sponge. Harris had always been a hard and dedicated trainer, and the speed Tom must have got from training with the sprinter was just what he needed in the run-up to the championships.

Cyril also rode on the track with Tom, showing him how to hold his line around the bottom of the bankings in a pursuit race and how to start, both skills that could knock seconds off his times on the big day. Cyril adds: 'While I was at it I showed him how to ride a distance race, how to position himself in a sprint and how to develop a sprint.' He would have constant need of these skills over the next few years and further in the future they would help him move seamlessly into the world of six-day track racing when he became a pro.

Harris and Cartwright also worked on Tom psychologically, and at the end of two weeks they had him believing that he would win the championships. This was no mean feat, and I mean both winning and making him believe it, for to become National Champion Tom would have to beat the reigning World Champion, and a whole boat load of super pursuiters.

Finally, the big day came. The press had really got behind this championships: track racing used to command far more column inches, even in the national papers, than it does now, and a huge crowd turned out expecting a battle royal. They were not to be disappointed. There were four potential world champions at least, as well as one actual one in the field and, as the first round approached, Tom was suffering, not unnaturally, a massive butterfly attack and very serious misgivings.

More than anything he needed a good ride in the first round to settle his nerves because, as we shall see, physically he was ready and in great form. Cyril Cartwright had done a fantastic job in the preceding two weeks, turning a raw novice into a world-class pursuiter. And world-class was what he would have to be, as his first opponent was one of the championship favourites, Pete Brotherton, a great track all-rounder from Barton-on-Humber.

Brotherton was very experienced, having won his first national title seven years previously, and Tom's riding as they got under way on opposite sides of the Fallowfield track reflected his nervousness. At first he fell behind Brotherton who had won sprint medals and was therefore a very fast starter, but by halfway Tom had drawn level. A terrific battle ensued as the lead swung first one way then the other, with Tom finally running out the winner. He was through to the next round and all trace of nervousness had gone.

His next opponent was none other than the reigning World Champion, Norman Sheil – enough to freeze the blood of any 18 year old, but not Tom. He beat Sheil easily and the crowd were astounded. Tom was through to the semi-finals.

It's fair to say that for various reasons Norman was not at his best that day, but he takes nothing away from Tom, and to this day has an abiding memory of him: 'He wanted to win so much you could taste it. He feared nothing and no one,' he told me.

John Geddes, in great form and in no mood to give way to an unknown teenager, now stood between Tom and the final; their match was the battle of the championships. There was nothing between them: Geddes tried to draw level with the fast-starting youngster, but every time he did Tom somehow found the power to go faster. Neither rider would give in and they pushed each other to faster times than either of them had ever done. On the final lap Tom just managed to keep ahead and won by one tenth of a second with a time of 5 minutes 10.7 seconds, the fastest 4,000 metres ever recorded on Fallowfield to that date. Tom was through to the final against the reigning National 25-mile Time Trial Champion, Mike Gambrill from London.

It had all happened so fast. In the course of one day Tom had progressed from a raw talent that some insiders were tipping for great success, to arguably one of the best pursuiters in the world. He had won his place in the final with some spectacular riding which had had the crowd on their feet several times. They had really taken to the young lad who was cutting ribbons through the established stars. It was the first time he had experienced such support and he hadn't had time to take in what was happening. As he sat there quietly waiting for the final, the enormity of it all hit him and the nerves came back. His mental state wasn't helped much, either, by a Liverpool fan getting carried away by the occasion and threatening to knock his head off for beating Geddes. So, all in all, by the time it came to go to the line for the final, Tom was a bit jittery, to say the least.

It was mental rather than physical strain because he made a good start against Gambrill and was ahead when, after three laps, he punctured. The race was stopped and a rerun ordered. This was terrible luck for Tom as he was very nearly at the end of his nervous tether, but he gave it everything he had in the rerun to draw ahead at halfway when disaster struck and he punctured again.

That was it, he couldn't take any more and broke down in tears. Another rerun was ordered, but he'd already given too much – try as he might he couldn't match Gambrill and had to settle for the silver medal.

Although Tom was at first bitterly disappointed he soon saw his performance in its proper perspective. Bad luck was certainly a factor in his final defeat and after a while he convinced himself that even though he hadn't won he had laid down one of George Berger's foundations; now it was up to him to build on it. He would get the opportunity because, before the dust had chance to settle on the championships, Tom was being talked about for the coming Worlds and the Olympics.

I asked Norman Sheil what was the effect of the appearance of this new boy on himself and the rest of the established stars. His answer surprised me. There was no 'we had to calm this young lad down and teach him a lesson', quite the contrary:

We learned from him; he raised the game and we had to follow. The same thing happened a few years before when I broke into world-class pursuiting. I did faster times and the rest had to adapt to my ways or get left behind. Tom taught us things, a new attitude. And let me tell you this: later he did the same thing to the Europeans. They learnt from him because they could see that he was seriously good; he could just ride them off his wheel and they had to adapt to him.

Jean Bobet echoed this point when in 1965 he said, 'Simpson only pretends that he is conquered by the Continent. He is actually the conqueror and we shall know it in a few years when his countrymen get hold of the yellow, pink, amarillo and rainbow jerseys that are the stamp of genius in cycle racing.' Alas, that didn't happen, and still hasn't. Not yet, anyway, but perhaps some talented kid is reading this book and believes ... well, let's hope, shall we?

3

THE SPARROW FLIES DOWN UNDER

Everything in his life had changed now that he was an Olympic prospect. For one thing the kitchen at his Festival Avenue home in Harworth would never be the same. Tom returned from Manchester determined to follow Cyril Cartwright's dietary principles to the letter, which meant that his mother, a good northern housewife accustomed to serving up wholesome stews, meat and two veg, and the like, now found herself having to prepare fruit salads, rare steaks, and complicated vegetable and nut concoctions. These didn't come cheap, either, but her son was an Olympic contender so, after 30 years being a housewife, she decided she'd help him in the only practical way she could: she got herself a job at the Glass Bulbs factory to earn some extra money.

Tom became totally single-minded about his bike. He stuck rigidly to his diet. He was also strict about getting enough rest and bedtime was nine o'clock, come what may. As for training he crammed as much of that around his job as he could. In later years, when he knew more, he became a bit more relaxed about diet and sleep, but training was always a serious matter. It had to be done, and his professional colleagues all remember that training times were rigid – you had to be there at the appointed hour, and the miles had to be done, whatever the weather.

It might not have sounded much fun, living like a monk, working and training, but Tom said later that this period of his life gave him the strength of character to hang on and keep at it, even when the going got tough. Many people have told me that Tom was so successful because he could push himself further than the others, but it was second nature to him; he learnt the discipline in his teens.

Another change which helped his Olympic ambitions was that, now a fully qualified draughtsman, he found a job in the Glass Bulbs drawing office in Harworth. This gave him more control over his training. For a start he didn't have a daily commute to take into account, so he could undertake more race-specific training sessions and use his time on the bike to better effect.

Glass Bulbs was to prove a good employer to Tom and helped with (unpaid) leave over the coming years. He also made good friends at the factory. They were very proud of him and helped with his Olympic expenses. Later, Tom's dad, who worked in the stores there, loved updating everybody about his son's latest exploits. The company have even kept some of his work in their archives and, now, as Demaglass, they have continued their link with Tom by sponsoring his memorial race, held each year in Harworth thanks to local organisers Joe and Dave Marsh, and, before them, Tom's friend George Shaw, plus Mick Brown, Gordon Harling and Barry Neilson.

After the National Championships Cyril Cartwright was busy trying to get Tom selected for both the Olympics and the Worlds, and he forgot all about road racing and concentrated on the track, anxious to prove to the selectors that his recent form was no fluke. All the track promoters wanted him, but Tom had now started charging for his services. Under guidance from George Berger he started asking for higher expenses than some of the established riders, arguing that as he was the up-and-coming man he was therefore the bigger attraction. He didn't always get them, though, but it showed that even at 18 he had his eye on the bottom line. He was going to do this for a living one day.

Benny Foster, as national track team manager, was the man who would have the final say in who went to the Olympics and the Worlds, so Cyril lost no time in lobbying him on Tom's behalf. At first, Foster was evasive – his concern was that although Tom had an obvious claim on a place in the individual pursuit at the World Championships, was he experienced enough to cope with it mentally? He tried to put Cyril off, saying Tom would have to have more trials, but Cartwright, ever protective of his young charge, replied, 'If you haven't seen enough now you never will.'

Eventually, Benny prevailed and got Cyril to forgo Tom's place at the Worlds in exchange for automatic selection for the Olympics. Benny was probably right about Tom's lack of experience, though; the individual pursuit can be as demanding on the nerves as it is on the body.

So Tom was selected to ride in the 1956 Melbourne Olympic games. Melbourne? He hadn't even been on a day trip to France yet.

His event would be the 4,000 metre team pursuit – in those days there was no individual pursuit at the Olympics. The team event is basically the same as the individual one, except that instead of individuals starting on opposite sides of the track and attempting to catch each other, two teams of four riders take their place, each rider taking it in turn to pace the others. The event probably suited Tom's temperament better at this stage, as he was very young and in his first major championships, so having team mates would help to share the pressure.

Before the games he had another adventure – his first trip abroad, and it was behind the Iron Curtain to Russia where, along with the team pursuit squad of Don Burgess, John Geddes and Mike Gambrill, plus Eric Thompson, Alan Dawson and Pete Brotherton, Tom was to compete in several track meetings against the Italian and Russian Olympic squads.

Cold-war Russia in the fifties was a daunting prospect for even the most seasoned traveller, but our gallant young Olympians just took it all in their stride. Their manager was Benny Foster, the man very much in charge of British international cycling at that time. Benny had assembled a group of riders around him that he called Foster's circus. They were regarded as a sort of chosen few and numbered all the above track riders as well as a road squad which Tom would meet at the Olympics.

They accepted him as a younger brother, but he had to pass the initiation of being the butt of their jokes, which included them throwing him into a Russian river. Years later Benny remembered being reticent at first about Tom: 'I didn't know what to make of so much class in one so young. He was full of talent. You could see it emitting from him. He took the others' jokes in good part and fitted in, but I was also impressed by the great feeling he had for his mother and father and his sister. It told me that Tom wasn't shallow.'

John Geddes has warm memories of Tom: 'We were together from June 1956 almost continuously until well into 1958, and it was a privilege. On that trip to Russia he came through as a showman: when the crowd got behind him they seemed to egg him on.' Benny Foster said the same: 'I believe that Tom's clowning was born at this time; he learned how to entertain.' He had some good teachers, too: Geddes was famous for his practical jokes. For example, Tom was so frail-looking and skinny that John used to make a joke of it and not allow him to walk anywhere, but pick him up, throw him over his shoulder and carry him about the track.

One thing that certainly started in Russia was the collection of hats that would become Tom's trade mark, from the Cossack one he bought in Leningrad, to the famous bowler he wore in countless photo opportunities after he became a professional rider. He eventually gave the Russian hat to his dad, who brought quite a hint of the mysterious east walking around Harworth in it on cold and frosty days.

Any thoughts of cold-war austerity were soon dismissed when the riders saw their accommodation, which in Leningrad was an old imperial palace, complete with servants to pander to their every need. They were ferried back and forth to the track on special buses, and what with John Geddes carrying him about once they got there no wonder he shone at the racing.

After Leningrad, the circus moved on to Moscow, where they did all the sights – Red Square, Lenin's tomb and the Kremlin. They even went to the Bolshoi Ballet, but Tom let the side down by managing to fall asleep during the performance. The Moscow crowds also warmed to him and he was nicknamed the 'Sparrow' by the press: they had never seen an athlete who looked so frail. The weather, though, was very cold on the big, open track, where an icy wind coming straight from Siberia whistled around the bankings.

Tom didn't just make an impression on the crowds, he brought admiring comments from the competition. The great Italian national coach, Guido Costa, for example, said to Benny Foster, 'Benjamino, one day your lad Seemson will be famous.'

The British team received a boost to their morale when they beat the Italians, hot favourites for the Olympic Games team pursuit title, in the final of that event in Moscow. This was revenge for Tom who had really set himself up to win the individual event, but was knocked out in the semi-final by the Italian future World Champion, Leandro Faggin.

Despite the apparent friendliness of their hosts on this trip none of the team felt completely at ease. Tension between the East and West in 1956 was high and every one of them felt that they could easily disappear without too many questions being asked. They were protected to some extent by the presence of Benny Foster, worldly wise and a father figure to the boys, but when he had to leave them due to business commitments back home, some strange things started to happen.

After Moscow the team was due to race in Sofia in Bulgaria. On the morning of their departure they were all picked up by the usual bus and taken to the railway station – that is, all except Pete Brotherton, who, for some reason they hoped would soon become apparent, was bundled into an unmarked car and driven away. Once at the station the Russian officials shepherded the party, minus Brotherton, onto the train, bade them farewell, and off they went. Six cyclists heading who knows where – no manager, no knowledge of the language and no tickets: Brotherton had them.

After about an hour trundling along in the dark and jokes about Siberian salt-mines having worn a bit thin, the train juddered to a halt in the middle of a field. To say the least, there was an air of apprehension in their compartment as footsteps approached. Then the door flew open to reveal none other than Peter Brotherton. It seems that he'd been taken by car to meet the wife of one of the officials and brought out to meet the train. However, all the riders thought that it was more a case of the Russians putting these boisterous British back in their place.

They had yet more problems when the train crossed the Romanian border and it was found that the riders didn't have a visa for that country. The upshot of this was that they were put on a train to Bucharest and had to spend 24 hours under house arrest at the British Embassy there, until all the paperwork was sorted out, eventually arriving in Sofia a day and a half later than they should have. It had been an interesting journey.

Their problems behind them, they had a great few days racing in Sofia. Again, on the surface, they were extended the greatest courtesy, but they were never allowed out of sight of their hosts and Tom was fairly glad when he got home, though he really enjoyed telling his mates at work about all his experiences behind the Iron Curtain.

Next stop Melbourne and the Olympic Games, but first he had to go to London to get fitted for his official Great Britain team uniform. There wasn't much time left before the Games and the training still had to be done: a missed weekend would have been disastrous now. So why not combine the two, thought Tom?

And that's just what he did. On the Friday afternoon he set off down the A1, with his knapsack on his back, to ride the 160 miles from Harworth to London! He writes about this ride in his autobiography, so I knew all about it, but John Geddes made a point of mentioning it when I asked him what in his opinion made Tom so good. He said:

Tom did everything to extreme, he did things that no one else would even think of doing. That ride to London, for example – I would never have done that. He trained so hard. I couldn't even train like him. Add this to his class, his determination and the better racing; when I got over there to France in the early sixties he was way out of reach.

Tom took about eight hours to do the ride, tucking in behind lorries as riders used to be able to do in those days because the lorries went a lot slower than they do now, and arrived at his sister Alice's house in Mill Hill none the worse for wear, or so he thought.

Next day he got fitted up in Central London and headed off in the afternoon back up the A1. It wasn't long before he started to feel the effects of his previous day's efforts and the journey home soon became a nightmare. Eventually, he had to give up, catching the train from Grantham for the rest of the journey home. Mad? Yes, but as John Geddes was hinting at, perhaps you have to be.

The Olympic Games were held between 23rd November and 1st December, so Tom celebrated his nineteenth birthday out there. He also celebrated crossing the equator on the flight to Australia and was given a certificate by the cabin crew to prove it, in the name of 'Thomas "the Sparrow" Simpson'.

The first stop on their journey was Singapore where they were put up in grand style at the famous Raffles Hotel. Once they'd settled in, the team wanted to be off on the town sightseeing. The Singapore riots had only just died down, so there was a fairly lengthy briefing from team officials about the area it was unsafe to visit. This over, our team pursuiters hired a rickshaw and headed straight there. They had an interesting time exploring the colourful markets and Tom bought plenty of souvenirs, including a brass camel of all things, which did for a present for his mum and dad when he got back home.

The serious work soon restarted when the riders got to the Olympic Village in Melbourne where Tom shared a room with that other precocious teenager on the team, 19-year-old Billy Holmes from Hull. They knew each other very well from their junior racing days in the north of England and it was very astute of Benny Foster to lodge them together, as it helped keep their morale up during what was to be a wonderful, but sometimes traumatic, Olympic experience for both of them. Billy Holmes takes up the story.

When we got there I was really put through the mill in training and I know the same thing was happening to Tom. I was in the road-race team, and the others were a lot older than me. I was very fast, but I felt I wasn't accepted by them, and they really tried to work me over in training. The first ride we went on, Stan Brittain said to me, 'You need three bottles today, we're going out for eight hours.' This went on: they kept trying to work me over, but I held on every day. It all came to a head one day when I was dropped near the end of a long run and was plodding back through the streets of Melbourne. I started to think, I can't do this; I can't race 123 miles; I'm going to ask if they'll send me home and send out Ray Booty. Many people at the time thought Booty, a more established rider, should have been picked instead of me. Anyway, I was going to tell Tommy all this when I got back to our room, but when I walked in I found him lying on his bed, crying his eyes out. I asked him what was wrong? And he said, 'I can't cope, I just can't go that fast. Do you think they'll send me home?' So there we were, two young Yorkshire lads going through the same experience. We pulled ourselves together, though, and both of us came through with medals.

In a letter home Tom told his mum and dad about the weather, the food, and who he was sharing his room with, then mentioned the training: 'Training isn't too bad, but seven days a week makes you pretty tired.' It must have been hard to make him mention it. He ends the letter: 'Well, as you know I can't write very good letters and I have to get ready for a ride. I'll say Cheerio. Keep the stamp.' Short, sweet, but he'd done his duty, bless him, and his mum wouldn't have to worry about her son on the other side of the world.

Benny Foster certainly put his riders through it. He had them out on the roads every morning, following them on a motor scooter to see that no one was slacking. Then, in the afternoon, they did more training on the track. Despite his private worries Tom was finding his feet amongst these older men and one day hatched a little plot of his own to catch Benny out. Somehow he'd discovered an alleyway between two rows of suburban houses, just wide enough to fit a string of cyclists down, but not a motor scooter. In one of the houses lived a loose and very dangerous dog. So Tom arranged with the others to shoot down this detour, whereupon he would call out to the dog. His timing was perfect – the cyclists got through, but Benny on his scooter got stuck. They had quite a laugh watching their taskmaster wrestling to free his mount whilst fending off his canine attacker.

On top of all the training, Benny arranged for the team to race in some Australian track meetings to keep them race-fit. The highlight of these was their appearance on the 200-metre Essenden track. There was a tremendous atmosphere at this meeting. The track was made from wood, not laid around the run of the track, but across it. The boards were painted white and loosely bolted down to allow for expansion. The rattling noise this produced as riders raced around added to the excitement, but it was nothing like the excitement Tom caused. One of the races was a one-lap flying time trial, where the riders do a couple of warm-up laps then go flat-out on their own for one timed lap. The lap record was held by none other than former World Sprint Champion, Reg Harris, but in his ride Tom, the skinny teenage pursuiter, equalled it and won the event. The Australians couldn't believe it.

Eventually, it was time for the serious stuff and the opening ceremony of the 1956 Olympiad, only you couldn't get these cyclists to take anything seriously, except racing, of course. When the time came for the British team to march on to the track behind the Union Jack, John Geddes got the cyclists to change the shape of their stylish Panama hats into bowlers, and out they went wearing them like that. The crowd appreciated it, but the other British team officials certainly didn't and Benny Foster once again found himself with the job of pouring oil on troubled official waters.

The British team qualified for the semi-finals of the team pursuit with ease. Their opponents in this round were the hot favourites, Italy, whom they'd already beaten in Russia. Confidence was high because the other teams left at that stage, South Africa and France, weren't regarded as much of a threat. The talk in the British camps was all gold medals, and it was doing Tom's nerves no good whatsoever.

In the semi Tom had a disastrous ride: he got dropped by the others and the team lost. He blamed himself for losing Britain a gold medal and said later that he'd suffered a terrible feeling of asphyxiation after doing his turn at the front. John Geddes remembers it well:

Tom did his turn at the front, and as usual with him it was 110 per cent. He wasn't like other riders I've ridden with who'd do enough to keep the pace going – they'd go 100 per cent, but not raise it. Tom did. He'd give everything every time it was his turn. But this time he was unlucky because I was in my very best form ever in that semi-final, and as Tom swung up I went through and did a full lap, very fast. I was the strongest I'd ever been in my life and Tom didn't get on at the back. He was very, very disappointed.

Nerves had got the better of Tom. Recalling those Olympics some years later Benny Foster said about managing him: 'In those early days I can only liken him to unstable dynamite. Within his long, slight frame was a dynamic power likely to erupt at any moment – unfortunately, it was often the wrong one.'

John Geddes told me, 'Tom really was unlucky that I was so strong when I did that full lap. We'd trained to do half laps. Also, we did our fastest ride in that semi-final, 4 minutes 40 seconds. In the ride-off for the bronze medal we were all on the same level and won it easily with a 4 minute 42 ride.'

John felt that Tom was being a bit hard on himself taking the blame; they came out with bronze medals and Tom, at that time, was probably the youngest cyclist ever to win an Olympic medal. And, to cap it all, his room mate, Billy Holmes, won a silver in the road team classification. The two young Northern lads had, indeed, come through.

Tom enjoyed the rest of the trip, attending the final day of the athletics to witness Chris Brasher win Britain's only gold medal of the Games, before flying home to England and all the fun of showing off his medal to family, friends, neighbours, and work mates in the two weeks leading up to Christmas.

4

DISTANCE MAKES THE LEGS GROW STRONGER

The rest and recuperation didn't last long because Tom had a plan. Possibly influenced by the training he and Billy Holmes had been subjected to in Australia, Tom had decided to continue this heavy duty approach in his preparation for 1957, but he needed a partner to keep him at it.

While Tom had been away, Harworth's other big prospect, Lenny Jones, had been earning quite a reputation for himself, including beating Norman Sheil in the 25-mile time trial on the Isle of Man. Norman must have wondered what was happening – he, a reigning world champion, getting beaten twice in the same year by two teenagers from the same North Nottinghamshire pit village. Anyway, Lenny was a very hard trainer, one of his favourite sessions being a solo ride from Harworth to Cleethorpes and back which, depending on his form, took him five to five and a half hours. Tom found out about these rides and thought Lenny would be an ideal partner for his own little training project.

What Tom suggested to him was that from the first Saturday in January they would ride for 100 miles together like a two-man team time trial, each taking his turn at pacing the other in order to keep the speed high. Tom told Lenny that these rides would ensure that they would be strong enough to last in any road race breakaway group, no matter how long.

Lenny, who was game for anything and nearly as mad as Tom, agreed. So that was what they did, every Saturday for nearly two months. The rides had to be done on Saturdays because Tom wanted to go weight training on a Sunday afternoon, so there was time for 'only' 60 or 70 miles of riding on Sunday mornings.

Riding for 100 miles as a two-man team time trial is a revolutionary training method even for today when, so the coaches would have us believe, riders train harder than they used to, so I was a bit sceptical when Lenny told me about these rides. I asked him if the rides hadn't been round trips of about 100 miles, with a bit of pacing thrown in now and again to keep the speed up. I was wrong: 'No, we used the A1 where all the time-trial courses were, so we would be sure of the distance, and we rode bit-and-bit for the whole way, hardly speaking for five hours. Sometimes it rained for the whole ride, but we still did 100 miles', Lenny recalled with pride.

For the rest of the week Tom trained on his bike every day and repeated Sunday's weight session on Thursday evenings in a little hut at the pit under the supervision of a local body builder, Terry Holian.

Tom's target for 1957 was the World Amateur Pursuit Championships. 'Every time we filled in a team questionnaire or gave our aims and ambitions, Tom's and mine were always the same,' recalls John Geddes. 'These were World Amateur Pursuit Champion, then World Pro Pursuit Champion, then World Pro Road Race Champion. That was how we thought it went. It was our dream.' In the spring of 1957 Tom thought he was going to get his foot on the first rung of their ladder because he was absolutely flying.

He won every 25-mile time trial he entered throughout that spring, sometimes winning by as much as six minutes over the next man home. His dominant riding made him the hot favourite for the National 25-Mile Championships held at the end of May, but on the day his form deserted him and he was well beaten by Norman Sheil.

Searching for an explanation for his defeat, Tom sought Sheil out after the event and without giving too much away, because he rated Tom too highly as an adversary to do that, Norman explained that he had taken his time with his preparation, coming to this big event ready both physically, and mentally. Tom realised that he had peaked too early and had been unable to hold his form. He also had misgivings about his winter training, thinking that it might just have been a bit too hard, especially after the mental and physical pressure of 1956. He'd been impulsive, and it wouldn't be the last time, but for now an important lesson had been learned.

A few weeks before the 25-mile championships, Tom and Norman had been on international duty together, representing Great Britain on a trip to Denmark along with John Geddes and John Entwhistle. Tom was still flying at this stage of the season and still feeling the benefits of all that work he'd done over the winter. John Geddes remembers it well: 'Tom was brilliant. He never forgot being dropped in the Olympics, though, and we rode this one team pursuit and Tom stomped over everyone. He rode like a man possessed, trying to show off to everyone that he was the best. Me and Sheil held on, but Entwhistle didn't know what had hit him.' Tom made an even bigger impression on John during that trip than he had at the Olympics:

He was a real all-rounder on the track, and he was just brilliant on that trip in every event, but his motor-paced riding behind the little derny motorbikes was fantastic. There were lots of races behind dernys during this trip and the local star was a guy called Palle Lykke, who went on to win loads of six-day races. The Danes did everything to help him win, but Tom kept beating him. I'll never forget his enthusiasm in these races, he just couldn't wait to get going. Because you had to ride a bigger gear behind the dernys the pushers-off used to run and push you, then when they couldn't go any faster they would give you one almighty shove. The idea was that you sat in the saddle while the pusher ran, then got out and gave it everything once he'd shoved you. I'll never forget Tom. In one race he was so fired up he was out of the saddle while the pusher was running alongside him, his nose was nearly on the front wheel because he was trying so hard. The poor pusher couldn't keep up to give him a final shove, so he had to let him go. He was so aggressive and anxious to get on. Everyone on that trip admired him – the crowd, the competitors and the officials.

Tom's second appearance for his country in 1957 was a lot nearer to home – at Fallowfield in an international meeting held the week after the 25-mile championships, and in it he ran into his second disappointment of the year. Well, it was more of a disaster, really. Whilst riding one of the events he crashed badly along with several other competitors. He fell very awkwardly and at first it was thought that he'd broken his leg. Dennis Lowndes, a photographer working at the track that day, recalls that it was an amazing sight, and a measure of Tom's huge popularity by then, to see the crowd of people who ran to his assistance: 'There was no one to help the others – they had to straighten their own bikes out and get back in the race, or make their own way to the first-aid tent – everyone was around Tom, concerned about him.'

Their concern was justified. The leg wasn't broken, but it may as well have been. Tom was off work for a month and off his bike for two, so badly was it twisted. All those 100-mile rides with Lenny had gone to waste, in the short term, at any rate.

By the time Tom got back on his bike another of his targets for 1957 was approaching fast – the National Pursuit Championships. Winning was by now a forlorn hope, but being eliminated in the quarter finals was a big disappointment and Tom left Fallowfield a very dejected young man. He was way behind where he wanted to be, and decided for a while to turn his back on the track and return to his first love, road racing.

To his great relief he found that although he couldn't get his speed back for the track, he was still strong enough to win a number of races on the road, some against semi-professionals of the calibre of Ron Coe who was to ride the Tour de France the following year. Many of these races were in the Peak District, just the other side of Sheffield, and Tom often rode to and from them, regularly chalking up 120 to 150 miles on a Sunday, including 80 to 100 miles of tough racing.

Not surprisingly, he was soon back to his old self. The speed was there again, too late for the track as the season was nearly over, but just in time for the hill-climbs where he had several victories leading up to the National Championships; and, typical of those troubled times, there were two of them.

The first was organised by the B.L.R.C. on the Mam Nick climb out of Edale, up on to the shoulders of Mam Tor in Derbyshire. Tom threw himself at the climb and won easily, greatly impressing the huge crowd that had turned out to enjoy the battle. One of their number was a 16-year-old schoolboy from Stockport, Gordon Hill, who now owns a bookshop in Clitheroe. Gordon had just taken up cycling. A typical young club rider, he was totally in awe of the occasion, which he described to me as electric:

There was one name on everyone's lips on that day, 'Tom Simpson'. There was a buzz in the crowd as he began to climb, you could feel it, and I remember this lad with a shock of hair thundering up the hill past me, carried on a solid wave of excitement. The overall feeling that day was that this was the future, this was the man to watch – Tom Simpson.

Ten years later, on 13th July 1967, his wife's birthday, Gordon was getting ready to take her out to dinner. He turned on the TV for the news and learned that Tom Simpson was dead, and he wept uncontrollably. He'd never met Tom, other than that day on Mam Nick. 'But he meant that much to me,' he told me in 1998.

Next was the National Championships organised by the R.T.T.C., yet another national cycling organisation, only this time dedicated to running time trials on the open road. This race was held on the infamous Winnats Pass, again in Derbyshire. The climb is right up the middle of a collapsed limestone cavern and is ferociously steep. Unfortunately, instead of winning, I think Tom fell victim of the ongoing B.L.R.C. versus the establishment battle. Anyway, I'll tell you what happened and let you decide.

Tom was called to the start-line with one minute to go as is usual in a time trial. He tightened his toestraps and settled himself down to concentrate on the effort ahead. The countdown continued and, as the timekeeper called ten seconds to go, up struts the chief judge and tells Tom that he hasn't got a locking ring on his rear wheel and will be disqualified if he starts without one. 'Three, two, one,' went the timekeeper. That was it, Tom had missed his start. He went ballistic, ranting at the chief judge, who just told him that if he calmed himself and found the missing piece of equipment he could start. Fair enough, it was in the rules that you had to have one on your bike, though most of the other competitors hadn't, but they weren't the new B.L.R.C. National Champion, were they? Things like that happened in those days.

So that was that, the 1957 season was over. Tom had won races, lots of them, including a national championship, but he'd planned to be world champion. It was time to think. First of all he needed a rest – he'd been at it since just after Christmas 1955, training and racing without a break – so he wound down slowly after the hill-climbs, and spent most of the winter just doing a bit of weight training and a few rides to keep in trim.

The serious stuff started at the end of January, and the rest must have done him good as he was soon back to full fitness. During this period his training became even more specific, and he spent a lot of time at Cyril Cartwright's home, using the track facilities to perfect his pursuiting technique. This year he was definitely going to win that world title.

His first major race of the year should have been the Good Friday meeting at the Herne Hill track in London, but there was a problem over his expenses. Tom priced himself out of the market and the meeting went on without him. In a letter written to him at the time, George Berger said that he was sorry Tom couldn't have ridden there as 'he would have certainly made certain gentlemen look silly.' They were obviously having a feud with somebody, but Tom always did have to battle against something; the harder the battle the better he went, and George probably realised this and encouraged it.

George went on to give Tom some training advice: 'Adapt the time of your training to the time (not distance) of your next event. It is also advisable to train at the same time as the race will be held.' All sound and sensible stuff. The next bit was more questionable: 'Try and eat a couple of herrings before you go out, and don't take a feeding bottle.' He called this an old Belgian method; and riders did this, training for long periods without drinking, thinking that it would benefit them during long, hot races, that they would go better because they were conditioned to ride without taking liquids. They were wrong, and it was a dangerous practice that was still prevalent in the late sixties when Tom died.

Tom's first big win came in the *Daily Herald* Gold Trophy at Fallowfield. Then, the following week, he dominated another meeting at Fallowfield, defeating all the best track riders in the distance race and even winning his heat in the international sprint.

After this came news of another trip abroad. Along with his old rival Norman Sheil, Tom was picked for a three-day international track meeting in Sofia, Bulgaria, where he had, of course, been once before. The world was getting a small place for Tom. The journey there was to be a new experience, though, because they travelled on the Orient Express.

The highlight of the meeting was a distance race called the Grand Prix of the Union of Physical Culture, a grand title for a race with an even grander trophy. Norman Sheil remembers this:

There was a huge crowd for this race, and this enormous cup. Tom was really taken with it, really excited and wanted to win it – he'd never seen anything like it. It was about four feet tall and made out of a strange metal – we both reckoned it was made out of a melted-down tank – but Tom wanted it. I was using the trip as training, as I'd set my stall out to win the Worlds at the Parc de Princes in Paris, so I said, 'OK go ahead,' and he won it.

Tom had to lug this thing home, but he was glad that he did because it had pride of place in his parents' home for years, where his dad found that the only way to clean it was to bath it in soapy water once a month. Perhaps that's how they clean Bulgarian tanks.

Norman and Tom really enjoyed their stay in Sofia, never more so than when they were taking a short cut though the showers and found the Bulgarian women's basketball team in there. Norman says that he will never forget Tom – carrying his wheels in one hand and frame in the other; he couldn't decide what to put down first so as to take his dark glasses off for a better look.

All good clean fun, but a problem arose after the three-day meeting when the Bulgarians refused to let the pair of them go home. They had made such a good impression that the authorities wanted them to take part in a meeting at Bourgas on the shores of the Black Sea some five days later. This was all well and good for state-sponsored athletes from communist countries, but Tom and Norman both had jobs to get back to, plus Tom was due to go to his brother's wedding. On top of this they couldn't get any messages back to Britain explaining what had happened, and even found out later that their normal mail, postcards and such like, hadn't been sent on by the postal authorities.

The result of all this was that their families became increasingly worried as each day passed with no sign of them, nor any word as to what had happened. Tom's mum was especially anxious, and it even made the national papers which ran stories about 'missing cyclists behind the "Iron Curtain".' It was Tom's second experience of communist high-handedness, and it left his mother with a deep mistrust of the East, as she was sure they were trying to get hold of her son. We shall see later that she wasn't far wrong, either.

Once the two of them realised that no amount of protesting was going to sway the authorities they actually started enjoying racing at Bourgas. Norman Sheil takes up the story:

We had a lot of fun there and rode lots of races, including a lot of Madisons. In one of them it started to rain. Now, the Bourgas track was painted cement, very slippy in the wet; riders were coming off all over the place, and every time I handed over to Tom I tried to get him to pack, but he wouldn't. Anyway, a couple of days later we rode another Madison on a very bumpy track and Tom was suffering with some kind of injury to his crotch; of course, on this bumpy track he was going through agony. Now he wanted to pack, but I wouldn't, getting my own back for riding in that rain. Then I missed a turn and stopped in the back straight, hanging on to the rails. He kept shouting at me to get back in every time he passed, but I just waved at him. The crowd thought it was hilarious, then he stopped coming past. I looked up and there he was, hanging on the rails on the other side of the track, waving at me. We didn't win that one.

Tom reckoned that the crowds were so big at the track because there was nothing else for them to see or do there. There must have been an army post somewhere near by because one afternoon about 2,000 soldiers took over the stands. They really enjoyed themselves and cheered anything that happened. Doing a lap of honour, Tom and Norman thought they would play to this gallery a bit, and instead of presenting their victory flowers to a pretty girl, as was the custom, they threw individual flowers to the soldiers who thought this was highly amusing, cheering their heads off and waving their flowers like mad. Yes, maybe he was right, there wasn't much to do in Bourgas.

With the trip over, Tom got the chance to play to a different gallery and said to a *Daily Mail* reporter when he got back to England: 'What's all the excitement about? I've only been having a little holiday by the Black Sea.' Already his sense of humour and skill in handling the press was starting to surface. No other British cyclist would do it better.

The Great Britain team mates were adversaries for their next race, the National Individual Pursuit Championships held at Herne Hill.

Tom won easily and Benny Foster later described him that day as being 'in a class of his own'. This was an important victory: it was the first of Tom's major racing ambitions fulfilled – everything before had been a stepping-stone. Next, he wanted the Commonwealth Games and World titles at this event and he wanted them both in 1958: there was no time to waste.

The Commonwealth Games were held that year in Cardiff, the track-cycling venue being the Maindy Stadium. The English selection for the pursuit was Tom Simpson and Norman Sheil. Because of his easy win in the Nationals Tom was the clear favourite, but he'd reckoned without the master tactician Sheil, and ended up losing the final to him by just one hundredth of a second. Tom really was bitterly disappointed with the silver medal. Even as late as 1967 he was still saying that it was the biggest disappointment of his career, and he'd had a few by then. I think he never really accepted that he had actually been beaten, it was that close.

I put this to Norman, who said: 'I actually felt sorry for Tom there. I wasn't really looking to win there, but was using it as preparation for the Worlds. I wanted to see if I could pick it up in the last lap, so in the final, knowing that Tom was a very fast finisher and Maindy a big track like Paris, I kept something back, and just got him. I felt really sorry for him and, you know, I really think he lost interest in pursuiting after that.'

The Commonwealth Games was also the scene of what Benny Foster very candidly admits was his only mistake in managing Tom: 'Tom had an exuberance that needed containing, but not stifling. I think that I only stifled it once, and that was in the Commonwealth Games when after narrowly losing to Sheil in the pursuit final I should have put him in the ten. I reckon that with Geddes he would have split the field and given us another gold,' said Benny when writing a piece about Tom soon after he'd won the World Road title in 1965.

He may have been right – Tom was very good at these ten-mile bunched races on the track. The Manchester official, Albert Hawes, who's seen them all, remember, told me:

Tom was the best ten-mile rider I've ever seen. He would always have a go at halfway, and if they brought him back he'd go again with about three laps to go. I saw him win loads of these races at Fallowfield. It was the last race on a Tuesday night and you would get as many as five national champions getting up for it, and remember Reg Harris once said that if you could win at Fallowfield on a Tuesday night, you could win anywhere in the world.

Next came the World Championships, where Tom and Norman were the automatic selections to represent Great Britain, and hot favourites to win the title. In his autobiography Tom says that he was dead keen to win the Championships: 'A world champion before I'm 21' was the thought that was uppermost in his mind, but Norman is not so sure:

I think Tom lost interest in pursuiting after the Commonwealth Games. There was something about him in the Worlds. I can't put my finger on it; it was like he didn't want to be there. He even rode the first round with socks on – nobody did that in pursuiting, then; bare feet gave you a tighter fit in your shoes. It was like he was saying that he wasn't serious, so if any of us beat him, we hadn't really done so because he wasn't trying.

Whether Norman was right or not, only Tom could tell us; he certainly prepared very hard for the event, spending as much time as he could with Cyril Cartwright, and had shown good form in British races. But bear in mind that Norman knew him well; he'd studied him, and to justify his claims about the change in Tom's attitude at these championships he told me: 'You know, you could sometimes beat Tom off the bike, before the race had even started, and it was just as well because it was a damn sight harder to beat him on it.'

As it happened all this was academic (though it does show a certain fragility in Tom's make up, as though the nervous energy that he could channel so positively, could also work against him) because Tom's assault on the title effectively came to an end in the qualifying round. He did get through to the quarter-finals, but his chances of making further progress ended during his first appearance on the Parc des Princes track.

In the qualifying round, Tom was drawn to ride against the reigning World Champion, the Italian, Carlos Simonigh, who at that time was the fastest amateur pursuiter ever. In the qualifying round it was the eight fastest who went through to the quarter-finals, and in their ride Tom and the Italian both qualified, but Tom crossed the finish line sprawled all over the track, having crashed dramatically in the last few metres.

What happened? Everything was fine with one lap to go: Tom was just ahead and had plenty in reserve. The fastest qualifying ride was on the cards when, coming out of the final banking, Tom was too close to the bottom of the track and his bike slipped into the flat concrete guttering. He had to get the thing back on to the track because the guttering was fast disappearing below ground, so there was nothing for it but to try to 'bunny hop' the bike sideways. This is easier said than done on a track bike travelling in excess of 32 miles per hour, and the front tyre hit a crack in the track with such force that it exploded, causing Tom's front wheel to collapse and skittling him across the line. He'd finished and qualified, but didn't find that out until after he'd regained consciousness in the track hospital.

A jaw that had been dislocated and put back in place whilst he was still unconscious, plus numerous cuts, bruises, and abrasions weren't at all soothed by the news that Benny Foster, the team manager, still wanted him to take his place in the quarter-finals. Tom, who, in normal circumstances, would have jumped down a dragon's mouth for Benny, replied weakly that he would have a go, but doubted his chances against New Zealand's Warwick Dalton. Benny agreed: Tom wouldn't beat Dalton, but he wanted Tom to ride against him as hard as he could so that he wouldn't get an easy passage into the semi-finals where he might come up against Norman Sheil, who was obviously now Britain's best bet for the title.

It all went according to plan. Tom rode against Dalton in what must have been the bravest effort of the championships because he only lost 100 metres to the New Zealander in four painful kilometres, and Norman eventually triumphed in the final to become World Champion for the second time in his career.

Tom was happy for him, but very angry at his own luck. Despite what Norman thought was going on in Tom's head at the Championships, Tom believed that he should have won, that he was the best rider in the world. He decided that the only way to prove it was to turn professional. He didn't have time to spend another year chasing the amateur pursuit title, not if he was going to emulate his childhood road-racing heroes, Coppi and Kubler, like he told his mother he would, just five years previously.

5

THE BRITTANY LANDINGS

To attract a sponsor on the continent he would still have to do something big. The world title would probably have done, but that was behind him now. Next best thing would be a world record, and the most famous of those is the hour. The hour record has been described as the blue riband of cycling. It is a simple test: a rider rides alone and unpaced on the track for one hour, and the distance he covers is recorded. It is a test of ability on a bike in its purest form. It requires concentration, tenacity, speed, economy of effort and style. Tom had all of those, but it also requires thorough preparation and he just didn't have time for that; he would just have to hope that he had enough of those other qualities to see him through.

So he decided to attack the World Amateur Hour Record as soon as possible and, as it was now November, it would have to be on an indoor track. Tom got in touch with Reg Harris who arranged for him to have a go at the record on the Zurich track. Of course he was going to succeed and would be snapped up by a pro team straightaway, so he left his job at Glass Bulbs, and set off for Switzerland.

Tom was due to make his attempt on a Sunday and turned up at the track on the Friday before, completely alone. There was no time to get used to the track, he just put his bike together, pumped his tyres up and gave it his best shot. In the end the record attempt was the longest period he got to spend on the track.

He'd previously written to Benny Foster informing him of his plans and asking for a schedule to ride to. Benny's reply had been short and sweet: 'Don't do it.' he said, but Tom wasn't listening. Benny tried to tell him he needed a lot more special preparation for such a record attempt, and to be patient – his time would come. Patience, however, was not one of Tom's virtues – his plans just didn't cater for waiting – and, in the end, he missed the record by just 300 metres.

Rock bottom again, a big effort and nothing to show for it, but Tom wasn't deterred. He never was deterred – ever. On Monday morning he packed his bags and headed off to the place that would eventually become his home – Ghent in Belgium – where he planned to stay with the man who would become one of his closest friends, and biggest supporter, Albert Beurick.

Those of you reading this who know Albert will have smiled, perhaps, when I described him as Tom's biggest fan, because he is a huge man and his personality every bit as large as his physique. Say what you might about Albert, you'll never forget him, and he was to be a very loyal friend to Tom, and to British cycling.

Albert's café was the Café den Engel in the Saint Amandsberg part of Ghent, a place that was to become home to hundreds of ambitious Britons in the sixties, over to try their luck and 'do a Simpson'. He ran the place with his mother, known to everyone as 'Ma'. They made Tom very welcome on his first stay, but he wasn't on holiday and Albert soon fixed him up with a ride at the Ghent indoor track, the Sportspaleis.

He was very fit and just too hot to handle for the local Belgian amateur riders he was up against. He lapped the field twice in the distance race Albert entered him for, and thought that this would see him in good stead for more rides at the venue, with the chance of picking up some more easy prize money. He had a shock coming.

Tom went to see the track director, Oscar Daemers, to collect his prize money only to be told that there was no way he was going to be given another ride in an amateur race in Ghent. Daemers told him that people had paid good money to watch the local hopefuls do battle, not to see them get their noses rubbed in it by some Englishman. It was unheard of! Daemers wasn't completely heartless, though. Once Tom had digested this particular fact of life he told him that he obviously had ability and if he came back as a professional there would always be a place for him in the six-day races held at Ghent.

There was nothing for it but to come home. His prize money covered his board and lodgings, and he arrived back in Harworth with just half a crown (12.5 pence for you younger readers) in his pocket. No world record, no pro contract and, of course, no job. So it was back to Glass Bulbs and some explaining to do.

They'd been very good before he went to Zurich; they'd accepted his ambitions to make a life for himself as a professional cyclist; they'd wished him luck; they'd even promised to give him his old job back if things didn't work out. What they didn't expect was to see him back after only three weeks and asking for a job. Not his old one mind, but a labouring one with plenty of overtime so that he could get some money together. You see, the plan hadn't been abandoned, just put back a bit. He was still going to make it, but had to concede that it might be just a bit harder than he had at first thought, that there wasn't a professional contract waiting on every street corner for some ambitious young Englishman to pick up.

He needed money behind him to weather the bad times and worked every hour he could get at the factory, sometimes around the furnaces where he got extra 'heat money'. This went on until February, when he was invited with a British team to take part in a series of events on the indoor track in East Berlin. He was off again and this time he would leave the factory behind for good.

The East Berlin track was notoriously hard to ride with its 56-degree banking, which Tom later told Benny Foster, 'frit me to death, Benny.' He made a big impression on the East Germans, and when the time came for the team to leave they wanted Tom and Karl Barton to stay on for one more week in order to ride in a six-hour Madison race, though this time the officials requested rather than insisted as they had in Bulgaria. Anyway, Tom jumped at the chance: he needed all the experience he could get now – the Germans were paying his expenses, after all – and there was no way he was going back to that factory – not again.

Karl Barton was basically a very good track sprinter so did not relish this six-hour test of stamina as much as Tom, but he remembers it: 'I told Tom to take it easy for the first few laps while we rode ourselves in. True to form, Tom came round for the first change half a lap up on the rest of the field. Now that's not my idea of taking it easy at all.'

Despite his reticence Karl must have found Tom's enthusiasm infectious because with 20 minutes to go they were still in with a chance of victory. Unfortunately, at this point Tom was brought down by another rider, so that was that, another trip to the track hospital, but with just cuts and bruises this time.

It was time to go home again, but not for long: Tom was now convinced that his future was on the continent. For some time he had been talking to George Berger about basing himself abroad. George suggested he look at Brittany, which has always been a hotbed for

French cycling. Also, he had contacts there in that he knew Louison Bobet's trainer, Le Bert, and his brother, Jean, all of whom were Bretons. But where in Brittany should he go? Tom had a friend, David Cooper, from Liverpool, who had raced in St Brieuc, and the previous year at Fallowfield; he had introduced Tom to two brothers, Robert and Yvon Murphy, who lived and raced there. So, as soon as he got back to Harworth, Tom was on to the brothers, and they invited him straightaway to go and stay with them for the start of their racing season in the first week of April.

It was all set then. Tom had just one more weekend of racing as an amateur in this country and then it was off to the continent to make his fortune. The big step that he'd planned almost from the first day he'd turned a pedal in anger was about to be taken, but the weekend was Easter and Tom was racing in all the big track meetings that mark that occasion in this country.

The first is perhaps the most famous of them all, the Good Friday Meeting at London's Herne Hill track, which, over the years, must have been the most popular track event ever held in this country. Crowds of cycling enthusiasts used to flock to the event, many by bike, and the pictures of thousands of bikes stacked together outside the track have to be seen to be believed.

Every year the promoters would engage at least one World Champion to keep the crowds happy and many of the world's greats have ridden there. They were also keen on trying out new events. So, in 1959, as well as having three World Champions on the bill, they had brought over the big pacing motorbikes from East Germany along with their amateur World Champion at this discipline, Lothar Meister.

This kind of racing has sadly declined in popularity in the last few years, and it must be said that races were, shall we say, open to a degree of collusion between the pacers, but there is no denying that it was spectacular. The pacing motors were huge and the pacers sat upright on them, clad in full leathers so that they could give maximum shelter to the riders, who rode on special bikes with smaller front wheels to get them closer to their pacers. The result was very fast racing; and the spectacle of six of these motorbikes, each with their rider furiously pedalling an enormous gear, flying round a track at over 50 miles per hour is a sight and a sound never to be forgotten.

This was the event Tom had been invited to ride. He'd ridden behind these motors once before in a training session whilst in East Berlin, otherwise he was a complete novice. The competition the organisers had brought over was very hot, for as well as the reigning World Champion they had brought over the silver and bronze medallists from 1958, Heinz Wahl and Arie Van Houwelingen, who, incidentally, went on to take the gold in the 1959 championships. Just by chance I recently met Arie in a bar in Amsterdam – it's funny how many ex-cyclists you meet in these places – and he remembers Herne Hill, and in particular the nickname Tom christened him with that day: 'Harry the Hooligan'.

Much to everyone's surprise, Tom beat all these specialists and won the event. The Germans couldn't believe it. They immediately offered to take him back to East Germany and train him for the 1959 Worlds, which they told him they were sure he could win.

What an opportunity! Tom was tempted and one or two British officials tried to encourage him to go, no doubt sniffing an easy gold medal and some reflected glory for themselves; but he wanted to be the best, and that meant being a professional roadman, riding the classics and big tours he'd dreamed about as a kid, so he politely refused their offer. They didn't let it stop there, though, and kept writing to his home in Harworth with improved offers, quite frightening his mother, who was terrified of him disappearing to the East for ever. She was still convinced that they'd tried to kidnap him the previous year in Bulgaria.

At the same time the Elswick Hopper cycle company made Tom an offer to join their team, which would be based in Britain. Tom would not have entertained this, but their manager was Benny Foster and Tom had a great deal of respect for him. Benny was at Herne Hill that day so Tom had a word with him about the two offers and, to his great credit, Benny put Tom's future in front of any personal gain by advising him to stick to his plan and go to France where he told him, 'You are sure to make it.'

Tom knew this all along, but it was nice to hear Benny confirm it. The rest of his weekend continued in the same way as Herne Hill. He won everything he entered at Cardiff, and did the same at Fallowfield on the Monday, though he was disqualified for forcing Norman Sheil to run off the track in their last event, but I think he was a bit demob happy by then and was messing about, though apparently Norman didn't think it funny at the time. Albert Hawes remembers speaking to Tom that day, and Tom told him of his plans: 'I'm off to France tomorrow. I've got £100 to get me by for a bit, so it's shit or bust.'

Tom was now leaving home for good, and not before time, because the day after he left he received an invitation to join Her Majesty's Armed Forces that he was now none too keen to accept. Conscription was still in force in the late fifties and Tom had been deferred once while he completed his draughtsman's training. He'd had a medical in the summer of 1958 and had been approached by the RAF who were on the look-out for athletes. Tom was quite keen to join then, but had heard nothing more, so got on with his life. His mum just sent his call-up papers back, and they both thought that would be the end of it. They were wrong.

It had been a busy time building up to his big move to live in another country – there'd been a lot to do and arrange, so much in fact that he'd forgotten to tell his mum and dad anything about it. There was only time for a hasty goodbye to his mum on the Tuesday morning of his departure and luckily he met his dad off the same bus that took him to Doncaster station, otherwise he'd never have had the opportunity to tell him where he was going.

So off he went with £100, all his worldly goods in a suitcase and a haversack, and his two Carlton bikes. Tom had been a good advert for Carltons with his exploits up till then, and to show their appreciation their two directors, Kevin and Gerald O'Donovan, kindly gave Tom the £100 he needed to set himself up in France out of their own pockets.

The Murphys' home was over the butcher's shop owned by their father, on the old road out of St Brieuc towards Lamballe. Interestingly, if you keep going a few kilometres past it you come to Yffiniac, the birthplace of Bernard Hinault. See what I mean about a hotbed? Anyway, Tom was given a warm welcome, but almost straightaway a problem emerged: he didn't speak a word of French, and Robert and Yvon only had a smattering of English. They managed to communicate by sign language most of the time, which must have been fairly sophisticated as Monsieur Murphy senior managed, through this medium, to inform Tom that the family name was inherited from his Great Grandfather, who was an Irish priest! Well, at least that's what Tom thought he said. But sign language wasn't nearly enough, not for a lad who, his mates back in England would testify, couldn't stay quiet for more than two minutes on end, and it started to get him down.

The language barrier also presented more practical problems. Once the racing started he had to find riders who would tell him where the lap prizes were and when the last lap was on. And, believe it or not, they didn't always tell him the truth.

He soon adapted to the racing over there, though; most of the events were held on small circuits and were very fast, as the riders fought for the lucrative lap prizes on offer. With his track-racing background and bags of speed in his legs, Tom quickly started winning the lap prizes and, very soon after, the races themselves.

To keep in touch, and I think to cheer himself up a bit, he wrote plenty of letters back home. Cyril Cartwright has one, dated 1st May 1959, in which Tom tells him, 'I have raced seven times on the road and had four wins and earned £150.' 'Not a bad start to a pro career,' says Cyril. Not a bad start, indeed – he'd only been there a month.

His successes, coupled no doubt with the fact that he was English, soon started to attract a lot of publicity, a fact not lost on one local businessman, the owner of Vins Santa Rosa who became Tom's first official sponsor now that he had received his independent (semi-pro) licence from the B.C.F. Now he had the opportunity to really show what he could do racing against men who had even ridden the Tour de France. He was soon beating them as well, but the language problem was really getting him down now. Then something happened that made all the difference in the world, something which, he once told John Geddes, if it hadn't happened, then he probably would have come home.

One day on returning from a training ride Tom found all the Murphys waiting for him and grinning like Cheshire cats. Sensing that the poor lad was a bit down in the dumps they were all excited because they'd found out a bit of news that was bound to cheer him up. With a great deal of arm waving and whistles and suggestive facial expressions, they got through to Tom that there was an English girl working as an *au pair* for a French family who lived on the same street as them, and they proudly produced a piece of paper bearing the address.

Great, thought Tom, somebody to talk to at last, and a girl, too. So, off he trotted clutching his piece of paper, but it wasn't quite as simple as that, and this only dawned on him after ringing some unknown Frenchman's doorbell. What if she didn't answer the door? How was he going to mime that one? No, he couldn't go through with it and ran off up the road like some schoolboy doing a prank, not daring to look behind in case someone had seen him.

Helen Sherburn, the girl in question, didn't know any of this, but she had been told about Tom by the family she was staying with, whose son was interested in cycling. So, one day soon after Tom's aborted visit, curiosity got the better of her and she set off to find this English cyclist everybody was talking about.

It was a sunny day, and when Helen arrived at the Murphys' she saw Tom sitting reading in the garden. Tall, dark and with very continental-looking sunglasses perched on his long nose, he looked to Helen nothing like an Englishman, so she asked him, 'C'est ici où le jeune Anglais habite?' Tom, not understanding a word of this and getting a bit fed up with the locals wandering up to the garden fence and peering at him as though he was the man from Mars (remember British cyclists were a rarity in those days, and ones that won races were even rarer), thought to himself, 'Oh no, not another nosy Froggy.'

If you can, imagine Helen's surprise when the gentleman she'd made this polite request of replied in a broad Yorkshire accent, 'Bugger off.' Then imagine Tom's when Helen calmly said, 'Oh it's you is it?' Not exactly Romeo and Juliet, was it?

They were even more surprised to find that since Helen's home was Sutton, a village just north of Doncaster, they only lived about fifteen miles from each other, but they both enjoyed a really good chat right there in the Murphys' back garden, and Tom was instantly happier for meeting her. He never really looked back after meeting Helen, and even though he was away racing a lot he visited her whenever he could. Also, being fluent in French, she was a great help with Tom's efforts at learning the language.

Never one to do things by half, Tom decided to take formal lessons from an Englishman in St Brieuc with the improbable name of Professor Batman. He didn't find it easy and, because of his hybrid Geordie/Yorkshire accent, struggled manfully with the pronunciation exercises the Professor gave him. He had to perform these in front of a mirror so that he could get the correct shape of mouth to produce the required sound, much to the Murphys' delight.

By mid May Tom had won 12 local races and got the chance to ride his first stage race, a four-day race around the Brittany peninsula, for riders under 25 years, called the Essor Breton.

The first two days were fairly uneventful – Tom's French was still not up to much and most of the well-meaning advice he was getting from various supporters was going over his head. Then, at the start of the third day, a funny little Frenchman came up to him (you know, the real stereotype – striped T-shirt, beret, and breathing garlic fumes) and he got it across to Tom that he had to attack in such and such a place.

Well, he did attack and, with a 75-kilometre break that eventually proved unsuccessful, he impressed everyone – everyone that is except the little Frenchman who was at the finish and gave Tom a proper telling off for attacking in the wrong place. Next day he told him he should attack at Le Faou, and just so that there could be no misunderstanding he would be there himself with a flag. He said that when Tom saw the flag it was time to attack.

Whatever his new friend thought, Tom had ridden well and greatly impressed the Breton journalist and former French Free Forces fighter pilot, Yvan Clech, who wrote the following about him in his paper the *Télegramme de Brest*: 'We sincerely believe we spent a privileged day today, watching the blossoming out of a real champion.'

Next day Tom nearly fell off his bike with surprise when the race got to Le Faou because there by the roadside, madly waving the Union Jack of all things, was the little Frenchman from the day before. What could Tom do but attack? So he did, making a series of attacks as they came out of the town with 40 kilometres to go. Only one rider went with him, the aptly named Bastard from Morlaix. Tom did ten kilometres on the front then moved over and waved this other rider through, but he refused, saying, 'I can't do it' which Tom mistook for a swear word so left him behind. Anyway, I'll let Clech take over now, because he was there:

The margin grew – 40, 45 then 50 seconds. Then came the final hill and Tom appeared in difficulties.
'How many kilometres?' he shouted to us.
'Fifteen,' we shouted back.
It was enough – fifteen kilometres, mostly downhill. Tom's style returned and he stayed away to win.

Tom ended up with that stage victory and second place overall, just two seconds behind the winner, so they would have been chasing him on that last stage, make no mistake. It had been a good race, and the first in which he'd made the headlines in France. The only downside was that he never saw his little Frenchman again.

Straight after the race offers of a ride with bigger teams came winging their way to St Brieuc. The professional Margnat Rochet team were particularly keen to get hold of Tom, but he turned them down in favour of getting a little more experience with the younger riders. Why? Because he'd received an offer which, in the long run, held far more promise than the one from Margnat. This was from the St Rapha/VC 12 club, the set-up behind one of the best pro teams of the day, St Raphaël-Geminiani. Their proposal was a place in their squad for the Route de France, an eight-stage race for under 25-year-olds from the French national and regional squads, and a good ride would put Tom in a great position for a full professional contract with St Raphaël, and that was what he wanted.

Meanwhile, it was back to earning a living in the local Breton races, where he carried on winning, and his popularity in the area carried on growing as his exploits became more widely known, so much so that when John Geddes went over to ride a few races there he remembers: 'Some tailor had made Tom a suit of clothes and was using pictures of him dressed in them on billboards all over Brittany. Wherever I went I kept looking up and seeing great big pictures of him grinning back at me, all toffed up in this suit. They really loved him over there.'

Another familiar face who turned up was Norman Sheil: 'Tom had asked me to go with him in the spring of 1959, but I was a married man by then and had commitments, so I couldn't go, but I did go over and ride some races there with him. You asked me what he was like, what made him different. Well, I'll tell you two stories that happened over there that illustrate what he was like.

Norman was speaking to me at the World Masters Track Championships in Manchester where he became a world champion once more, this time in the over-65 category. Old bike-riders don't even fade away, you see! He went on:

In one race he crashed and ripped the whole of the back of his jersey off and skinned his back. He just got straight back on and won the race. Won the race, mind! Another time he attacked on a descent and flew down this hill, faster than anyone else dared. Anyway, we went round this bend and it was covered in new loose gravel. There was a pile of it on the outside and when Tom got to it he was going so fast that he just went straight across the bend and buried himself in it, bike and everything. That was Tom: he took too many risks, risks other riders wouldn't take. One day, some years later, I even told him that he would kill himself on his bike. I really thought that he would kill himself the way he went down mountains, or the way he drove. I would never, ever get in a car with him.

A couple of years later Norman was back on the continent riding full time for the Helyett-Leroux team. About his experiences of Tom then, Norman told me:

By then the Europeans, the best ones – I mean Anquetil, and the like – had serious respect for Tom. He could ride them off his wheel and really made them think. I saw this, being in a rival team; the managers respected him and when they were handing out jobs no one wanted to mark Tom, they didn't want the responsibility. That's what they thought of him.

This was in the future. Tom now had to raise his game for the Route de France. This was a different league from what he had been used to. Most of the guys in this race were going to become pros and it was a shop window for them, so they weren't going to hang about.

They didn't. The first stage was 196 kilometres, run off through the pouring rain at an average speed of 27 miles per hour, and Tom sat in the middle of the bunch all day, terrified that he might not last, as this first stage alone was the longest race he'd ever ridden. But he came through it unscathed, ready to face the test of the next stage. And what a test it was – his first taste of the high mountains.

Like today's Tour de L' Avenir, the Route de France saw itself as an apprenticeship for potential Tour de France riders and, as such, included in its itinerary a trip into one of France's great mountain ranges, climbing the same passes as the big Tour. In 1959 it was the turn of the Pyrenees.

Tom was completely unsure of how to ride these mountains, so on that first day he sought the advice of the team mechanic. His French still not being up to scratch, he had a lot of difficulty understanding what the mechanic was saying to him. Eventually, the exasperated spanner man mimed a slow pedalling action and said the words, *'Touriste, touriste,'* which Tom took to mean that he should climb the mountains very easily, like a tourist.

What he was most probably trying to tell Tom was that he should ride within himself and not make violent efforts from which he couldn't recover. This is sound advice when climbing these 10- to 15-mile passes or cols as they are known in France, but Tom took him too literally, and once he got to the giant Tourmalet climb, he just stuck it in bottom gear, and pedalled gently upwards.

He really enjoyed himself, climbing the 2,000 metres up to the snow banks at the summit and admiring the views along the way, but from being in a small break at the bottom of the climb, he arrived at the top nearly ten minutes down on the last man, having hardly broken into a sweat. Once up there and informed of his position in the race Tom realised that this couldn't have been how the mechanic meant him to ride, and over the rest of the race he got more into the tempo of racing up mountains.

His lack of understanding of the language got him into trouble off the bike as well. Wanting to learn as much as possible, he insisted on asking his own questions of hotel staff or race officials rather than have someone do it for him – it was the only way to learn. Unfortunately, cyclists being what they are and fond of a practical joke, sometimes his team mates would provide him with phrases that were less than helpful. For example, in one of the Route de France stage towns he wanted to ask the lady at the reception desk of a rather posh hotel where the bathroom was. Armed with the phrase his mischievous mates had given him, he approached the lady, blurted out a rather vulgar request of her and was very taken aback when she brought her husband out to him. Very embarrassing, but all was explained and it did Tom no harm with the race journalists who were always interviewing him in the hope that he would let slip other little pearls.

Tom got through the mountains relatively unscathed and on the last stage still had a lot in reserve. This wasn't his typical way of racing, but it was so important not to get dropped and look outclassed in this company that it had affected his style of riding. It wasn't until just under 50 miles to go on the final stage that Tom knew he would finish and, therefore, still be in with a shout for that contract with St Raphaël. Now it was time to show what he could do. He did – he attacked and time trialled his way to the finish, spending the energy he'd been hoarding over the previous seven days. The whole bunch was after him, but he just held them off and greatly impressed the people involved with the VC 12 organisation, including the *directeur sportif* of the St Raphaël team, Raymond Louviot, who summoned Tom to Paris so that he could have a good look at him.

Louviot had been a good professional rider in the 1930s with victories in the GP des Nations and had been French National Champion; he was an even better *directeur sportif*. This is the man who in professional cycling largely directs team tactics, both in pre-race briefings and out on the road from the team car. Of course the riders have a say, but less so the further down the pecking order they are. Anyway, Louviot was one of the best and also had an amazing memory. He remembered everything about any race he was involved with and his prowess was legendary. Sometimes riders in his teams used to test him by saying things like, 'Let's ask him about such and such a race in 1935 and see if the story changes this time', but it never did.

Louviot told Tom that he was very happy with his riding and asked him if he would ride for the team again, later on that year in the Tour de L'Ouest. He told Tom that this was a big professional stage race and some of the biggest names would be riding. He gave him two tyres and a St Raphaël jersey saying, 'Now go away and make sure you are properly prepared, and don't lose too many races in the meantime.' Tom was on cloud nine.

A few weeks later they met again when the Tour de France was in Brittany and Tom went to the hotel where the British team were staying to visit Brian Robinson, who rode for St Raphaël, and was riding the Tour. Robinson really is the father of British cycling success on the continent – just the previous year he had become the first Briton to win a stage in the Tour de France, a feat he repeated in 1959 – and he was to have a huge influence on Tom in the coming years. Of this first visit he remembers having a 'laugh and a joke, as you always did with Tom', and introducing him once more to Louviot, who by then had done much more homework on Tom, and had decided to sign him up with the team full-time after the Tour de L'Ouest.

After the Tour de France Tom got his first taste of the big time when he was contracted to ride in a track meeting at Landerneau in Brittany against some of the professional stars who, only the previous day, had finished the big Tour. Now, the idea behind having some local talent in these races is to provide a bit of home-town interest for the crowds, so they can see how they fare against the big boys. They are not supposed to win! But nobody had told Tom, and it went down none too well with men like Jean Stablinski who had won the Tour of Spain in 1958, and Jean Graczyk, winner of the green points jersey in the Tour de France, when he won most of the events at the meeting. Tom had cause to realise his foolishness the following year when he finished his first Tour de France a near physical wreck.

Also riding this meeting was a real larger-than-life character who was more famous for his antics off the bike, or during the quiet parts of races, than he was for his victories. Roger Hassenforder, the 'pedalling clown' as the press dubbed him, was a real entertainer whose practical jokes were legendary. It didn't matter how he was riding – although he was good, make no mistake about that – he could send the crowds home happy. So he was a must at track meetings like this, or round-the-houses criterium races where the public have to pay to watch. In the end he earned a fortune playing the pedalling clown, a fact not lost on Tom who, though he never got up to the standard of Hassenforder's pranks, developed his own crowd-pleasing tricks over the years and consequently was popular with the people who handed out the contracts for these races.

You could write a book on Hassenforder's antics, but my favourite story is about the fat gendarme who used to work with the motorbike escort on all the big races in France. This guy was a real pest, always scrounging food, even from the riders. As soon as they'd passed through a feeding station, and were transferring the rations from the *musettes* the team helpers had handed them to their pockets, he'd be around asking for anything they didn't want. Well, Roger got fed up with this and one day rode up behind the gendarme carrying a bulging musette which he told him was specially for him. The gendarme took it, of course, and feeling its weight was drooling in anticipation at the feast within, only to find that it contained a large, dead cat!

At last the big day came and Tom took his place with the Rapha team in the Tour de L'Ouest. They were a mixed bag of young and experienced riders, and on the first two days worked well together to put one of their number, Pierre Everaert, in the leader's jersey. Everything was fine – a Frenchman at the head of a French team leading a big French race.

The *status quo* was preserved for the next three days. Then, on the sixth stage, the Rapha team let things get a bit out of hand when a breakaway group built up a lead on the road over Everaert that threatened to put him out of first place on the overall classification. Tom, who'd been playing the ideal team mate role to perfection, decided to act, and tried to pace Everaert up to the break. Unfortunately, the Frenchman couldn't keep up, so Tom innocently thought that someone, at least, from the Rapha team should get up there and pressed on without him, soon bridging the gap.

Meanwhile, back in the bunch, all hell was breaking out. Pete Ryalls from Sheffield, a friend and rival of Tom's from their junior road-racing days, was riding this race with a rival team and he takes over the story:

> The Rapha team didn't want Tom to win; they wanted a Frenchman to win, so they had to get him back. Their team manager went round trying to get other teams chasing because they couldn't be seen to be doing it themselves. But this wasn't enough, so eventually all the Rapha team were chasing, as well. I tried to block them because, obviously, I wanted Tom to stay away, especially with what was happening behind, but they were going so fast it was all I could do to hang on. The whole race was chasing Tom.

They didn't catch him, though, and he made contact with the break with just one kilometre to go and went straight past them to win the stage and, despite the efforts of his team, take over the yellow jersey of race leadership. He couldn't believe it: some of the biggest names in the game were riding that race! It was a big win, especially for a 21-year-old Englishman.

Next day he tightened his grip on the overall standings, proving that he was the strongest in the race by winning the time trial stage to establish a lead of nearly three minutes on the second-placed man overall. He looked a safe bet to win with only one more stage left, the longest of the race, from Brest to his adopted home town of St Brieuc, but there were dark forces at work.

Tom wasn't supposed to win this race. It might be hard to understand now, when the world is a much smaller place, but in those days the cycling establishment wasn't falling over itself to welcome outsiders; they didn't mind plucky triers, but winning was different. The Rapha team simply didn't want Tom to win, not yet, anyway: he wasn't accepted yet. So they hatched a plan to use this long stage to defeat him.

Very early in the stage Jo Morvan, an experienced pro and himself a Breton, got a small break going and nobody from the field chased them. The lead grew to six minutes, and Tom got more and more concerned. He kept trying to get his team mates, who were, of course, all in on the plot to do him down, to chase, but they kept assuring him that the break wouldn't last to the finish. Then fate stepped in and he punctured. One of his team, making a good show of it, gave up his bike, but it was too big, so in the end there was nothing Tom could do about the situation under his own steam. He eventually finished in the main field and Morvan, who'd been working like a maniac in the break, stayed away and took the race overall.

Tom had learnt a bitter lesson: he knew now that it wouldn't be enough to be as good as or even a bit better than the Europeans: he had to be a lot better; he had to force acceptance on them, and this realisation affected the way he raced from that day on. He had made some friends, though: the journalist, René de Latour, for example, was particularly scathing of the Rapha team's tactics and wasn't afraid to say so when writing about the race. Louviot was also sympathetic, and perhaps sorry for what had taken place, and straightaway offered Tom what he had always wanted, a full pro contract with the Rapha-Gitane team. He was to be paid the princely sum of £28.50 per month, and just to show his fairness, and that he hadn't necessarily agreed with what had happened to Tom on the Tour de L'Ouest, Louviot personally raised this by £7.50 per month to try and make amends. No doubt, he was also anxious to ensure that nobody else could come along and lure away his 'discovery'.

Tom had now arrived at the highest levels of the sport – cycling's Premier League. It had taken him just four months to get there from being a raw novice ex-track rider, winning his first local races in Brittany. Now he was about to make his debut in his first world championships as a professional. He would ride two events. First, on the track in the pro pursuit, then – the jewel of the crown – in the pro road race. And it would be one of the best debuts at this level the cycling world has ever seen.

He had left behind him an interesting legacy in Breton cycling, though. This was discovered a couple of years later by Lenny Jones when he went over there to try his luck:

> I went over to St Brieuc in 1962, and Tom wasn't popular with some of the British riders over there, I can tell you. Quite a few riders from the south, especially teachers, used to go over there for a sort of racing holiday in the summer. They weren't brilliant riders, but could pick up enough money in third- and fourth-category events to get by. Anyway, this all stopped after Tom had been there, and if you were British they automatically used to make you a first-category. They thought everyone must be as good as Tom. Well, these blokes couldn't win anything as first-categories, so Tom had ruined their holidays.

Lenny chuckles at the memory, though I must tell you that it didn't affect him – he won plenty of races over there in 1962 and '63.

Just before the Worlds Tom spent a little time training in Italy. It was another country so a good opportunity to write home. In a letter dated 29th August Tom tells his mum and dad: 'Well, I'm professional now so there's no turning back. Now I am fixed up with a contract for next year I am quite secure. If I keep in reasonable form I can expect about £75 a week.' Not bad for 1959, when his dad wasn't on much more than £10. He ends the letter in typical style – he always was much happier speaking than writing: 'Well, I can't think of much more to say except for you to wish everyone all the best from me and tell them I am having a good time, but it's harder work than the factory.'

It was the turn of Holland to host the World Championships in 1959. The track racing would be on the big open-air Amsterdam track, and the road racing on the nearby motor-racing circuit at Zandvoort. In accordance with the tradition of the time the track racing started off the championships and Tom was very confident about his chances in the pursuit, despite having done no special training for this specialist event. He reasoned that it was only a year since he was up with the best in the amateur event and that, after a year of hard road races, the longer (5,000 metres) distance of the pro pursuit would suit him.

He qualified for the quarter-finals with the third-fastest time in beating the Swiss rider, Max Wirth. Then he faced Belgium's Brankaert, a specialist pursuiter and time triallist. Now his lack of specialised training showed as he lagged behind Brankaert for the first 4,000 metres; then his strength came through and he started gradually to gain on his opponent. If the race had been 5,100 metres he would have won, but it wasn't: Tom was beaten by just 0.3 seconds, so he was out.

To say that he hadn't expected that is an understatement. He was distraught and once inside the changing rooms fell into the arms of Tommy Godwin, the British team manager, and wept like a child. He really had expected to win, but Godwin, like the good manager and experienced competitor he was, got to work on him straight away. He convinced him that he couldn't have expected to beat the specialists who'd been preparing just for this race, not with all the road racing he'd been doing, What Tom had to do, said Tommy, was get himself back together ready for Sunday's road race – then he'd show them all just how good he was.

He did, too. At 180 miles, the Championship was the longest race Tom had ever ridden; it was also the first professional single-day race he'd ridden. The best in the world were assembled on this wind-swept circuit amongst the sand dunes on the Dutch coast, all in their national rather than trade team jerseys, and all dedicated to getting one of their men into the rainbow jersey which the World Champion is entitled to wear for the year following his victory.

So, his World Championships: Tom should have been overawed, but he just didn't have time. He never gave himself time to think this way, which was one of the reasons for his success. Almost from the start a break of ten riders formed. It looked a promising move so, after 63 miles, Tom bridged the gap across to this break and started to work hard – very hard.

This was all new to him: he only knew the name of one rider in the break, the Dutchman, Geldermans, who had been on the Rapha team in the Tour de L'Ouest. He didn't know that he was showing his hand by doing too much work; he didn't know that the blond-haired French rider in the break was none other than André Darrigade, a multiple Tour de France stage winner and one of the best roadman sprinters in the world; nor did he know that Darrigade had paid the Dutch riders there to try and prevent Tom from winning.

As the finish approached their lead began to dwindle, so Tom went on the attack, only to be brought back each time by a Dutch rider and, anyway, the strong wind was making it unlikely now that a lone rider would succeed. It was going to come down to a sprint, but whose wheel should he follow for a good lead out? 'Belgians are good sprinters,' he thought, so he sat on Fore, but Darrigade produced a blistering sprint to win with Fore in third place, still followed by fourth-placed Tom.

In the end he had been just too shattered to raise a sprint, but fourth place in the Worlds, after just weeks as a pro, and at 21! Just to put that in perspective, in the whole history of this race only one British rider has finished higher – ever! And that, of course, was Tom when he won it in 1965. I know I'm labouring this a bit, but it's difficult to get across what an achievement it was. Perhaps only someone who has ridden the World Pro Road Race can do that, so I'm going to let one try.

Dave Lloyd was the best British rider of his generation. He was a member of the famous T.I. Raleigh team, backed by British money, with a mixture of British and continental riders under the management of a Dutchman, Peter Post. Their aim was to win the best races – the classics and national tours – but within five years Post felt that the only way they were going to do that was with a full compliment of continental riders. That is, except for Dave Lloyd – he was the only British rider Post kept. He was that good. In 1975 he rode the World Road Race at Yvoir; he finished twenty-third, the only British finisher from a full team. And this is how he remembers it:

It's the hardest race of the year, just a constant selection, a wearing-down process until only the strongest are left. I was flying, the fittest I'd ever been. I'd been racing with the best over there all year. It was hilly. We had to climb the big hill 21 times. Towards the end, a break went away containing Gimondi, Zoetemelk, and Kuiper, who won. I thought that was it, so I chased and got across to them. Almost as I got to them it came together again. Then the pace went up again, the race went up a gear, and I just couldn't follow. Perhaps I shouldn't have chased, but I thought it was the winning break. But those guys, even some in that break, just went again. You should have seen me at the finish: I was as thin as I'd ever been. I was just shattered. Next day, I was in bed, and Kuiper was racing again.

There, that's how Dave remembers 'his' Worlds. Every year is the same. It starts fast then gets faster, a constant selection until the race finds somebody good enough to be called World Champion.

Meanwhile, back in 1959, Tom was getting huge praise in the press for his good ride. Darrigade was particularly generous, saying that their break only stayed away because of Tom's strong riding. He also did what he could to make sure that Tom got some good contracts to appear in criterium races. So, even though he didn't earn a medal for his efforts, he was still able to earn some serious money, and that's what it's all about.

Harworth Cycling Club: Tom is back-row right; Harry is in
the front row, second from the left. (*Author's collection*)

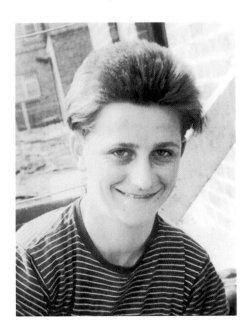

Tom, aged 16
(*Author's collection*)

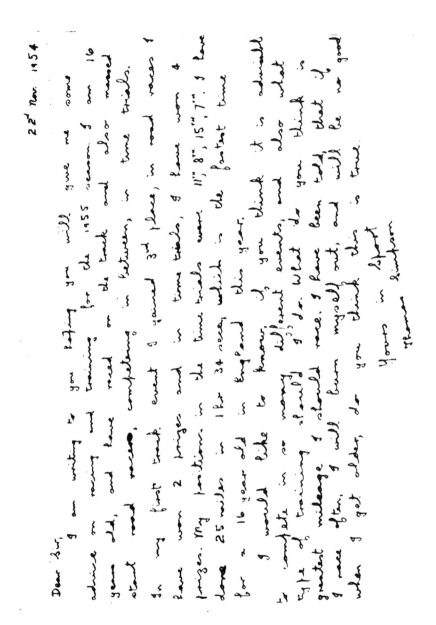

Letter written by 16-year-old Tom to Charles Pélissier, director of the Simplex training camp, and passed on to J. B. Wadley who was assisting at the camp. Wadley published the letter in *Sporting Cyclist* after Tom became World Champion in 1965. (*Cycling Weekly*)

On the wheel of Ron Coe in a race in Derbyshire, 1957; Tom is wearing the Italian national jersey which he acquired for his team from the Scala Wheelers.
(*Author's collection*)

Tom's last race as an amateur: Fallowfield Track, Manchester, Easter Monday Meet, 1959. Mr McCann, MP for Rochdale, presents the *Daily Herald* Gold Trophy with Meet organiser, Norman Grattage, in the middle.

Tour du Sud-Est, 1960: first professional stage-race victory.
(*Cycling Weekly*)

Master and apprentice:
Brian Robinson and Tom.
Tour de France, 1960
(*Cycling Weekly*)

Tour de France, 1960: time trial. (*Presse Sports*)

First Classic victory – Tour of Flanders, 1961:
Tom winning the sprint from Nino de Filippis.
(*Cycling Weekly*)

Tour de France, 1962; end of the stage 12 at St Gaudens and Mr Tom wears the *maillot jaune*. He eventually finished sixth overall in Paris.
(*Central Press*)

6

CLASSICS, MONUMENTS, MARRIAGE
AND THE TOUR

Tom also walked straight into the Rapha first team for the two end-of-season classic races, the Paris–Tours and the Tour of Lombardy. The classics are the name given to a number of single-day races that, because of their geography or history, have captured people's imaginations, and evolved to be bigger and more special than the rest. To win one makes you part of cycling history. Within them, five are called 'monuments'. Win one of those and you are immortal.

Tom's first was the Paris–Tours, the sprinter's classic. A flat to undulating run south-west from Paris to finish on the straight and wide main boulevard in Tours. The race traditionally favours that rough, tough and fast breed of cyclist who can win a race in front of a massed, flat-out, elbow-to-elbow sprint. In the action all day, Tom finished sixteenth in a bunched sprint just a few metres behind the winner, Rik Van Looy of Belgium.

There, we're getting to some legendary names now, aren't we? And, in his last race of 1959, the Baracchi Trophy, Tom had the honour of riding against the biggest legend of them all, his boyhood hero, Fausto Coppi. This sadly turned out to be Coppi's last race: a few months later the cycling world was shocked by the news of his death from a tropical disease, contracted whilst away on a hunting trip. Tom finished this two-man time trial in a very creditable fourth place, riding with his French team mate, Gérard Saint, who was himself killed in a car crash six months later.

Just before this race Tom made his first acquaintance with one of the monuments, Italy's race of the falling leaves, the Tour of Lombardy. Van Looy won again here, completing an amazing Autumn double that only one other man has ever achieved – the Dutch rider, Jo De Roo, and he did it in consecutive years, 1962 and '63.

Lombardy would see some inspired racing from Tom in later years, but by now he was feeling the effects of a long season and, although he finished the race, his riding was rather subdued. For once he had things other than cycling on his mind. As thoughts about racing left his head, thoughts of Helen had filled it and he was sure now that 'she was the girl for me'. Not that he could do much about it as she had now gone to work for a family in Germany; but on his return to England he put in some groundwork by visiting her parents, all togged up in his new suit in an effort to create a good impression on them.

Tom enjoyed relaxing a bit with friends and entertaining them with stories of his exploits in France. He always was a good storyteller and a natural entertainer with perfect timing, just like the comedians he listened to as a kid, though, as John Geddes recalls, 'he sometimes changed his stories to suit a particular set of circumstances' .

This ability, and his new-found fame, meant that he was very much in demand as a guest speaker at cycling club dinners. Early in 1960 at the Sheffield Racing Club's big night, Dick Snowdon, the famous local cycling journalist who was the first person from the media to predict great things for Tom way back in his junior days, asked him about his plans for 1960. Tom said that at that stage he wasn't planning to ride the Tour de France – the team didn't want him to – but they were going to give him some experience in the Tours of Italy or Spain instead. Dick also asked Tom if he was looking forward to returning to the 'hectic pro racing game in France which some British champions had described as tough, gruelling and near killing'. Tom replied: 'It's nothing like that. I enjoy it now that I have got the confidence.' There it is again, that attitude: Tom never would let himself make things out to be tougher than they were. If he made the wall out in his mind to be too high, then he knew that he never would be able to climb it.

Tom's life was rather like a British summer. Optimistic plans would follow bright sunshine, only to be ruined by rain; and dark clouds were rolling towards him now in those first few days of January 1960. The question of his call-up raised its ugly head again. Everything had gone quiet after his mum returned his papers at Easter, but someone was making waves now that Tom was back in England and very much in the limelight. A jealous English cyclist? It could have been. Anyway, just after Christmas he was summoned to yet another medical.

This was bad news. Eighteen months in the RAF could have ended his career. For some reason the knives were really out for him and even the national press, sensing a scandal no doubt, got hold of the story. Throughout the year, Tom was to find this episode being raked over time and again, usually after he'd had a victory, and he was constantly on the defensive trying to explain himself.

Luckily, the RAF's wheels turned a lot slower than Tom's did, and after being assured by his enlisting officer that 'they would soon have him in', once more they missed him by a day. His call-up papers arrived the day after he'd left for France to attend the Rapha training camp in Narbonne. His mum returned them, but the press stories continued and even she was interviewed in her home by journalists searching for the 'truth' about 'The Man Who Refused To Fight For His Country', as one paper had it.

Tom was picked up in Harworth by his new team mate, Brian Robinson, and together they travelled to Narbonne. Older and more experienced than Tom, Brian had already done some of the things Tom wanted to do: he'd won two stages in the Tour de France; he'd finished on the podium of a monument with third place in the 1957 Milan–San Remo. It's fair to say that he was the first British rider to force acceptance on the continentals, to break down their prejudices. Without Brian it would have been more difficult for Tom and, I think, for all the English speakers who followed – those who made their mark on the sport and won big races, all along the line from Shay Elliott and Barry Hoban to Millar, Yates, Lemond, Kelly, Anderson, Roche, and up to the present day with Chris Boardman and Lance Armstrong.

Brian's greatest asset was his intelligence. It was why he was able to make the most of himself physically and to adapt, both to the circumstances of a race, and to a different life from the one he'd lived at home in the Yorkshire mill-town of Mirfield. He is a serious and careful man who could read a race as others would a book. He was just what Tom needed in his first full professional season, someone mature, who'd been around the block and knew his way back, someone who could help channel his prodigious talents, but Brian wistfully admits: 'I would have gladly swapped a little experience for some of Tom's energy and enthusiasm.'

Training camps serve two purposes: an obvious one in getting fit, and a more subtle one in ensuring that the team gets used to the communal living that is forced upon them at times during the year. To be a cohesive group they must get on together, and not fitting in can be as harmful to a young rider's prospects as bad results. The Rapha camp went like a dream. Spirits were bound to be high as Roger Hassenforder was there and he found a willing accomplice in Tom. It was just like being back with the 'Foster circus' in Russia, learning the ropes and getting accepted. Fitting in was second nature to Tom. John Geddes remembers him 'just being able to live anywhere: he used to stay at my house and all over the place, and this was when he was a teenager, remember. He could just get on with people and didn't seem to need support from home – he was a very independent kid.'

The serious stuff had to be done, too, and plenty of training and early season races on the Côte d'Azure got Tom into shape for his first big challenge of the year, the Milan–San Remo classic. This is a big one, a beautiful race, Italy's other great cycling monument; known by the Italian word for spring, 'Primavera', it is traditionally held on or about 19th March, St Joseph's day. It is famous for its big field, always well over 200 riders, and its dramatic course up and over the 'capi' of the Italian Riviera with spectacular views over the blue Mediterranean Sea.

That year, 1960, saw the first inclusion of the famous Poggio climb, almost in the streets of San Remo itself. Not particularly long or steep, but its proximity to the finish means that it has been the scene of some of the most memorable moments in the history of this race. The winner has got to be able to climb the Poggio with the best because its helter-skelter descent empties almost directly out onto the finishing straight, the Via Roma, and by then it's far too late to make up any lost ground.

The race is also famous for its length, at least 280 kilometres, but that didn't worry Tom as much as the huge field of riders, most of them Italian, and most of them wanting to be seen at the front of their classic. Consequently, they ride shoulder to shoulder, sometimes bouncing off the rockfaces at the side of the climbs. Barry Hoban, riding his first Milan–San Remo a few years later, said, 'You can't fall off because there isn't room: the riders are packed in too tightly.' The typical Simpson solution to this problem was simple: clear off on your own. So he did.

Tom attacked at the foot of the first climb, the Turchino Pass, right at the end of the flat run across the Lombardy plain from Milan, and right at the end of the wide roads. At the top he was one minute clear and, after turning right at the coast to begin the run westwards towards San Remo, his lead had grown to two minutes. He was really enjoying himself now, as the road twisted and turned around rocky headlands and over winding climbs like the Capo Berta, always with the blue sea over his left shoulder, and always following the lowering sun.

He forged onwards, but he'd made a big mistake: he was basing his effort on a shouted distance check from the team car. He thought they'd said *'soixante-dix kilometres'*, whereas, in fact, they'd said *'cent-dix'* – 110 not 70 – and Tom was flat-out thinking he'd only 70 kilometres left to ride, and two minutes in hand – enough to win his first classic.

Those missing 40 kilometres were his undoing, and he was caught and dropped on the Poggio climb by the eventual winner, René Privat. Next, Gastone Nencini got up to Tom and led him over the top, but on the twisting descent they were both caught by the main field, and that was that. His gamble hadn't quite worked. If there had been only 70 kilometres left then maybe he'd have won, because he was caught well after that point. But 'ifs' and 'maybes' don't win races.

Milan–San Remo signals the end of the first phase of the professional cycling season. The races in the mild Riviera climate of the south were over and now it was time for the northern classics. It was, also, after two months of living out of a suitcase, time to put down some roots and find a more permanent base.

Being the 'senior pro' Brian got on with this job and found them a small apartment to share in the Porte de Clichy area of Paris, not far from the centre of the stylish French capital. Tom loved this, and while Brian got on with the practical stuff like paperwork and buying furniture, Tom enjoyed his first few days there, cruising the shops and trying to look as sophisticated and Parisian as he could in as short a time as possible. It was all over too quickly and the treadmill beckoned once more with a race which, coincidentally, started in the two British boys' new home city, the Paris–Roubaix.

Well, it starts just north of Paris if you want to be pedantic, but it is some race, nevertheless. There isn't another one quite like it; of all the monuments it is surely the most monumental. It's not the distance – all the big races are long. It's not the hills – there's hardly a change in elevation along the entire route. Sometimes it's the weather – you can't hold a bike race at Easter in northern Europe and expect the sun to shine. No, it's quite simply the roads; more particularly the dreadful cobbled cart tracks that interlace the pan-flat beet fields of northern France.

The race starts innocently enough, nowadays, from Compiègne, and bowls along northwards on wide, well-surfaced main roads. But as the riders approach St Quentin a sense of urgency takes over because everybody wants to be at the front when the carnage begins on the first cart track, known throughout the cycling world almost affectionately as *pavé*. This is a simple and all-encompassing word for a cobbled road, but it does nothing to convey the hell Paris–Roubaix has in store for its contestants. No, it doesn't even go half-way to describing the treacherous bone-jarring surfaces that wait to trap the unwary or the weak. The only way to ride over their cambered surface, with a profile like a set of bad teeth, is to attack them hard and fast in as big a gear as possible. This requires strength – you have to do it time and time again, and each time a few riders blow and they are gone; only the strongest survive – only the strongest and the most acrobatic, because if it rains the surface becomes like ice. If you can't ride them, then you can't ride them: it's as simple as that. The famous stretches such as Mons-en-Pevele, Wallers-Arenberg and the Carrefour de L' Arbre are just as big in cycling folklore as the Galibier and Tourmalet mountain climbs and, like them, just as special in the demands they make of a rider – though, of course, the greats can ride them all.

At first, Tom didn't think he'd be able to ride on them at all. As a kid he'd eaten up pictures of Coppi and Van Steenbergen racing over the roads of the 'Hell of the North'. Now, in a training session during the week running up to the race, he was all at sea on the *pavé*, which he described as 'cart tracks that haven't been repaired since Napoleon's army marched over them'. But Tom in training and Tom in a race were two different people.

On the Sunday of the race, as always on a big occasion, he was inspired. As soon as he smelt the cobbles he was off on his own, just like Coppi. Now he found that at race speed he could ride them. This really was history in the making because the 1960 Paris–Roubaix was the first race ever to be televised live and put out over the Eurovision network. Nowadays, even in this country, we're spoilt for cycling coverage, thanks to *Eurosport* and the very venerable David Duffield, but this Sunday in hell was the first coverage of the kind we've grown used to, with mobile cameras on motorbikes, and helicopter shots beamed live into people's homes all over Europe. The broadcast was of the last hour of the race, and who filled the screen for 56 minutes of that hour? Tom Simpson.

He went like a bomb, riding over those terrible cobbled surfaces like they were the smoothest indoor track. In fact, he went further in that hour than Roger Rivière had when he set the track one-hour record. Tom looked as though he'd been riding the *pavés* all his life, as he switched smoothly from one side of the road to the other to find the flattest bits. Crouched low over his handlebars, sitting well back in the saddle so that he was nicely balanced on his bike, powerful yet relaxed. It was a wonderful effort and one that instantly made him a household name all over Europe, probably more so because it ended in defeat rather than victory.

Almost at the gates of the Roubaix track, where the race finishes, he was caught by the winner, Pino Cerami of Belgium, a remarkable man who got his career the wrong way round and only started winning big classic races when he was 38 years old. More riders caught and passed Tom on the track, his strength completely gone by now. Eventually, he crossed the line in ninth place, shattered, but famous. The crowd demanded that he did a lap of honour and gave him a standing ovation as he rode round that cold, concrete track.

People all over Europe actually cried when Tom was caught – his ride had captured their hearts and their imaginations. This was the heroic stuff of which bike-racing legend is made. It hadn't done the Rapha name any harm either – 56 minutes of historic publicity – and it didn't end with the broadcast, far from it.

It's hard today to gauge the impact Tom must have made doing what he did on that historic day, both for himself and for British cycling. Jean Bobet, who by then was a journalist and presenter with R.T.L., saw its effects at first hand and sums them up perfectly:

> Before that Sunday when Tom Simpson appeared on millions of TV screens, the continent did not really know much about British cycling. Sure enough, we had heard of one Reginald Harris in the late forties, but there had always been something unreal about him. Harris was a wonderful athlete who rode two or three laps on the track, then disappeared for months on

end. His name was printed on the World Record tables, but not on the hearts of the people. And then Simpson came.

There was more: French journalists couldn't believe their luck with this photogenic young man. Tall, slim and a snappy dresser, Tom looked just like they thought an Englishman should. They took pictures of him all over Paris, dressed in a city suit, reading *The Times*, and all topped off by a bowler hat. Tom Simpson had become Major Thompson. He was a mythical English gent, an ex-cavalry officer, now something in the city, who was created by the French writer, Pierre Daninos, and who first saw light of day in the newspaper, *Le Figaro*, in 1954. He was everything the French liked about the English – tall, elegant, quirky and permanently fascinated by the French. His adventures were very popular over there and he did a lot for the career of his young compatriot.

The press also made a lot of him having the same birthday as Winston Churchill, and one particular magazine even had a front-page picture of Tom smoking a twelve-inch cigar and giving Churchill's famous V-for-victory salute.

Tom was famous and in cycling fame means money. Everybody wants you to ride their race or promote their product, and for that they have to pay. Now he was really earning and, for the first time in his life, he had the chance to indulge himself a bit.

Ever since they first met Tom and Bill Womack had been mad about cars, and the one car they wanted above all others was an Aston Martin DB2. Well, he had the money now, so he bought one, a 1953 model. Brian Robinson, who'd been away racing elsewhere while Tom was making his name, had cautioned him to look after his money, but on his return to the flat there was the gleaming sports car parked outside. Brian instinctively knew it was Tom's and even today remembers thinking, 'Aye-aye, Tom's been impulsive again.' But he drew his power from that impulsiveness, that ambition, and Brian knew it. Bill Womack got his, too, a bit later than Tom did: he worked hard at the family business and he got his Aston Martin.

With these trappings of success his character was developing. He saw, through the Major Thompson episode, that his Englishness could be an advantage. If you can ride, that's one thing, but if you can ride and be different, interesting, then that's another. Also, if your personality extends beyond your handlebars you will be far more popular with the press. This means fame and, as I've said, fame means money.

Tom cultivated his image and he cultivated the press – he was learning quickly. Just how quickly you can see from the following extract from an article written by the celebrated journalist and Olympic Gold Medallist, Chris Brasher, shortly after Tom's death. He was writing about their first meeting in Paris, about the time we are at now in this book:

> I can still remember him seven years ago, uncoiling himself from a low chair in a Paris shop, revealing an immaculate Prince of Wales check suit, a silk tie and Italian hand-cut shoes, and suggesting that we dine at a restaurant whose name was world famous. I am sure he knew that I had expected to meet a tough northern lad bumming his way round Europe, and yet here was a complete man, the complete athlete, one of the greatest figures of British sport this century.

I am sure that is what Tom thought as well. He loved to stand people's preconceptions on their heads; that way, they would remember you. It was part of his charm, part of a character that even succeeded in raising the awareness of cycling as a sport in his own country to a level that no other person has ever come near to achieving.

Anyway, back to the racing. Tom was flying after Paris–Roubaix and won the Mont Faron hill-climb, beating the 'Angel of the Mountains', Charly Gaul, the 1958 Tour de France winner and, incidentally, a great friend and inspiration to the 1998 winner, Marco Pantani, and it was a superb win because Gaul was a really fantastic climber. Small and light, he was typical of that breed of riders, the *grimpeurs*, who seem to take on an ethereal quality as they dance lightly up the great mountain climbs.

Tom's spring classics campaign continued with seventh place in Flèche Wallonne and eleventh, a few days later, in Liège–Bastogne–Liège. I'll tell you more about these two races later in the story when they were the scene of two epic attempts by Tom to win them. He never did, but his seventh in Flèche Wallonne, at the age of only 22, and in his first full pro season, shows that they were made for each other, and that, but for the tragedy of 1967, Tom must surely have added at least one of these two beautiful classics to his list of victories.

Then it was on to his first full professional stage race, the Tour du Sud-Est. Brian Robinson, who was at his best in stage races, was riding this event with Tom and remembers him struggling for some reason in the first couple of stages. Tom's morale was low, and when that happened he was at his most fragile. He wanted to stop, to retire from the race, but Brian nagged him into continuing, telling him that it would be easier the next day. It wasn't, but these things can help a rider when he's struggling: they give him a thought to hold on to, something to pin his courage to.

Well, it worked: Tom stayed in the race and, by the final stage, had climbed his way into the first ten places overall, about two minutes behind the leader. His problems of the first two days were behind him; he was full of fight and his manager, Louviot, had a plan.

A small breakaway had gone up the road and gained about six minutes. In it was the Milan–San Remo winner, René Privat, and one of Tom's team mates, Raymond Mastrotto. Louviot drove alongside Tom in the team car and told him to wait for the steep climb coming up out of Toulon, then to attack hard. If he went hard enough then the race leader would be unable to follow, and Mastrotto could drop back and help him to gain enough time to win the race.

The plan worked like a dream. Tom flew up the climb and launched himself off down the road towards Marseilles, and the stage finish. Mastrotto played the perfect team mate, although he had to be threatened with a pay-cut by Louviot first, and he almost stopped in the road to wait for Tom. Once they linked up they worked together like crazy and got the lead Tom needed to take the race overall – his first stage-race victory as a professional.

This was a different Rapha team from the one in the Tour de L'Ouest – then they weren't quite prepared to accept him, but now they could see he was a winner. Tom had forced acceptance on them with his sheer class. This didn't mean that it would always be easy, that he would be on the same footing as other French, Belgian or Italian team leaders. It was just that Louviot, as an individual, was very fair and brave in his dealings with Tom. It wouldn't always be so with others, as we shall see.

However, that's not to say that he didn't have his work cut out managing Tom: it was still like managing dynamite, and they were to clash on several occasions. The first was over Tom's participation in the Tour de France. Louviot was dead-set against it. Tom was far too young for this, the hardest race in the world, and he told him so, with typical Gallic bluntness, even before he'd signed him up. As Louviot explained his plans in the winter Tom had been happy to go along with it, but now it was different: he was all fired up and he'd just won his first stage race. Of course he could manage the Tour, even at 22. What did Louviot know? Anyway, it wasn't up to him: in those days the Tour was disputed by national teams and Tom accepted his place in the British one without hesitation. Three weeks later, at the finish, he desperately wished he had listened to his manager.

Tom had one very narrow escape just before this. He'd been riding a lot of contract races and had received one to ride in the international professional race that used to be held on the Isle of Man as part of its famous cycling week. He was really looking forward to this – it was the nearest he'd get to a home crowd all year – but at the last minute he got a tip-off that the authorities had just got very serious about his call-up and it might be better for him if he gave the race a miss. He did, and it was just as well because the Military Police were waiting for his plane, all ready to arrest him and march him off to the barrack square.

The Tour de France in 1960, starting from the northern French city of Lille, was what is called a 'transitional' Tour. There was no clear favourite casting a dominant shadow over the event. The days of three-times winner Louison Bobet were over. Jacques Anquetil, the brilliant young winner of the 1957 event, could not yet be sure of the undivided support of the French team, so he refused to ride. The previous year's winner, the Spaniard, Bahamontes, could win again, but as a specialist mountain climber he was vulnerable to being hijacked on a long, flat stage in the wind. So it was an open Tour, and because of that it was going to be an extra hard one – they always are when several riders really believe they can win.

Into this cauldron of ambition and emotion stepped Tom Simpson. Was he overawed? What do you think? On the first stage he found himself in a fourteen-man breakaway that gained over two minutes on the rest by the time they sprinted it out together on the cinder track in Brussels. Unfortunately, Tom was one of two riders to crash on the track, but he was given the same time as the winner, and luckily only had a few scrapes and bruises to show for it.

That wasn't the day over, though: there was to be an afternoon shift – a 37-kilometre time trial – with just time for a meal and a short rest before this important test. Tom was following everything that Brian Robinson did. He was an old hand at this event by now, and it suited him: he thrived on stage races because he was so methodical, always getting to the hotel first, keeping on top of his washing, and the thousand-and-one little things that have to be taken into consideration on a three-week tour which mean a rider can get more rest, and suffer less stress. Tom wasn't a bit like this. Left to his own devices, he'd be chatting away to other riders or journalists, or the spectators, anybody who'd listen, really. It was just his nature, but he knew he had to learn from Brian.

The time between these two stages was ideal for one of Brian's little naps – nothing recharges the batteries more than a little sleep. So that's what they did: they had a little kip on the grass outside the Heyssel stadium. It was a good plan, but, unfortunately, the team masseur, who'd been given the job of waking them up, only remembered just before they were due to start. There was no time for a warm-up and it took Tom all of the first part of his ride to get his legs going. This was a shame because he recorded the fastest time for the second half of the time trial and finished in ninth place, one minute and 23 seconds behind the winner, the Frenchman, Roger Rivière.

What a start! Tom ended the day in fifth place overall, just one minute behind the yellow jersey, Gastone Nencini of Italy. Next day it got better. It was an incredibly fast stage from Brussels to Dunkirk, so fast that once the race reached the coast road, with the wind whipping in from the North Sea and over the sand dunes, Bahamontes simply couldn't cope, and retired. Tom had proved at Zandvoort that he could ride well in these conditions and attacked a number of times, finally getting away with several riders including Darrigade, the World Champion.

This was a great opportunity: Tom was the best-placed rider in the group, so if they stayed away and got just over a one-minute gap on the bunch then he would take the yellow jersey, and that was all he could see as he flogged himself all along the road to Dunkirk. But the break was carrying passengers: the riders from the French national team wouldn't work because their leader, Rivière, was back in the bunch. Then, just at the point when Tom made history and became the leader of the Tour de France on the road, back in the bunch the Italian team started to work flat-out, and the lead began to dwindle.

As they approached the stage finish Tom got another lesson in the brutal reality of cycling tactics when the non-working French national riders started to take turns attacking him. No sooner had he brought one back than the other would attack and he'd have to chase again, only for it to happen once more. Obviously, he couldn't keep this up, and eventually René Privat attacked and Tom just could not answer. Privat won and Tom was out-galloped for second place by the crafty French sprinter, Jean Graczyk, who'd had an armchair ride at the back of the group all the way. This was tragic. If Tom had taken second place he would have been given a 30-second time bonus, enough to have taken the yellow jersey in his first Tour de France. As it was, he ended the day lying in second place overall, 22 seconds behind Nencini. It was still a fantastic start.

Tom had made his mark on the race, but wanted to do more, and to do that he would have to relax a bit and save something for the Pyrenean stages coming at the end of the first week. Unfortunately, he relaxed a bit too much and missed the vital move on stage six between Saint Malo and Lorient which gained many minutes and virtually decided the race. Tom fell to ninth place overall that day. Another lesson learned. There was nothing for it now but to see how it went in the mountains.

Stage 10 from Mont-de-Marsan to Pau crossed the Aubisque climb. Tom went up this very well in a group at the head of the race containing all the favourites – Nencini, Rivière, Adriaensens and Junkermann. From the summit it was mostly downhill to the finish. He had a good chance to move back up the classification: all he had to do was stop with this group. But Tom being Tom, he had to do more, so he attacked on the descent and then the inevitable happened when a rider throws caution to the wind: he crashed. Rivière won the stage, Nencini was second and Tom fourteenth. He wasn't badly hurt, but he had lost time when he should have gained it.

He still had good morale, though, and was looking forward to the next day's stage between Pau and Luchon. It started off so well. At the summit of the Tourmalet Tom was in the second group with Nencini. It was the same over the Aspin, except they'd been joined by Rivière, Massignan, and a few others. Tom was starting to think that the Tour de France was like any other stage race, that you just got on with the racing, took every day as it came and didn't think too much about it being three weeks long. He felt good every day and recovered every night. What could possibly go wrong?

He started the last climb, the Peyresourde, by attacking his group. Nencini reacted and by half-way there was just Nencini leading, followed by Tom, followed by Rivière. Then it happened: all of a sudden he couldn't breath. It was just like a recurrence of what had happened at the Olympics and he had to let the other two go. More riders went past as he made his way to the top, but Tom couldn't match the pace of any of them – all his strength had suddenly gone. One minute he'd been fine, the next he was empty. The Tour had got him. It simply wasn't like any other race, after all.

The star of that day as far as British interests were concerned was Vic Sutton, who did an amazing ride to finish well up with the best in thirteenth place, one ahead of Rivière. He did another good ride in the Alps, too, finishing the Gap to Briançon stage in sixteenth place.

The Luchon stage was it for Tom: he was only a shadow of his former self afterwards. Still, that shadow managed to take a defiant third place on the difficult fifteenth stage from Avignon to Gap, only four seconds behind the winner, Michael Van Aerde. The next few days, though, were purgatory, but he hung on hoping to ride through his difficulties when he probably should have stopped. He was determined to get to the finish in Paris; he eventually did, in twenty-ninth place overall, but at the cost of his health. Of the rest of the British team only Brian Robinson got to Paris with Tom, doing a typically mature ride for twenty-sixth place overall.

Tom really was on his knees by the finish: he'd lost nearly two stone during the race and he didn't really have anywhere to lose it from. What he needed was a rest, but it didn't work like that, not in 1960 it didn't. In those days the Tour was followed by a series of races held all over Europe where the promoters charged people to come and watch the racing – unlike the Tour de France, where you just stand by the road and the race comes to you. These races are called 'criteriums', and are held on small circuits in towns and villages. Because the spectators are paying they want to see the best. That means classic winners and, in France, riders who have just performed in the Tour. Tom had almost taken the yellow jersey, he was popular and twenty-ninth is not at all bad for a 22-year-old in his first Tour, so the contracts to ride criteriums came flooding in.

The first one was for the evening after the Tour finished, at Evreux in Normandy. Imagine that: you've just raced for 28 days, in all weathers, on fast and flat stages, over mountains, in time trials; then, when you've digested all that, you start all over again. These criteriums were no joke, either. Local riders got a chance to shine. Ambitious ones were capable of making the Tour stars very uncomfortable, too. Remember Tom at Landernau the previous year? On top of this, France is a big country, and the races were held for the convenience of the public not the riders, so very often there was a long drive from one event to the next. But everyone wanted to ride them – wages from sponsors weren't as high as they are now and the criterium promoters paid well, plus the prize money was good, and the locals could be relied upon to put up money for sprint prizes. Pro bike riders regarded the criteriums in the same way as high-street shops regard Christmas, and they made a big proportion of their money in the month or so after the Tour.

In no fit state, Tom rode at Evreux, then had to go to Milan. From there it was on to Turin, then Sallanches in the French Alps, then Lyon. Up to Belgium next, for a week of races there. In every town a tough ride with up to 100 laps of a small circuit and distances much greater than the criterium races we see in this country, perhaps 100 to 150 kilometres.

After finishing the last race in Belgium Tom had just over 24 hours to get to the start line of another in Nice, more than 1,000 miles away! He drove alone through the night, napping when too exhausted to go any further, and arrived in Nice just in time to drag his bike to the line, check that he was facing the same way as the others, and off for another two or three hours of flat-out racing. He lasted just three miles! He was dead, but couldn't lie down. A night's sleep and another drive saw him racing again in central France where a crash put an end to his misery. This couldn't go on: he was out on his feet.

When you speak to people who knew Tom they may have different memories of him, different stories to tell, but at some stage they will all use the same word when describing him. It's a word that's perhaps a bit unfashionable now; perhaps we live in less heroic times. The word is 'brave', but no amount of bravery can take you anywhere if you've nothing left in your body, and Tom was empty – in fact, he'd been running on empty for a month.

He returned to the Paris flat, alone and unwell. Brian was away racing and Helen back in Germany after being at the finish of the Tour to welcome her boyfriend. He needed rest and recuperation to recharge his batteries, and as always he needed some company to keep his morale up. So he took himself off to the doctors and paid for a private room at the local hospital so that he could get put to rights by the experts. He was very glad he went private, too, because one day two men calmly walked into a public ward, armed with machine guns, and shot dead two patients. It was the time of the French troubles in Algeria – a terrorist killing – but you don't want to be in the next bed to that, do you?

Tom still had contracts to fulfill, but was in no state to do so. This was a problem. If breaking into the criterium circuit was hard, then staying there was even harder; he just could not afford to let these people down. He could almost hear people saying, 'Oh well, what do you expect from an Englishman?' Luckily, Brian Robinson was still in good shape – he had those extra years as a pro to support a heavy programme – so he took over Tom's contracts as well as his own. Things were starting to look better. A week in bed saw him ready to get back on his bike, though perhaps not ready for his next scheduled race, the World Road Championships.

These were held on the Saxonring in Germany. As ever, Tom was in a positive mood, Raymond Louviot having spent a lot of time trying to psyche his boy up. It was wishful thinking on both their parts, though; I doubt whether any of the opposition had come to the race straight from a Paris hospital bed. Anyway, fate took a hand at the end of the fourth lap and Tom was put out of the race by a freak accident: coming through the finishing straight one of his shoe-laces snapped, so he eased himself to the back of the group and stopped in the road to put matters right. He should have got right to the side of the road because one of the following car drivers wasn't paying attention and ran straight into the back of him, throwing him over the handlebars, and his head made sharp contact with the road.

The end result was five stitches inserted into a nasty head wound, and a monumental telling-off from his manager. Raymond Louviot went crazy: he was already exasperated by Tom not listening to him over the Tour de France; now he said that Tom had thrown away a world-title chance just by being careless. John Geddes was in the British pits when Tom returned from having his head attended to, and he remembers the incident between Louviot and Tom vividly:

> Louviot attacked him – he was actually trying to hit Tom and had to be held back. He was shouting at him, 'You don't pay attention. You could have been World Champion.' He was really mad, really going for Tom, actually trying to hit and kick him. I couldn't believe it. Tom said to me, 'Let's get out of here,' and we went off for a walk round the circuit.

He was a very volatile character, Louviot, but even taking this into consideration his actions that day still seem excessive. Why did he get so mad with Tom? I think that it was because he knew he had got someone very special on his hands and he really didn't want Tom to do anything to waste his talent, or his opportunities. Like I said earlier in the book Tom could be exasperating and push people's patience; he could be flippant, facetious even. It was a mask he hid behind sometimes, and maybe this was one of those occasions. Remember what Norman Sheil said about his changed attitude towards pursuiting at the 1958 Worlds? Louviot, though, was Tom's best manager and he really thought Tom was one of the greatest. This is what he said about him in 1965, just after Tom had become World Champion, when he was *Directeur* of the Ford-France team and, for reasons beyond both their control, Tom was the leader of their rivals, Peugeot-BP.

> I wish Tom was still under my direction. I am not saying that because he is World Champion, but because he is the kind of rider I prefer – a man who fights until he lays in the gutter. There are few who have the guts for that and no matter how many times they fail I prefer this attitude. Tom failed many times, but it is because he tries so often that his record is so beautiful. Had it been up to me, he would still have been one of my riders. I did not let him go willingly. He is intelligent and he does learn from his mistakes.

Louviot understood Tom and liked the way he raced; we shall see that his second manager did not. Louviot was also one of the many on the continent who believed Tom could win the race he wanted most, the Tour de France, and he told him so. But more of that later.

The 1960 season was by now drawing to a close. They were still talking about Tom, though. In the press Jean Bobet paid him a huge compliment when he compared his style to that of Coppi. He must have been thrilled by that.

He didn't do well in any of the autumn classics, but remained hard at work cashing in on his earlier successes, riding criteriums and track meetings. He was still tired and very relieved when his final race was over. He was also glad it was over because he really wanted to see Helen again, and with work out of the way for another year he had the opportunity. Cyclists live a strange life: for almost nine months a year they are either racing, recovering or travelling. Consequently, they have only three months at the most to live a normal life and do what the rest of us take for granted: go out with their mates, spend time with their kids, or visit their girlfriends, for example. Helen was still in Germany, but now with his own transport he could do something about it. So it was off in the Aston Martin to Stuttgart where, at the end of November, they were able to celebrate Tom's twenty-third birthday together.

The next day he set off for England. He was going home for Christmas and he hadn't a care in the world: Helen would be returning to her home in Sutton; he was to be best man at his friend Bill Womack's wedding; he was off to see his parents, and he had a beautiful motor car to enjoy and show everybody back home – the fruits of his first year's labour, the fruits of already being the most successful bike rider this country had ever seen. It was a happy journey.

Despite Tom's busy race schedule and Helen's work in Stuttgart they had seen each other as often as possible. Tom had already decided the previous year that Helen was the girl he wanted to marry, so it was not really a surprise when they got engaged on Christmas Eve 1960. The official plan had been then to wait ten months before they got married, but for two young people in a hurry, who had made their minds up, it seemed daft to wait. As soon as the church was open for business, the day after Boxing Day, Tom took Helen to see the vicar and asked him for the first available date that they could get married. This turned out to be the following Thursday. So that was all decided then – only Tom hadn't told his parents.

He'd told them about Helen, of course, but they had no idea how serious he was. Their next stop was Festival Avenue in Harworth where Tom introduced Helen to his mum and dad, and with the introductions quickly out of the way, told them that he was going to get married. Helen has never forgotten his dad's reply, delivered in his broad Geordie accent, 'We tee, lad?' which means 'Who to?' It had all happened so quickly. Tom had taken up cycling, gone to the Olympics, Russia, Bulgaria, then living in France, then become the country's best pro rider, now he'd turned up on their doorstep in a racing car and with a prospective wife. My poor grandad was having a fair bit of difficulty following the plot.

The day after their wedding the couple were due at the *Daily Mirror* Sportsman's Dinner. No one knew about the wedding and Brian Robinson had to be shown the wedding ring before he believed them. It was yet another occasion for him to think, 'Aye aye, Tom's been impulsive again,' but, as ever, he tried to counsel and help with fatherly advice, though he knew Tom probably wasn't listening to him.

From London it was off to Paris and a few days to themselves before Helen had to go back to her work in Stuttgart and Tom had to head south for the team training camp in Narbonne.

He was a relaxed and happy man, newly married with a promising career in the sport he loved in front of him; so he began to train with renewed vigour. He had responsibilities now. He worked hard, but it didn't show in the first few races on the Côte d'Azure, where he spent a lot of time with the French journalist René de Latour. René wrote for the British magazine *Sporting Cyclist*, so had more than a passing interest in Tom.

About his current form Tom told René: 'I'm not brilliant at the moment, but why hurry? There's plenty of time yet.' What's this, Tom being patient? Married life had mellowed him. 'I'm older now,' he continued, 'and I realise that I made lots of mistakes last year, but I was getting so much conflicting advice.'

Latour tried to get Tom talking about his exploit in the Paris–Roubaix, but Tom wanted to talk more about the Tour de France. Already it seemed that he had decided that this race was the only one that really mattered. It was as though he knew that he would win a classic as a matter of course, but the Tour would always be different and would demand more. In summing up his 1960 Tour he told Latour, 'In my first Tour I was fighting too much from the start: using too much energy. I thought I was OK, but the bad time came.'

The first races were soon over and, like Tom said, he did OK. Mainly he was using them as training for his first big challenge of the season, the Paris to Nice stage race. Helen had finished her time in Germany now and they were able to spend a few days getting the Porte de Clichy flat organised, and getting used to living together in the City of Light.

The race start came round all too quickly and it was time for Tom to get on with carving out a future for them. The Paris–Nice is known as 'The Race to the Sun' because it takes place in March, when Paris can still be in the grips of winter, and travels in stages to Nice on the Côte d'Azure which is the sun bit, hopefully.

Tom's form had improved no end; Paris–Nice is a big race and he was always better at big races. On the first day he got into a break that gained time over the others. Next day, the stage ended in a bunch sprint at Montceau les Mines; then, in the afternoon, there was a team time trial around the lake at Montceau.

Tom's team, now back riding under another of their sponsors' trade marks, St Raphaël, was then one of the strongest in cycling, with people like Geldermans, De Haan, Otano, Annaert and the great Rudi Altig riding for them, and, boy, could they go in a team time trial. On this occasion their strength worked to Tom's benefit as they won the stage and he took over the leader's white jersey by three seconds from the Belgian, Armand Desmet. In the future this would prove a 'double-edged sword', with too many leaders causing Tom to defend when he wanted to attack. Never mind that now, though – he had the leader's jersey in a major stage race, another first for his country.

Next day, on the road to the capital of the French cycle industry, St Etienne, Tom lost the jersey, but said at the finish that he was not unduly worried as he was really more interested in testing his form out against Jacques Anquetil in the time trial at Avignon, rather than defending his overall lead. Was this his Tour de France ambitions surfacing again? Anquetil had already won the race in 1957 and he was expected to be the man to beat in the coming years. The reason behind this was that Anquetil was a superb time triallist: by 1961 he had won the only classic run as a time trial, the G.P. des Nations, six times, and time trials are a big part of the Tour; so if Tom had designs on the Tour de France, he needed to show up well against Anquetil in a time trial.

Tom might have been in good form, but he'd underestimated Anquetil's power at this event and how he could successfully raise his game to ride a time trial within a stage race. The course at Avignon was twisting and hilly, and the day windy – just how Jacques liked it. He really was the master at gauging his effort over such terrain, keeping the power on over the top of hills, choosing the right line and gears both into and out of corners, and powering into the wind where his low position on the bike proved to be a huge advantage. Equal second place with Rik Van Looy in this time trial was an excellent performance for a second year pro, but, nevertheless, Tom was astonished at the margin with which Anquetil beat him: 2 minutes and 34 seconds over 26 miles.

That beating really deflated him. Anquetil had done nothing in the race before the time trial and was nowhere near the form he would have in the Tour de France. Before the stage Tom was sure that he would have been closer to Jacques, maybe even have beaten him. That ride shows us what a master Anquetil was against the clock and how he was able to exercise such a grip on stage races in the first half of the 1960s.

The final stages fell into a predictable pattern. Once in the overall lead Anquetil set his team the task of shutting the race down and chasing every attack. Tom went away many times, but was always brought back – Anquetil's Irish team mate, Shay Elliott, being particularly active in chasing him down. Eventually, Tom finished the race in fifth place overall – a good ride in itself and, as a bonus, his fitness had improved in the race. He had also learned something: if he didn't know it before he knew now just how good Anquetil was, and how good he'd have to be if he wanted to beat him. There was no time to sit back.

Next came the first classic of the year, Milan–San Remo, the scene of one of Tom's brave lone efforts the year before. And, with good legs and more confidence, he was looking forward to doing better in this year's event. Unfortunately, once the race got under way he fell victim to the other side of St Raphaël's double-edged sword when one of his team mates, Annaert, went with a small break very early in the race and they were never seen again by the others. This meant that, in spite of his ambitions, Tom had to play the loyal team mate and use his good form to chase down riders trying to get across to Annaert's group. To add insult to injury, Annaert didn't win and Tom had to settle for twenty-fifth place, which was a good 24 places behind where he really wanted to be.

Milan–San Remo is a race that is still very much with us today, still a monument of the sport and fought for as hard as it ever was, but one race that is no longer on the calendar is Menton–Rome, a short stage race which, in 1961, started the day after Milan-San Remo. Before the first stage, Tom confided to René de Latour: 'I am really going to try and win this one. I don't think that I have ever pedalled with such ease.'

The first stage was from Menton, on the Côte d'Azure, to Mondovi, and though Tom was confident about his form he was again upstaged by a team mate and had to ride shotgun in the bunch. This time it was Geldermans, but at least he won the stage and, in turn, the race. Tom realised that in future he would have to change his tactics and get his move in first – and that is how he tried to race for the rest of his life.

He had his moments in this race, though, especially in the time trial where he got his revenge on Anquetil, beating him by 90 seconds and taking second place on the stage in the process. The Tour de France dream was alive again. He followed up this performance with another second place on the stage to Bologna where he lost in a two-man sprint to Guido Carlesi, a very classy Italian who, like many after him, was being hailed as the new Coppi, but who retired from the sport only a couple of years later when he was still quite young.

The good form was there and Tom would need it. Two days after the finish of Menton–Rome he was to take part in another monument, the race that is the pride of the Flemish people, the Tour of Flanders. To them this is the race, bigger even than the Tour de France. It is an expression of the Flemish character, and a festival of their history and their language. The winner of the Ronde van Vlaanderen, whatever his nationality, becomes an honorary Lion of Flanders overnight, entitled to be mentioned in the same breath as Brik Schotte, Eric Leman, Johan Museeuw and the other great Flemish winners of this race. I say Flemish winners because in the 44 editions before 1961 only seven victories had gone to non-Belgians.

The race, in those days, was one of three distinct phases, each presenting a different face of the Flemish countryside. From the start in Ghent the race headed out on a long, straight road, northwest over the flat farmlands towards the coast. Here, the view across endless fields was only broken by the occasional line of poplars that sheltered squat farm buildings from the wind which, at that stage of the race, was the riders' only enemy, as it attacked them head-on.

On reaching the coast, the road turns left and heads south, past sand-dunes, still-closed seaside resorts, and the busy port of Ostend. Here the wind blows from the sea on to the riders' right shoulders and, instead of keeping the group together, can blow them apart if it has any strength, and it often has at the beginning of April. Here, too, the tactics change as the riders use the wind to gain a lead over their rivals by riding in an echelon formation, which is the most efficient way to combat these conditions. Anybody who has serious designs on victory has to be at the front by now.

Near the French border the race turns inland and heads for a little ridge of high ground which defines Flanders itself. It runs east to west, just south of Oudenaarde and just north of Renaix. This is the ridge on which the famous bergs, monts and murs are located – those short, sharp, cobbled climbs where the race is decided. On one side of the ridge they speak French, on the other Flemish. The famous hills – the Kluisberg, Kwaremont and Mur de Grammont, plus as many more with equally guttural names as the organisers can find – are all on the Flemish side. Each brutal climb is followed by a quick sprint in the cross-winds along the top of the ridge, then a bone-jarring plunge down an equally precipitous and cobbled descent on the same side. It would never do to go over to the French-speaking side – it's not their race.

This was the menu for the 1961 Tour of Flanders. Throw in over six hours of racing, the very best riders in the world, and in particular the Flemish guys who would sell their own mothers to win this race, and you've got the picture. As ever, they attacked from the start, and it wasn't a group of no-hopers just looking for publicity, for the first break of the day contained Rik Van Looy, Arthur de Cabooter, and Jos Planckaert who, incidentally, for all you students of cycling, is not a member of the famous family of the same name that was to provide two winners of this race in the future, but he was a very good rider, none the less.

The break worked well and quickly got a good lead. Van Looy was unlucky and fell, hurting his wrist, but Daems, Stolker, Le Menn and Tom's team mate, De Haan, got across to swell their numbers. It was the winning move, and Tom was experienced enough now to know it. He was so sure that he could win the race that, despite having a team mate up there, he knew he had to get up to them. Team work is critical in pro cycling. If a rider takes the initiative like Tom was going to do and chases a team mate, he has to be sure of winning. When he attacked, Louviot's heart must have been in his mouth because the only rider who could follow him was the Italian, Nino de Filippis, and he was one of the fastest roadman sprinters in the game. What's more, Tom gave him an armchair ride up to the others as he crossed the gap in no time.

It looked like a very naïve move, but this was Tom Simpson at his very best. These big races did something to him and if his morale was good he was unbeatable. This was to be the first day he would prove it. Once with the leaders Tom worked with them for a while, but with about five miles to go he decided to increase the odds of victory by attacking to get rid of some of them. It was his second attack of the day and it was too good for all of them, apart from that man again, de Filippis.

As they approached the finish at Wetteren, a small town close to Ghent, it soon became obvious that they wouldn't be caught. It also became obvious to Tom that since the run to the finish was absolutely flat he wasn't going to be able to drop de Filippis. In short, he was going to have to contest a sprint with one of the fastest men in the world. Not many in the crowd were betting on Tom.

The finish was after three laps of a small circuit, so they would cross the line twice, then sprint for it. Riding round the circuit Tom knew that, even though he wasn't a bad sprinter himself, particularly after a long, hard race, to beat de Filippis he was going to have to come up with a bit of tactical 'sleight of hand'.

So, on the last lap, coming up to the line, he started his sprint with about one kilometre to go, but not flat-out. De Filippis was content to follow, nicely sat on Tom's wheel, sheltered, poised, ready to launch his sprint. With about 300 metres to go Tom slowed slightly, as if his effort was over, and Nino fell for it: he thought Tom was finished and overtook him on his right, but as he did Tom started sprinting again, moving across to Nino's right. Just before the line the Italian, thinking he had a comfortable lead, looked over his left shoulder, expecting to see Tom, but he wasn't there. Confused for a moment, he slowed. It was all Tom needed and he galloped past on Nino's right for his first classic victory.

The Italian just could not believe it. He'd lost a race he should have won. How could he, the crafty veteran of so many Giro d'Italia and Tour de France sprints, have been tied up in tactical knots by a young Englishman? He could not accept what had happened, and immediately lodged a protest, claiming that the finish banner had blown down and therefore he didn't know where the line was. The banner had certainly blown down, but the line was clearly marked across the road and, what's more, they'd crossed it twice before the final sprint; so that didn't wash with the judges.

Next, de Filippis's manager appealed to Tom, trying to get him to agree to a shared victory: they told him that an Italian hadn't won a classic since 1953 and this was a terrible thing for Italian cycling. What they actually meant was that Nino was likely to get lynched in the Italian press the next day. Tom wasn't having any of that – a Briton hadn't won a classic since Arthur Linton in the Bordeaux to Paris, and that was in 1896. No one was going to take his victory, the first by a Briton in one of the five monuments of the sport, and he is still the only English speaker ever to have won this race. Four-stone Coppi had won the Tour of Flanders, and that was that!

Let's now just pause for a moment and look at this win from two perspectives because it will help us understand just how good Tom Simpson was. First, from the perspective of British cycling. In this country cycling is not a major sport; it never has been. In Europe, however, it is up there with football and in certain regions it's even more important. Somehow, in our country, it never took hold. Then along came Brian Robinson and he got his foot in the door, only for Tom to blow it off its hinges. Tom raised the game and won a monument; he would go on to win three out of the five. No other British rider has managed to win one since.

After Tom's death there were some honourable performances. Barry Hoban and Robert Millar had podium places in Paris–Roubaix and Liège–Bastogne–Liège, and both distinguished themselves in the Tour de France by playing to their strengths. That can also be said of Chris Boardman: in one particular aspect of the sport he is the best in the world, but it's not the stuff of legends; it's not the stuff that excites the fans, like victory in a race as big as the Tour of Flanders.

Now let's look at it from the perspective of world cycling: a 23-year-old, second-year professional winning the Tour of Flanders is something you don't see very often. Frank Vandenbrouke is the hottest young property around at the moment and he's been a pro for four years, but he couldn't do it in 1998 when he was the same age as Tom, and he was a Belgian trying to win a Belgian race on the roads where he cut his teeth. Frank had to wait one more year before winning his first monument, the 1999 Liège–Bastogne–Liège. I know that comparisons are odious. I'm not really making any; all I'm trying to do is set Tom against some kind of background that we can all relate to.

And didn't he win it well? He only attacked twice in that race and both were decisive moves. He was, as the French say, *imperiale*. At the finish he told reporters, 'It's not any harder to win a race than to lose it, and I didn't suffer a tenth of what I had to go through last year when I lost Paris–Roubaix in the last five miles.'

In saying that he was setting himself up for his next objective because on the following Sunday he would get his chance for revenge on that race; but there are a lot more variables in Paris–Roubaix than there are in the Tour of Flanders. To win it a rider needs great legs – that is the same for every big race. No, Paris–Roubaix demands that little bit extra, everything other races need plus, for want of a better word, a little bit of luck. Not that anybody has ever had a lucky win in this race – luck is probably the wrong word – but there has to be just enough good fortune to avoid the unseen and the unexpected which can hit in this race like no other. So, for want of a better word, we'll call it luck. In 1961 Tom had the legs, but not the luck.

As soon as he reached the *pavés* he launched an attack and went into an early lone lead. Just like last year, but Tom Simpson in 1961 was a different proposition: he'd won one of these races, and now he was going to batter this one into submission. Or so he thought.

Once in charge and at the head of things he settled down to a rhythm, searching out the smoothest bits of road, taking the best line through all the corners, nice and controlled, just enough to stay clear. Then he got news that Raymond Poulidor, already a winner of Milan–San Remo that year, and a threat in any race, was chasing. Tom didn't want him for company and, anyway, he reckoned that because he wasn't used to them he could ride faster over these roads on his own, so he increased the pace – so much so that he started to catch up the race vehicles in front.

The result was pandemonium as officials on motorbikes tried to clear the vehicles out of the way, but they could not go any faster on the cobbles than Tom, so he found himself overtaking them in a desperate effort to stay away from Poulidor. Then the inevitable happened: a press car, swerving to avoid a pot-hole, forced Tom off the road and into a ditch. His front wheel was wrecked and he'd banged his knee, although he hardly noticed that ... at the time. All he wanted was a new wheel and to get on with the race, but the road was completely blocked by now. The rest of the race had caught up and Tom had to walk back through the convoy to find his team car, and a new wheel.

They don't let the cars on to the *pavé* now; only motorbikes are allowed down them and race service is provided by moto-cross bikes with special racks for carrying wheels. The team cars and most of the other vehicles are routed around the worst of the cobbles, but the journalists don't miss anything because the cameramen are still there, and a helicopter still clatters away above the riders' heads so every detail can be captured for us at home.

The mess was eventually sorted out, but by the time Tom got his wheel he'd been passed by dozens of riders. He set off in pursuit, only to crash twice more. Once at the back in Paris–Roubaix a rider can fall victim to the misfortunes of others as well as his own while he tries to pick his way past riders in varying stages of fatigue and through the general carnage that more resembles Napoleon's retreat from Moscow than a bike race. He had such a bad time that he eventually reached the Roubaix velodrome, the scene of his special lap of honour only twelve months before, almost half an hour behind the race winner, Rik Van Looy.

Paris–Roubaix has its variables, you see. You have the form of your life, you go like a train, you get an early lead and then you end up 30 minutes down with nothing to take home but a bad knee.

7

DARKEST BEFORE THE DAWN

The knee didn't seem too bad at first, but the pain grew worse over the next week and was really making itself felt by his next race, a short stage race in Spain, the G.P. Eibar. In spite of this Tom was still in good form and he overcame the problem to win the second stage, but to do so he'd gone deep – too deep. Next day the knee was really hurting and he felt completely drained. In the end, he had to abandon the race which had been held throughout in torrential rain.

Once home he developed a nasty rash and deep muscular pains. This was eventually diagnosed as food poisoning. After a short rest the symptoms were gone, but the painful knee refused to go away so easily. He was contracted to ride the Bordeaux–Paris, a race that I will tell you a lot more about later, but, for the moment, suffice it to say that it's not something that can be tackled on one leg. Tom rested, then tested his knee by riding behind a derny pacing bike on the Friday before the race – as late as he dared leave it – but it was no better and he had to scratch from this 365-mile marathon.

The problem just refused to go away and it marked what was to be the most difficult time in Tom's career. He was in his second year as a pro bike rider – a year when it is vitally important to be consistent; a year which is important even if you are a French rider on a French team, but for an English rider on a French team, in the early sixties, well, there were just too many people with a vested interest in writing Tom off. Despite them he had broken in, but now, through reasons beyond his control, it could all be over.

He became desperate to get the knee fixed and hiked it around various specialists. Their potions and creams proved useless. Tom couldn't race, there was no money coming in, and what cash he and Helen had was going on medical fees. The future looked very bleak indeed. Nowadays, the team would probably have taken control of this process, especially if the rider in question had just won the Tour of Flanders, but there simply wasn't the money for that in 1961. Sure, there was money in the sport, but you had to win it in races, and from your victories get appearance money and endorsements. If you weren't riding, then you couldn't earn – it was the law of the jungle – and I think it is fair to say that this was even more true if you were a 'foreigner'.

In desperation, Tom accepted his place in the Great Britain team for the Tour de France. He had to – his performance in the Tour could affect his earnings for the rest of the year. He was in no fit state to start, but he just hoped that a miracle would happen, that somewhere along the route the pain would go and the knee would right itself. Then he could do something. Then he would be able to earn again. If he'd stopped at home and it got better he'd have missed the boat. What could he do but start and hope that the miracle would happen somewhere along the road?

It didn't. At the start in Rouen the team was the biggest ever sent from this country, a mixed bag of 11 riders, including the very experienced Brian Robinson, Vin Denson in his first Tour, the Irish rider Shay Elliott and Pete Ryalls from Sheffield. Only Robinson, Elliott and Ken Laidlaw would finish the race: an Englishman, an Irishman, and a Scotsman.

Pete Ryalls and Tom didn't get any further than the fourth stage from Roubaix to Charleroi. Tom's knee was by then making it almost impossible for him to pedal. Pete was eliminated on that stage for being outside the time limit because the previous day he had pushed Tom for almost the whole of the stage and, consequently, was totally exhausted. He had helped Tom get one day further in the race than he would have done, one day nearer that hoped-for miracle, and in the process sacrificed his own chances of getting any further. Pete still races today with the veterans, but there's something about him, a certain look that marks him out from the rest. You see, Pete Ryalls once rode the Tour de France – only four stages, but it was the Tour de France.

The Tour went on without them. Tom was back in Paris coping with the huge void which all Tour abandons talk about, an unreal feeling that you should be some place else. On top of this he had his knee problem. His situation was now serious. He had ground to a halt. he was a racing cyclist who couldn't race. He had to get it fixed now, or it could all be over for him.

Just when things looked at their blackest Tom had a bit of luck. Someone suggested he visit a Dr Creff at St Michael's Hospital in

Paris who, Tom was told, had successfully treated similar injuries in the past. He got straight to it and diagnosed the problem simply as arthritis, and gave Tom a series of 16 injections directly into the knee to get it under control and bring down the inflammation which had gone unchecked now for three months. He warned Tom, though, that he would always have to take particular care of the joint, especially when racing in wet conditions. Tom followed his instructions to the letter and, over the coming years, if you see a picture of him racing in the wet you will always see a warming plaster on his knee – a little white reminder of how near it came to ending his career.

With his knee fixed Tom could get his career back on track, and show those people who'd been writing him off that he was far from finished. Also, he needed the money – times had been very hard. Apart from his wages from St Raphael he had only managed to win £500 all year and had received no more than seven contracts for the criteriums, whereas he could have expected four times that number if he'd had a good Tour de France. He wasn't going home, though; if he'd been determined before, then he had to make it now. Failure was not an option.

Through all his troubles Tom never once doubted his ability: he never had and he never would. I'll tell you a little story that his father-in-law told me which illustrates this. Frank Sherburn knew nothing of this world his daughter had married into, so during this bad time in 1961 he thought he would have a fatherly word with Tom about his future. He was naturally worried for his daughter and whether Tom could make a life for her by riding a bike. For a Yorkshire farmer it must have seemed a very tenuous way of making your 'brass'. One day when he had Tom on his own he brought the subject up. But he didn't get very far: Tom stopped him short, looked him straight in the eye and said, 'I am one of the best cyclists in the world, and one day soon I'll prove it.' Frank was a shrewd man, he'd been around a bit, but the way Tom said this just stopped him in his tracks; there was no arguing with it. Frank told me, 'I'd never heard anybody so convinced by what they said in my life – it was so intense – and, do you know, from that moment I was sure myself that Tom would make it.'

Those few short words convinced Frank that his daughter had married someone very special indeed. Having got his body fixed, Tom set about training for the World Championships which were held that year at Berne in Switzerland. Two weeks before the event Tom and Helen went there so that he could finish off his preparation with a mini training camp. And I mean 'camp' literally, because that's what they did – camped in a tent by the lake.

By now, Tom was feeling physically fit for the first time in months. However, this did not mean that he had the race fitness that only comes from a period of regular racing and training. Never mind, his head was right once more and that counted a lot with Tom. He tried his hand, or should I say legs, at the pursuit again, and qualified with the fourth-fastest time, but lost in the quarterfinals to the Dutchman, Peter Post. He wasn't as disappointed as he had been in 1959, though – he'd just used the ride as a test and was very pleased that things appeared to be going in the right direction at last.

Next was the road race. He had no particular ambition, but was sure that the distance would do him good. It was a strange race, run off in oppressive heat, and under the equally oppressive control of the Belgian team, all riding for one man, the defending champion, Rik Van Looy.

Eventually, a group of 17 got clear, including Tom, Van Looy, and several of his team who countered every attack. These 17 sprinted it out at the end with Tom finishing ninth and predictably, Van Looy, who had a tremendous sprint, taking the victory. For once he didn't care about Van Looy – ninth in the Worlds is not bad. Remember Dave Lloyd's little story: Tom was back in business.

He now had his sights set on 1962, and he made a vow to give nothing away to other riders or, indeed, anyone, particularly those he knew had turned on him when he was injured and not performing well. He was starting to get hard. Everything he would do from now on would be for himself, and for his family, because he'd learned that in the end that's all you've got, and his family was about to increase.

Helen was pregnant, and they were both delighted, but there was a big problem: there were 110 steps to climb to get to their tiny apartment. They needed a bigger place, but hadn't the money for the higher rent. Albert Beurick, whom Tom had stayed with in 1958, had been telling him for a while that they would be better off living in Ghent than in Paris. It was cheaper and was at the hub of Flemish cycling. In Ghent a pro bike rider was somebody special, somebody people wanted to help and be associated with, Albert argued. Also, in those days, there were hundreds of races for professionals in Flanders:

the whole country lived and breathed the sport. Tom was bound to thrive in such an environment where every road and cart track had felt the touch of a racing tyre. So they decided to move.

Ghent had a fairly big British community, and Tom was able to rent a small cottage by a canal from one of the customers of an Englishman, Ken Dockray, who ran a garage close to the city centre. It needed fixing up, but the rent was very low, so Tom and Helen moved in at the beginning of October 1961.

What money they had left was spent doing up their new place, so the first few weeks there were very hand to mouth. They were only saved from serious financial hardship by Tom managing to get a number of contracts to ride one-day meetings at the Ghent, Brussels and Antwerp tracks. Things were looking up and they could start planning again.

There was just one more problem to solve: the St Raphaël team. Tom wanted to be their number one, the team leader, the one the others work for in all the major races, but it was full of talented riders and this had already caused him problems at the start of 1961: he'd had to defend the chances of others when he had the legs to be off up the road, winning the race for himself. These problems were nothing, though, compared to the ones he would have with St Raphaël's star signing for the 1962 season, Jacques Anquetil.

Not that Tom had anything against Jacques personally; quite the opposite, he admired him. And it was mutual; in fact, over the coming years, they became friends. But he knew that if he stayed put, given his ability, he, the younger man, would be seen as an ideal helper for the French superstar. He would have made good money from it, too, but there was no way that this was what he wanted. Yes, he was talented, and he was going to use that talent for one person only: Tom Simpson.

So, he let it be known that he was 'on the market' and, despite his recent problems, he was offered a place in a new team for 1962, Gitane-Leroux. This was a combination of bicycle manufacturer and coffee producer, and the team would contain a lot of people Tom knew. The established star was to be André Darrigade, but he had always been very fair with Tom and had helped him. Anyway, after the 1959 Worlds – which André won, remember – he had offered to pay Tom for the work he'd done in the break. Typical of the uncanny maturity Tom could display at times, he'd told him then that he wouldn't accept money; he would rather have André owe him a favour, which would be worth more in the long run. So now he was sure he could rely on his support when he needed it. The team manager would be Raymond Louviot and, as we already know, Tom had absolute confidence in him. He was with people he could trust and was looking forward to riding with them.

The team's training camp was at Lodeve in the Herault region of southern France – a very scenic and tranquil place with lots of testing climbs: just the place for early season training. Here, the riders concentrated on getting a good base in preparation for the team's first big objective of 1962, the Paris–Nice. Tom rode an aggressive and very confident race to finish second overall to Joseph Planckaert. It was a mature performance and one that gave him a lot of confidence for his major 1962 ambition, which was a good showing in the Tour de France.

Disappointment came next when the Italian organisers, getting ever more desperate for a home win, limited the field in Milan–San Remo to Italian teams only. It wasn't very sporting of them, and it didn't work, either, because Emilie Daems, a stocky little Belgian rider in the Italian Philco team, popped up and won the race. So Tom took his good form back home to Ghent, gave his legs a try-out by taking a brilliant sixth place in Ghent–Wevelgem, then sat on it, waiting for his next big race: the Tour of Flanders.

Of course, he didn't sit about waiting. As ever, the training had to be done and Tom was able to combine this with one of his first business ventures with Albert Buerick. They ran a training course in Ghent for British amateurs from 18th March to 2nd April. Thirteen riders travelled from this country to attend, and they trained each day with Tom and the great Australian six-day track rider, Reg Arnold. They also attended lectures on everything to do with bike racing, given by Tom, Reg, his old six-day partner Alf Strom who was a *soigneur* by then, and the double World Pro Road Race Champion of 1928 and '29, Georges Ronsse. It was one of the first camps of its kind for British riders. Today there are lots of them, although you're more likely to find them in Mallorca than Ghent, which is not renowned for gentle weather in March.

Tom was the defending champion in the Tour of Flanders, he was fully fit and his troubles were behind him; now he would show them that his victory last year was no fluke. He wanted to win again, but so did Van Looy. Remember he had bad luck the previous year: he had crashed whilst wearing the rainbow jersey of World Champion, the jersey every Flandrian cyclist dreams of winning their race in. Now he had another chance, and one way or another nobody was going to stop him.

Van Looy in 1962 was at the height of his powers. If you were to get a computer to design a rider to win the Tour of Flanders it would come up with Van Looy. Compact, muscular, fast and aggressive, his style on a bike was made for thundering over awful roads, powering up short and steep hills, then killing everybody off with a devastating finishing sprint. On top of this, he was a natural-born winner, and because of the number of races he won, and the way he won them, he was known by his fans as the 'Emperor'. He was a very formidable rider who, in full flight, looked quite capable of eating one or two of his less robust rivals.

Well, he wasn't going to eat Tom, not without a fight. Van Looy got the first blow in and attacked after 50 kilometres, causing a group of 49 riders, containing Tom and most of the other race favourites, to draw clear of the rest. The race was now over for them, as Van Looy's devoted team, known as the 'Red Guard', put the brakes on the bunch and the escape group started to build a commanding lead.

Van Looy's next attack came on the first of those notorious cobbled climbs, the Kwaremont. This was a real selection, and only Tom, Planckaert, Fore, Van Aerde and Van Kerkhove could follow the furious pace Van Looy set. But, towards the top, Tom drew alongside him while he was in full flight, then sprinted ahead to take the hill prime. He was trying to tell Rik something in the only language he was sure to understand – with his legs.

Once over the top he waited for Rik and the others, but from that point he began to dominate the race. He matched Van Looy pedal stroke for pedal stroke; he did more than his share of the work to keep the break away, with longer and harder turns at the front, filling in when others missed theirs. He took the prime at the top of every climb but one, and easily won the climber's prize. It was as though he was trying to impress on Van Looy that he was the man to beat if he wanted to win the Tour of Flanders.

The group stayed away to the finishing circuit where Rik and Tom were seen deep in conversation, or was it negotiation? Then Van Looy unleashed his fearsome sprint to win, wearing the rainbow jersey, just like he'd dreamt of doing since he was a paper boy. Tom was fifth, apparently exhausted by his earlier efforts to dominate, but he was back in the news, and he'd burned it into the riders' minds that Tom Simpson was the man to beat again one way or another.

He was very much back in the promoters' minds, too. Ironically, his victory the previous year had ended up earning him nothing, but in 1962, on the strength of his fifth place, he got a load of contracts. All of a sudden, it seemed, continental bike racing had accepted him – for the time being, anyway.

The following weekend Van Looy continued his triumphant march through the early season classics when he won Paris–Roubaix. Tom wasn't in his way this time, though: he had crashed just like the year before when in the thick of it at the front of the race. Fortunately, he wasn't badly hurt this time. He might have been getting accepted, but he hadn't yet found a way of defeating the devils and demons which lurk in the 'Hell of the North' .

It was mid-April now. Helen had gone home to stay with her parents in England for the last few weeks of her pregnancy, and the couple spent a fortune telephoning each other while Tom was travelling from race to race. Despite keeping in touch, he actually learned that he'd become a father from reading a newspaper just before the start of a race. He couldn't wait to get finished, then to travel back to England to see their baby daughter Jane for the first time. He didn't get much time to experience the delights of fatherhood, though, and was soon back on the road working for their future.

Cycling is a sport filled with tradition. The order in which the races appear on the calendar is set in stone. There have been some recent minor changes, but even today the season is split into three distinct phases, just like it has been since the early 1900s when all the great races began.

It all starts in February with a series of single-day and short stage races in the run-up to the spring classics: Milan–San Remo in March, then the Tour of Flanders, Paris–Roubaix and Liège–Bastogne–Liège in April. At the same time in northern Europe there are a number of races, not quite of the status of these monuments, but non the less hard-fought and demanding, known as the semi-classics.

Once the last of these is over, attention turns to multi-stage racing, with events of varying length and importance held throughout

Europe, culminating in the Tour of Italy and then the biggest of them all, the Tour de France. Then the spotlight returns to one-day racing, apart, that is, from the Tour of Spain which was recently moved from its traditional May date to September.

The big races of this autumn period are Paris–Tours, the Tour of Lombardy and three races which count towards the season-long World Cup points competition, though none of these can really aspire to classic status – they haven't set fire to people's imaginations yet, and that takes something extra, more than just time because the Championships of Zurich, which is one of them, has been on the go since 1914. Also in this period is the biggest prize in single-day racing, the World Pro Road Championships. It's a long season, February to October, and during it riders can clock up 20,000 to 25,000 miles on their bikes, and even more when travelling between the races.

One of the first stage races in the run-up to the Tour de France is the Four Days of Dunkirk, which is actually six days long. Don't ask me why, it just is, right? This is a very important race in France and because of Tom's second place in Paris–Nice he was one of the hot favourites to win it.

Despite the lack of mountains which are usually associated with stage races, the race is a difficult one and uses such obstacles as can be found in the Pas de Calais to maximum effect: cobbled pit roads of the mining areas around Lille and Lens are combined with short, sharp climbs up near the Belgian border to make it an uncomfortable race for anybody not in form; Mont Cassel, a brutal little hill with a village on top, is visited at least once during the race, and the organisers can chose from other such delicacies as the Mont des Chats, or a particularly nasty piece of road between Berthen and Boeschepe, when selecting a course for the race.

Incidentally, one man who wasn't on form was the 'pedalling clown', Roger Hassenforder. He was coming back after a bad crash and this was his first race, so he was dropped in the early part of most of the stages and had to continue on his own because he still had to get the miles in his legs. Also, as his sponsors were a local company, he didn't want to let his poor form stop him getting as much publicity as he could for them. So he just rode the whole race bringing up the rear with a 'running-in' sign pinned on to his back, just like they used to have on new cars in those days, much to the delight of the press and spectators, and with the sure guarantee of getting his picture in the paper.

On the first stage Tom missed an opportunist break which quickly gained time. It soon became obvious that this move was not going to be caught, so he decided that he would have to get up to it. He attacked and crossed the three-minute gap on his own in just 30 kilometres, but, just as he was joining the leaders, he crashed.

It was, indeed, the winning break, and Tom eventually finished the stage more than six minutes behind it, though much of this time had been lost fighting off an over-enthusiastic first-aider who was bandaging him up as he was trying to get back on his bike, and then continued trying to drag him back towards the race ambulance.

Tom decided to use the rest of the race as training, eventually finishing in twentieth place overall. However, he had enjoyed entertaining the press and his team mates with his account of the furious ambulance man chasing him down the road while he was trying to remove bandages, sling and splints from an undamaged arm.

Next came the Tour of Luxembourg, and at the end of the second day Tom was in the lead. Even though his lead wasn't big, he probably should have watched the others and got his team to chase down any attackers. Instead, desperate to make sure he won the race, he decided to try and increase his lead, and attacked. It could have worked, but it didn't.

Only two riders were able to follow him, Joseph Planckaert and Armand Desmet, both very strong and both riding for the same team. Now Tom found himself in one of the hardest of all situations in cycling, a three-man break with two good riders from the same team. Get into this position and you are just asking to be worked over. What happens is that one of the two attacks and, if you don't chase, he rides off to victory. If you do, his mate sits comfortably in your slipstream while you go after him. Once you get there, his mate attacks and the whole process is repeated until you can't react any more, and one of them wins. This is just what happened to Tom: the two Belgians worked him over in this way until he was so shattered that he had to retire from the race, whilst still in the lead.

So why did he get himself into that situation? Well, long before he knew he was riding this race he'd accepted a contract to ride the

Manx Premier race on the Isle of Man, and the two races overlapped. He loved riding in front of a home crowd and never really got many opportunities. It gave him a welcome chance to bask in the new-found glory of being one of the top pros in the world, the best his own country had ever produced. Tom loved that. Yes, he was a bit of an exhibitionist, but it was that desire to show off that made him try so hard and consequently achieve so much. If, however, he could make sure of winning the Tour of Luxembourg long before the last stage he would have stayed in that race and given up on going to the Isle of Man. That is why he went on the attack when he already had the lead, and that is why he ended up getting worked over. It was that impetuous streak again.

Sadly, the Manx Premier disappeared from the professional calendar in the seventies. Held during the island's cycling week, which is still going strong, this race had brought some of the very biggest names in the sport to the island. Fausto Coppi rode it in the late fifties, and in 1962 no less than 33 riders were flown in from the continent, including Jacques Anquetil, Jean Stablinski and Rudi Altig.

Unfortunately, for the riders and the thousands of spectators who'd come to see them, the weather on the island, which can at best be described as capricious, was, on the day of the race, downright awful. A force-eight gale was blowing freezing rain across the Clypse circuit and of the 81 starters only 23 finished.

Of course, Tom wanted to win. When didn't he? It was always especially important for him to win in Britain. He wanted to show everybody just how good he'd become. Also, we shall see that Tom increasingly saw himself as a shop window for British cycling because he wanted to attract a rich British sponsor into the sport. This would enable him to put together a team of British riders that he could depend on. Then he could take on the might of Europe on an equal footing. So, it was more than just a matter of pride that he rode well here – he was trying to ensure his own future as well.

Alas, despite trying his socks off, he couldn't quite win this one. He made typical repeated efforts to get away, including a 'do-or-die' stint over the last four laps into the teeth of that force-eight gale and lashing rain. He was finally caught, barely one mile from the finish, by a battered group of just 16 riders – all that was left at the head of the race. It was Anquetil who was the main force in bringing him back, aided by Tom's old pursuiting mate, John Geddes, who did a fantastic ride that day. Anquetil's efforts were for the benefit of his team mate, Rudi Altig, and he sprinted from the group to win. Piet Damen was second, and Alan Ramsbottom, a very strong rider in his first year as a pro on the continent, who always went well in long, hard and hilly races, was third. Tom finished sixth.

8

THE MAJOR WEARS YELLOW

The 1962 Tour de France was Tom's big target for the year. His ambition was to win this race one day, and this year he intended to prove, to himself as much as anyone, that it was possible. To do this he would need to achieve as high an overall position as he could, and ride the whole three-week race as a contender. The Tour started almost straight after the Manx Premier, so along with most of the other continental riders who'd been riding on the island, he flew on a specially chartered plane to the start in Nancy.

This year the race was to be contested for the first time since 1929 by trade, and not national, teams and, together with the experienced Darrigade, Tom was designated as leader of the Gitane-Leroux squad. The team had good morale, a great manager in Louviot, and a belief that between them, Tom and André could really do something in the race. This would mean that they would all earn good money and there is nothing like that for ensuring a pro bike rider's loyalty. So, they were on the attack from the start.

After Tom had finished ninth on the first stage from Nancy to Spa in Belgium, Darrigade won the second stage and took the yellow jersey of race leadership, with Tom not far behind in sixth place. The result had caused a huge upset in Belgium, for the stage ended in the town of Herentals, home of the 'Emperor', Rik Van Looy, and neither he nor his fans were very pleased with the outcome. This meant a very uncomfortable afternoon for his 'Red Guard' because there was a team time trial in Herentals, and Van Looy flogged his Faema-Flandria squad to victory over the Gitane-Leroux boys. The 'Emperor' had preserved some of his dignity, but he hadn't changed much in the race: Darrigade was still in the lead, with Tom in seventh place.

Though aiming for a high overall place, Tom found it difficult to curb his attacking nature and, next day, on a long, hot trek from Brussels to Amiens, he made several attempts to get away. Eventually, he forced a group clear as the race crossed the First World War battlefields, and then attacked again with five kilometres to go, making a brave effort to score another historic victory there for a 'British Tommy', but he was caught and had to settle for seventeenth place.

Down through Normandy and Brittany he was involved in several similar skirmishes until, on the stage from St Nazaire to Lewçon, he forced a split of 30 riders which gained a significant amount of time on the rest. Darrigade was also there, so they both worked hard to press home their advantage. The group stayed away, with André taking over the jersey once more, and Tom just behind him in second place.

Some of the advantage Tom had worked for was lost on the very next day, a time trial, where the early starters – those lower on the general classification, because that's how time trials are run on the Tour, with the last starting first and the first starting last – had the best weather conditions. Anquetil, who hadn't made a move in the Tour up to then and so was quite low on overall classification, made the most of this and won. Tom, who'd started second to last, had to ride in wet and windy conditions, and could only finish eighteenth on the stage. It didn't affect his overall place, though, because he still beat those around him, including Darrigade, by a good margin, to stay second overall.

He had one or two disparaging things to say about time trials though, after his ride: 'I don't know why the French call these "the race of truth" when two riders can end up riding over the same roads in different conditions. At least in a bunch race everybody rides in the same conditions.'

Next day, to Bordeaux, everyone was caught out by a surprise lone attack from Willy Schroeders which resulted in him taking the lead and Tom dropping to third place. Never mind, the race now stood at the foot of the Pyrenees: there would be a big shake-up tomorrow, minutes gained and lost where previously there had been only seconds. Tom had worked hard all week to be in a position to make a move on the race leadership. It was part of his plan. He was going for a good position overall, but he'd been far more active than the other race favourites during this first week. There were two reasons for this: he wanted to show that he could lead the race, not just finish well up by following others; and a British yellow jersey would be a real attraction for the criterium promoters, and therefore greatly increase his market value.

The first mountain stage, from Pau to St Gaudens, was a big one, including as it did three of the great set pieces of Tour de France history – three mountain passes: the Tourmalet at 2,115 metres; the Aspin at 1,489 metres; and the Peyresourde at 1,569 metres. If he was going to take the jersey Tom had to make his move today; he couldn't afford to let the other favourites take the initiative.

Predictably, battle commenced as soon as the riders reached the Tourmalet and, predictably, Tom was the first to attack. A small group formed around him containing, among others, Anquetil, Geldermans and the man known to all as the 'Eagle of Toledo', Federico Bahamontes, a fantastic mountain climber who was to win the King of the Mountains title in this race a record six times. Towards the summit the 'Eagle' attacked to take the points in this competition, and went over the top a handful of seconds in front of Tom and the others.

On the twisting and steep descent off the mountain Bahamontes was caught. But, as soon as they hit the next climb, the Aspin, he was off again, this time with the German, Wolfshohl, for company, attacking the climb's famous hairpin bends as if he had, in fact, sprouted wings.

With the 'Eagle' climbing as only he could, and soon ridding himself of Wolfshohl's company, the group behind had grown, but for the time being they were only concerned with not letting Bahamontes get too far in front. Tom was there, climbing well, and climbing in great company as they had been joined by the man with that other evocative nickname, Charly Gaul, the 'Angel of the Mountains'.

At the top, Bahamontes again took the points and, then, on the descent, tried to press home his advantage. His lead started to increase and, sensing that they might miss out on a stage victory, Wolfshohl and Massignan attacked and caught up with him. They worked well and had a 40-second lead over Tom's group at the foot of the long, straight and steep climb to the summit of the Peyresourde. From there to the finish at St Gaudens was a long way, so Tom wasn't too worried about this move; he was content just to watch Geldermans, the closest rider to him in the overall standings. A pointless chase of Bahamontes at this stage would be as good as handing the yellow jersey to the Dutchman on a plate.

On the Peyresourde, Bahamontes steadily turned the screw on his breakaway companions, dropping them before the top where he again took maximum points, thereby tightening his grip, or should I say talons, on his fourth 'King of the Mountains' title. Behind him, Tom's group had split, with Tom and Geldermans still watching each other in the front half.

Despite this, they caught Bahamontes on the run in to the finish, where Cazala won the stage and Tom took over the yellow jersey, leading the race by 30 seconds from Geldermans. It had been a cool, controlled and professional performance. Tom had worked for over a week to get within spitting distance of the jersey, then used the terrain available and a combination of aggression and discipline to take it. Now he was the first Briton ever to wear the jersey – cycling's 'Golden Fleece'. It would be 32 years before another, Chris Boardman, would wear it. And, remember this, Tom is still the only Brit to take it when the battle for the race is at its height, where the favourites come to the fore and the race finds its winner – in the high mountains.

The scenes at the stage finish, however, certainly weren't cool and controlled. 'Un Anglais' in the yellow jersey, leading a French institution! It was 'incroyable'. What a moment! Ever the showman, out came the bowler hat and the people of France were treated to the spectacle of Major Thompson wearing the *maillot jaune* with their breakfast croissants. Every newspaper in France was carrying that picture.

But you can't please everybody. Louviot wasn't happy with Tom: he berated him for not sprinting for the stage. He told him that if Geldermans had won, and therefore got the available time bonus, then he, and not Tom, would have been leading the Tour. Tom replied that he hadn't wanted to risk a fall in the sprint and, anyway, he'd been watching the Dutchman. Still Louviot wasn't happy. Remember the 1960 Worlds? Louviot thought Tom was brilliant, but sometimes he infuriated him. He wanted Tom always to think like a champion; he didn't want him to miss a chance to make the most of himself. At times, maybe, he took things a bit too far, and perhaps this was one of them, because, in his anger, he might just have made a mistake with Tom the following day, a mistake that lost him the jersey, and possibly much more.

Tom wasn't going to let Louviot spoil his moment, though – he was ecstatic. When asked by a journalist how he felt about defending his jersey the next day, which was the thirteenth stage of the race, he replied: 'Both my wife and my daughter were born on Friday the thirteenth, so perhaps thirteen is my lucky number.' It wasn't, not by a long way.

Stage thirteen of the race was an individual time trial up a mountain climb to the ski station at Superbagnères. The road climbs by some very steep hairpin bends to a height of 1,804 metres. Tom was the last rider to start the test, resplendent in his yellow jersey and surrounded by a convoy of press, official and television vehicles. And, in case they missed anything, a helicopter would be clattering away above his head, slowly ascending the mountain with him.

He desperately wanted to keep the jersey – every day he wore it meant more money in the bank – but soon after he started it was obvious that something was wrong. He was constantly breaking his rhythm by getting out of the saddle, then sitting back down again. He was making a tremendous effort, but appeared to be fighting his bike rather than powering it up the mountain; and he was visibly losing ground on the other favourites.

Eventually, he finished his ordeal in thirty-first place, 5 minutes and 40 seconds behind the winner, Bahamontes, and nowhere near where he should have been. There had obviously been some sort of a problem because a fit rider doesn't lose form that quickly, and for the only time in their relationship Tom blamed Louviot.

He had wanted Tom to use higher gears than he was used to, higher gears than the others were riding, so he ordered his bike to be fitted with 49- and 45-tooth chainrings, and 24- and 26-tooth bottom sprockets. After his ride, Tom said, 'I was all right up to half-way on 45 by 26, but then Louviot came up alongside me in the car and told me to go on to the 45 by 24, then the 49 by 26. I just lost all my rhythm and about three kilometres from the summit I just couldn't give any more.'

He had lost the jersey, and with it a little bit of confidence in Louviot, but typically he saw the funny side. I may have gone down in history as the first Briton to wear the yellow jersey, but I must also have been the rider to wear it for the shortest time: he said afterwards. He didn't think for one moment that he would never wear it again.

Tom had fallen to fifth place overall and took it easy on the next stage, but set about redressing the situation on stage 15. It didn't work. He put in a big attack on the last climb of the day, only to be caught on the outskirts of Montpellier, where the stage finished, and gained nothing. He would have to wait for the Alps.

The first Alpine stage that year took them from Antibes to Briançon. Big decisions were being made again. Tom climbed with the best of them to finish ninth on the stage with a group that contained all the race favourites, and moved up to third place overall. The challenge was back on.

There was just one more day in the Alps, but the overall order was nowhere near decided. There were still a number of riders who believed they had a chance of winning, so the stage saw an enormous battle taking place, no one willing to give an inch. Tom fought through, defending his third place with great class, and a final place on the podium was beginning to look certain. Still, it wouldn't hurt to gain some more time on his rivals. He saw his chance on the descent of the last climb of the day, the Col de Porte, and took it.

He dropped like a stone, drawing away from the others on each hairpin bend, out-braking them into it, then sprinting flatout on the straights. It was desperate, daredevil stuff – he was even trying to slipstream the press motorbikes at over 50 miles per hour. It was a gutsy move, throwing all caution to the wind, taking the race to the others, but he pushed his luck just a little too far. Rounding a bend he hit a patch of loose gravel and his bike slid from underneath him. Still with his feet strapped to it, both he and the bike disappeared over the edge.

It could have been the end for Tom. Luckily, however, a tree prevented him from falling hundreds of feet. He slithered down the trunk, but his bike was still stuck up in the branches. Now these athletes can do superhuman things, but climbing a tree, towards the end of an Alpine stage of the Tour in cycling shoes is, I imagine, beyond most of them. It was certainly beyond Tom. He was left standing by the side of the road, without a bike, and third place in the Tour de France disappearing down the mountain.

A cameraman came to his rescue. He'd seen him go over the edge and was able to climb out on to a branch and get his bike back. A quick check: nothing seemed damaged, and so he was on his way again. The bike might have been alright, but Tom wasn't. He had cuts and bruises all over his body, and had broken the middle finger of his left hand. None of this hurt as much as falling to sixth place overall by the end of the stage, after he'd limped the last few miles home.

To add to his problems, he had no time to recover as the next stage was a long time trial, in which he would be forced to make a big effort to stay in contention, rather than cruise in the bunch and recover. He suffered deeply that day to limit his losses, and retained his sixth place, despite being hardly able to hold his handlebars because of the plaster cast on his finger.

This cast was to cause a final bit of panic on the last stage into Paris. There was a minor tumble in the bunch and Tom found himself lying on the road on top of the race leader, Jacques Anquetil. As they sorted themselves out Tom realised that he'd got his plastered finger stuck in Anquetil's back wheel. It took him quite a while to extract it, by which time someone had given Jacques a new bike.

The race finished on the Parc des Princes track which was packed with people who'd come to celebrate Anquetil's third victory in the race. Tom was still sixth, but it could have been higher. Should he have attacked on that last day in the Alps when in third place? Surely, if he'd been content to follow he would have been on the podium in Paris? Maybe, but Tom just couldn't race like that; he saw his chance and went for it. Anyway, could he be sure of doing a strong enough time trial to keep third place? There were too many unanswerable questions, but there was one thing that he was absolutely sure of after this Tour de France: one day he would win it.

The last day was full of lovely surprises. A party of English club riders had flown in to cheer their hero on his lap of honour at the track. Helen was there. But the biggest surprise of all was that the *Daily Express* newspaper had flown Tom's mum over to Paris for the celebrations. It was a proud moment and she was staggered by how popular her son was. 'He had to go round and round the track. There were more cheers for him than the winner,' she recalled, years later.

It was a great moment and there was huge publicity for Tom's achievement in France. A third-year pro taking sixth in the Tour is always going to be news, but an Englishman doing it ... Well! Pictures of Tom, Helen and his mum, even, appeared in *Paris Match*, a very chic, glossy magazine. Such was the fame of this Englishman who, when asked by the press how he'd celebrated taking the yellow jersey, replied, 'by having my pot of tea, and jam and bread in bed after the stage'.

Now it was time to cash in on all the hard work and suffering. The Englishman in yellow was in demand from every criterium organiser in Europe. This time, though, Tom survived them well; he was a lot stronger now than in 1960. The downside of all this activity would probably mean him not having much form for the Worlds in September, but at this stage of his career money would have to come first, even though making it was far from easy.

Tom took every contract he was offered during this period. On one occasion he had to race in northern Italy, quite late in the evening, then drive without sleep to the far west of France to ride in one of the notoriously hard criteriums in Brittany. Lenny Jones was riding in Brittany by then and he remembers going to watch his old club-mate in that race: 'Tom was so tired that he was lapped in that race, but he couldn't pack because there was a clause in his contract which said that he had to finish the race to get his appearance money.' No wonder Lenny had second thoughts about becoming a pro rider.

Not surprisingly Tom was exhausted by the time the World Championships came round, but a couple of days rest saw him slightly recovered. He didn't know what to expect from the race, but he was prepared as always to give his best in Salo, northern Italy, the scene of the 1962 pro road race.

The vital break went early, so with 40 miles to go Tom decided to try and get across to it. He was gaining quite nicely, but having to dig deep to do so, when, just 50 metres from catching them, what little form he had deserted him. That 50-metre gap may as well have been 50 miles because, try as he did, Tom could not close it. He flogged himself silly, but it was no good, and, in any case, he was now so shattered that even if he'd caught them he would have been in no state to contest the finale of the race, so he had to abandon. English-speaking cyclists did, however, make another step forward in that race when Ireland's Shay Elliott took second place to the French winner, Jean Stablinski.

Despite having no realistic form for this race, Tom was bitterly disappointed with his performance, especially so because in the World Championships, as always, he was wearing his national, rather than trade team colours, and he always wore the Great Britain jersey with pride. Also, though things were starting to go better (he'd worn the yellow jersey, had good placings in big races and was making good money) he hadn't won a big race since the Tour of Flanders in 1961, and Tom was a winner. Professionally speaking, everything was going well, but he couldn't be satisfied with that; he had to start winning again, and winning big.

For the time being, though, he had to put these ambitions on the back burner because there was still money to be earned, still chances to cash in on the races he had won rather than planning for those he might win. It was a harsh fact of life in those days that, for the vast majority of riders, it was only possible to earn big money from racing – no one was going to pay you much to go training. So it was on with the slog. Still, towards the end of the 1962 season Tom found a new opportunity to earn money in a different kind of racing. He went back to the track, but to a form of racing that was a far cry from the Olympic events in which he'd first come to international notice back in the fifties.

Most of the top road men in the sixties, if they had any kind of track background at all, would try to ride at least their local six-day race. This form of racing was still a very big affair then, and promoters could be sure to get extra bums on seats if they were able to sign up a good star roadman or two for their race, as well as riders who were specialists at this kind of thing. Some, like Van Looy, van Steenbergen and Peter Post could ride both, and did so with great success. At first Tom thought that one or two of these, because they are held on indoor tracks throughout the winter, would help him cash in on his summer successes and keep him fit, but he really took to them, becoming, later, a permanent fixture on the six-day scene.

Six-day racing first started in 1878 when a professional cyclist, David Stanton, was bet £100 that he couldn't ride 1,000 consecutive miles in six days. He won his bet, riding around a flat track in London's Agricultural Hall on his penny-farthing bicycle at an average speed of 13.5 miles per hour.

Inspired by him, riders were soon taking part in races over six days. As their bicycles and speeds improved it soon became necessary to build banked tracks to accommodate them. However, these races between individuals were still basically tests of endurance and the spectacle of a gaggle of shattered riders wobbling their weary way round a track for six days soon started to pall with all but the most sadistic race-goer.

To increase the speed and therefore excitement of these events the promoters decided to have them contested by two-man teams, one resting whilst the other raced, the winner being simply the team that completed the most laps in six days. The riders would agree between themselves when the race would be on or when it would be neutralised so they could get a good rest and be fresher, and therefore faster, when the crowds were at their biggest. During these fast periods both riders stayed on the track and relayed each other into the fray with pushes and handslings. This kind of race became known as a 'Madison' or an 'American race', because it was devised at the Madison Square Gardens venue during the New York six-days of the 1920s. Six-day racing was very popular in America then.

By the sixties, its popularity across the Atlantic had dwindled, reputedly because of too much interest in the outcome being shown by certain 'sporting' gentlemen fond of wearing spats, carrying violin cases and driving round in big, black Buicks. However, the sixes were still going strong in Europe, particularly in the north – Holland, Belgium, and Germany – where they were a social as much as a sporting occasion, with music, dancing and, in particular, beer drinking being nearly as big an attraction as the racing.

To keep the increasingly sophisticated audiences happy, the promoters had, by then, introduced races within the race: motorpaced and sprint races, record attempts and elimination races to spice up the evening's entertainment; but the Madison was still the core of the six-day. That is where laps could be gained and lost, and that is where the race found its winning team, as ever the one who had completed more laps than the others. In the event of a tie, the points earned in the interim races count to produce a winner.

These races were still tough – they still are – but by the time the sixties had come round only one of them required at least one of the riders to be on the track for the full 144 hours that make up six days. That was the Madrid Six, and that was the race in which Tom made his debut in early October 1962.

Thankfully, Tom's partner for his first event was the very experienced and very fast Australian rider, John Tressider, who had already won the race in 1960, adding it to his victory in the Lille event. Believe me, experience is everything in these events, even if you're only watching one!

Tom and John prepared for it by racing and training at the Ghent track. Here they met a young amateur rider from Norwich, Dave Nice, who was trying his luck at the racing there. Nice needed money, and Tom and John needed someone to look after them in Madrid. Dave also wanted to see Spain, so he said that he would do the job.

Unfortunately, they arrived and left in the dark, so the only thing Dave ever saw of Spain was the inside of the Palacio de Deportes in Madrid.

They travelled to the race in Tom's brand new Mercedes, the biggest you could get at the time. Tom loved cars; he later started a small collection of old ones, and always had the latest and most luxurious model to travel to races in. This was actually good sense as a professional cyclist in the sixties spent nearly as much time at the wheel of his car as he did on his bike.

Getting into Spain wasn't as easy then, under Franco, as it is now; it took them ages to convince suspicious customs officials at the border that you needed four bikes and twenty pairs of wheels just to ride one race. They managed it, and it was another story for Tom to tell, but the delay meant that they were only just in time for the start, and it really was like jumping in at the deep end.

The first night's racing went on until four in the morning, at which point the race was neutralised. From then until ten o'clock no one was allowed to race, but one rider had to be on the track, so they divided this period into two shifts, one riding for three hours while the other had a sleep, then swapping round at seven o'clock. From ten the race was on again, a more or less continuous Madison race which got faster and faster as the crowds started to build up.

It was a tough and sleepless schedule, so you can see that the riders' main preoccupation was getting some extra rest. This was where Dave Nice came into his own. From a distance he looked a lot like Tom, who had the bright idea of dressing him up in his track suit, plonking his Russian hat on his head, wrapping a scarf round the lower half of poor Dave's face, then shoving him out on to the track for the neutralised session while he went back to bed. This outfit didn't look out of place because once the paying public left, the promoter turned the heating off.

The scheme worked well for two days, and both Tom and John got some extra sleep while their exhausted helper plodded gently round the track. Unfortunately, on the third day, the track manager, himself an ex-bike rider, decided to have a little ride round and a chat with the boys. Knowing Tom spoke French he drew alongside Dave and was soon rattling away to him in that language, of which – yes, you've guessed it – Dave understood not a word. It didn't take long for the manager to tumble, and he whipped the scarf off Dave's face, then marched over to where Tom was sleeping and tipped him out of bed. He kept a very close eye on them after that.

Despite the lack of sleep, Tom really took to this form of racing. He had natural speed and was now a strong roadman. Plus, he knew how to entertain a crowd, both with displays of spectacular riding and by getting involved in the numerous pranks the riders played to brighten up the quiet moments of the race. By the penultimate night John and Tom were in the lead.

There was a full house for the final night: 20,000 people packed into the stadium, and nearly every one of them had come to see the home team of Poblet and Bover win. The only problem for them was that the Anglo-Aussie combination weren't going to give up their lead without a fight.

They had their problems, too. John had broken his hand in a race in Germany and was having increasing difficulty relaying Tom into the race. Tom had fallen in this race, his back landing heavily on the pedal of Henk Nijdam's bike as he did so, and was in great pain. On top of this, the partisan kitchen staff at the track were proving difficult and refused to prepare the meals Dave Nice had ordered for his team. This meant a quick trip out to the shops for fruit, chocolate, and anything else he could find just to keep them going on that long and hard final night.

They eventually succumbed to the pressure of practically the whole field riding against them to ensure a Spanish victory. Inevitably, they lost their lead and ended the race in third place. Once the crowd had 'their' victory they gave John and Tom a huge ovation when they did their lap of honour. Despite his bruises and the accumulated fatigue of pedalling round and round a 176-metre track for six days during which he and Tressider had completed a staggering total of 2,200 kilometres, Tom was very happy with his debut race. Third place overall is very good for your first attempt at one of these races and Tom was instantly in demand for others.

So much so that as soon as they'd finished in Madrid, they had to drive straight back to Belgium for a race in Ghent. Another 27 hours of shared driving with poor Dave Nice, who'd been awake for practically the whole six days, curled up on the back seat, fast asleep.

One-day meetings at Ghent and at Brussels followed, then a contract to ride in the Ghent six-day at the end of November. Just before this Tom had to make an appearance at the Cycle Show at London's Earl's Court. So, to save time, he moved his track bikes and all his equipment into the Sportspaleis before setting off for London, only to be met there next day with the news that the Sportspaleis had burned down during the night, taking with it all his track stuff and his contract, and any money he'd hoped to earn.

More problems came when Leroux suddenly announced that they would not be sponsoring a team in 1963. On the face of it, Tom was unaffected because he was contracted directly to Raymond Louviot, who was to be the manager of Jacques Anquetil's St Raphaël team and would have gladly taken Tom with him. But Tom had transferred from St Raphaël to avoid that particular scenario only the previous year. Now that he'd felt the yellow jersey on his own back, he certainly wasn't going to take a backward step and start working for Anquetil. Certainly, he'd have made good money, and certainly Anquetil would have allowed him to be leader for a lot of races he didn't want for himself. It would have been a safe move, but this was a man who never played safe. No, he needed a team where he was the number one in every race, not just someone who was allowed to pick up the crumbs from Anquetil's table.

As is usual at this time of year, there was a lot of speculation in the press about the destination of various riders, the make-up of teams, who wouldn't work with whom and all the other intrigue that goes on to fill the sports pages during the winter months when there's no actual racing on the roads. Tom was linked with a new sponsor, a biscuit manufacturer going by the name of Nutsy. He was quite taken with this: the thought of riding in a jersey with the word 'Nutsy' emblazoned across the front and back appealed to his sense of humour. In the end, the team wasn't allowed by the cycling authorities, who deemed that the company had too close a commercial link with St Raphaël, and therefore there was too great a possibility of collusion.

Peugeot, the French cycle and car producer, had plans to expand their team for 1963 with the help of a link-up with the giant BP concern. So, without him having much of a say in it, they bought Tom's contract from Louviot, though Tom didn't receive a formal contract from them until the following year. He didn't care, really; at least he had a team in which, in theory, he would be the number-one man.

The team was huge: 29 riders, of whom 15 were Frenchmen and 14 foreigners, many of them big names, though not as big as Anquetil. In many respects, Tom would be rather like the head of a chapter of gangsters with this lot, each ready to replace him if he should falter, but he felt he could handle the situation. They were none of them Anquetil after all. By then, I think he was the only rider Tom really feared, the only rider that he was not sure he could beat – yet.

Nevertheless, there were some strong riders in the Peugeot team: classic winners in Jean Forestier and Pino Cerami, some promising youngsters like Rolf Wolfshohl, Emile Daems and Ferdi Bracke, and the biggest name, former Tour de France winner, Charly Gaul, trying to stage something of a comeback. Tom would have a job controlling this lot, but looked forward to the support of his mentor Brian Robinson, although this didn't happen, in fact, as Brian decided to quit racing before the season started.

Never mind, he was a big boy now and was sure that he'd cope with things at Peugeot. He did, very quickly, though it would be a bumpy ride and he would never again have people round him like Louviot and Robinson, except on the few occasions he rode for the Great Britain team, when, although it was never as strong as the Peugeot squad, at least there was nobody there who would double-cross him. However, the 1963 season was still a couple of months away. Now it was time to bask in some of the glory he'd earned in 1962, and there was a chance to visit the folks back home.

All over Europe cycling holds its awards ceremonies in the month of December. The biggest one in Britain in the early sixties was the Champions' Concert held at the Albert Hall in London. Past events had seen the great Fausto Coppi as a guest of honour and plenty of cycling's aristocracy, including the Tour de France organiser, Jacques Goddet, and three-times winner Louison Bobet who attended the 1962 event, which, quite naturally, celebrated Tom's ground-breaking performance in the Tour. Vic Jenner, as master of ceremonies, told the audience 'The Story of the Yellow Jersey'. Tom was presented to them wearing the jersey. Then Bobet was interviewed on stage and told everybody that he thought 'Tom could certainly finish in the top three of the race, provided he had good team support'.

It was a great occasion, enjoyed by all. Next day, Tom drove the two French celebrities to Heathrow Airport wearing a new addition to his collection, a chauffeur's hat. A couple of days later he turned up on our doorstep at Harworth, wearing this hat, and ushered me and my mum into the back seat of his big, white Mercedes, and then drove us up the A1 to visit our relatives in Durham, wearing the hat all the way. I was six years old.

Just after Christmas, Tom was a guest speaker at a British Cycling Federation training weekend in Bolton. His input provoked some lively debate, particularly his suggestion on improving a rider's power on hills by riding 'no hands' up long drags. Also during this weekend he found out that he had been voted the British Cycling Federation's Personality of the Year for 1962.

But 1962 was over now, and he had to move up a gear in '63. Tom and Helen were expecting another baby. They'd moved to a bigger house in the St Amandsberg suburb of Ghent. A lot had changed: he had responsibilities to make a good life for his young family and to satisfy his own destiny; he had to start winning races and they had to be big ones. So, he set about training for the new season with a dedication that surprised even him.

He was very happy with his new home in Ghent, where they had lived for over a year now.

'There's something about the atmosphere here in Flanders that makes you want to win. Also, when I'm training, I go out every day, even between races, and even in bad weather. The Belgian people love cyclists and if you are a champion you are treated like a king.'

That is what he told the British *Cycling* magazine.

9

THE LION GOES FROM STRENGTH
TO STRENGTH

Tom's first race in 1963 was Paris–Nice, He'd missed the early season races on the Côte d'Azure in favour of extra training and consequently was a bit behind some of the others in terms of race fitness. This situation wasn't helped by a series of punctures and bad luck in the first few stages. By stage five, though, he'd found his race legs and was in the action all day with fellow British rider, Vin Denson.

Earlier, Vin and his wife Vi had moved into the little house by the canal that Tom and Helen had just left. Although Vin was riding for a French team he saw sense in becoming the second member of Ghent's British pro racing colony. It was the start of a close friendship between Vin and Tom, who came to regard Vin like a big brother over the coming years.

Vin had good legs in Paris–Nice and, next day, finished well up in a time trial to take an eventual tenth place overall. Tom, on the other hand, was still short of form: he was using the race as training, Unfortunately, he took this training idea a bit too far, and did something he would have cause to regret later in the year: on the last day he decided to give himself a short, sharp test, then retire, and save himself for his next race, Milan–San Remo.

The stage started at Nice and, following a brief warm-up, Tom attacked after just a couple of kilometres on the La Turbie climb. He gave it everything, and tore the field to shreds – over 30 riders retired from the race that day. Rudi Altig, protecting the interests of race leader, Anquetil, went after him and was furious when he caught him, but Tom took no notice and attacked again. By the top, he'd built quite a lead, so he coasted down to Monaco, stopped by the roadside, and waved at the decimated field as it went by in small but furious groups to cover the rest of the 180-kilometre stage. Then he set off along the coast road back to Nice in delightful spring sunshine, as happy as a bird in the air. He should not have done that.

In the short term, his training session worked, and he was starting to show the kind of form he would need to get another classic victory: his performance in Milan–San Remo showed that everything was on track for that big win.

He rode with great assurance in this race, forging an early lead with a group containing Balmamion, Schroeders and Denson, which gained just over three minutes by the 95-kilometre point in the town of Novi Ligure, close to the birthplace of Coppi. This provoked a reaction from the bunch, and a group of four, which included Tom's team mate Rolf Wolfshohl, set off in pursuit. A bit later, just as these four were joining, Tom punctured, but Wolfshohl stopped to wait for him and, after a furious chase, the pair got back to the front of the race.

By now the race was on one of the biggest climbs on the route, the Turchino pass. On the descent, Tom looked behind and saw that the chasers were closing on them. He decided that he must attack to draw the strong ones away with him. Unfortunately, Wolfshohl prevented this by making lots of little attacks himself and getting brought back. Tom got fed up with him, so, as it was obvious that Wolfshohl was going well – he had after all won the World Cyclo-cross Championships earlier that year – he told the German to save his strength for one big attack on the Poggio climb.

Unfortunately, Wolfsohl's legs were working better than his ears that day and he attacked on the flat, just before the climb, killing everybody off but a fast Frenchman called Joseph Groussard. He clung to Rolf's wheel and managed to outsprint him by the narrowest of margins on the Via Roma to win the race. After that, Tom made a little deal with himself: he would always help one of his team mates, but only after he'd tried to win the race himself.

Back in Belgium he put himself through an intense period of training and racing in the tough Belgian semi-classics which abound in March – such races as the Across Belgium, the Circuit of Eleven Towns, and the Circuit of the Flemish Ardennes. The weather was often cold and blustery, but this didn't prevent him putting in rides of at least 50 miles each day between races, and a weekly long ride of 100 to 120 miles. I should add that all the races were above 120 miles and that there weren't too many days between them either.

If your body can take it, a schedule like that is bound to bring results. Tom's home life was very secure, with Helen doing everything she could to support him. Already an excellent cook, since their marriage she had managed to work some of the weirder things Tom ate into tasty and nourishing meals. By the time of his next big race, the Ghent–Wevelgem at the end of March, Tom was flying, ready for anything, and ready to win.

This race was as important then as it is now, although it was staged just before the Tour of Flanders and Paris–Roubaix rather than between them, but this meant that all the favourites for these two monuments had to ride it to make sure they had the legs for the big two. Also, a victory in Ghent–Wevelgem is itself no small feather in a rider's cap.

A huge field started the 140-mile race, and almost from the off 57 of them got away, switching all over the road as the surface changed from *pavé* to concrete to cycle path, then back again. These were all Belgians, hungry for victory in another race they'd made their own; only one non-Belgian had won it in the 29 years it had been on the go before 1963.

Very sensibly, Tom wasn't getting involved in this particular brand of nationalistic mayhem. He sat back in the main bunch, biding his time with the other race favourites, while the battle raging up front ensured that 27 miles were covered in the first hour, and into the wind at that.

The race loops out towards the coast, then plunges down to a little range of hills just to the west of Kortrijk, whose names are synonymous with the First World War – none more so than the one-in-five slopes of the Kemmelberg, where thousands of French soldiers resisted a last push by the Germans and in doing so lost their lives in the final days of the conflict.

By the time these hills were reached most of the early aggressors had been mopped up by the main field, which itself was starting to split over successive climbs under the forceful riding of the race favourites. All of these men were now at the front and watching each other like hawks for some sign of weakness. The job of their *domestiques* to get them there was now done, and it was time for the big boys to take the stage for the finale.

With four kilometres to go Van Looy punctured, and the race was on. Van Meenen jumped away and Tom, Benoni Beheyt, Van Aerde and Van Geneughden went after him. They caught him with just 400 metres to go and Tom eased in order to have a good look round at just who was left. He didn't take long to decide that Beheyt, a very good sprinter, was the danger man. Despite him, Tom was still sure that he could win. Yes, Beheyt was fast, but after a long race so was Tom: ask Defilippis, and ask Rudi Altig.

Beheyt was from Ghent and a member of the Gentse Velosport Cycling Club, as was Tom, So despite being in a different trade team he cheekily asked Tom to lead out the sprint for him. Tom wasn't having any of that and braked slightly to get Beheyt to take the lead. Now they were close to the finish and Beheyt could not afford to finesse any longer: he went for it and, as he did, Tom started his sprint. He was just on the point of overhauling the Belgian to win the Ghent–Wevelgem when the line flashed beneath them. One metre after it, Tom's front wheel was past Beheyt's, but, on the line, where it counts, Beheyt had got it, with Tom second by a centimetre.

Tom was sure that he had won it and suspected a plot when the judges gave it to Beheyt. Was this a case of a home-town victory, he asked? No, the photo finish proved that Beheyt's last, desperate lunge was enough to win, but Tom wouldn't accept it until they actually showed him the photo.

Almost as soon as he had finished, Tom had to take his disappointment on the long drive down to St Raphaël on the French Riviera for the three-day Tour du Var. Despite the long journey, his form held up well and he won the first stage in an uphill sprint from a small breakaway group containing Gilbert Desmet 11 (who was second on the stage), Foucher, Messelis, Cazala, and Henri Anglade, and had gained over five minutes on the rest. It was looking good – he had the leader's jersey, and would only have to keep his eye on four others. Little did he know that, the very next day, he was going to receive a big pay-back for messing everybody about on the last stage of Paris–Nice.

The second stage of the Tour du Var was to St Tropez and, though Tom was now in the top flight of his profession, he made a novice's error. He thought the race finished there. It did, but once in the town there was a final five-kilometre climb that had to be negotiated, and guess who hadn't looked at the race profile that morning? Tom had spent a lot of energy chasing down attacks all day because his lead over Anglade wasn't that great. In the streets of St Tropez, he imagined he had saved the leader's jersey, then he was faced with that climb. Before he could think further, Anquetil attacked, taking Anglade and Jo Groussard with him.

Anquetil thundered up that final climb, never once relinquishing the lead to Anglade or his team mate, Groussard; never once, in fact, asking them to lead. He won the stage and, in the process, dragged Anglade into the overall lead, taking 1 minute 5 seconds out of Tom, who finished fourth on the day. He was furious – Henri Anglade was no friend of Jacques Anquetil, so why had he handed victory to him on a plate?

Tom challenged Anquetil about this, and received what seemed at first a very enigmatic reply from the great Frenchman: 'The penny has two faces, you know, Tom. Good deeds are repaid and bad ones, too.' But then he went on: 'Do you remember the last stage of Paris–Nice? You would never have lost this race if you hadn't played around then and made a monkey out of everyone.'

Tom knew then that, perhaps, he'd got just a bit too big for his boots. He'd learned two timely lessons: one, always check the race route; and, two, no matter how good you are, you don't need to make enemies, particularly not ones as powerful as Jacques Anquetil. Tom had a lot more professional respect after that day, and paid more attention to details.

Next day, Tom attacked repeatedly, but Anglade's Pelforth team were ruthless in chasing him down, ably assisted by Anquetil who must have wanted to make sure that the lesson had been well learnt. It had been, and Tom had to be satisfied with second place overall.

Never mind, it was the Tour of Flanders on Sunday, a race he'd won, and a race in which the distance and terrain suited his attacking style. On the day he was incredible. The author of ten attacks, he made the winning move with six kilometres to go – Altig, Fore and Melckenbeeck being the only riders who could follow him – but he'd done too much, again, to get himself into a winning position, and could only salvage third place behind Fore and Melckenbeeck, He really had tried to win this one – there was no 'hidden agenda' like last year, Tom was desperate for a big win and probably trying too hard, trying to shape the races on his own, rather than using the efforts of others. In the course of ten days he'd been second in Ghent–Wevelgem, second in the Tour du Var and third in the Tour of Flanders, and in that last race he had finished in the first five for three consecutive years – some record. But he wasn't winning the big races he needed for himself, and to impress upon his team that he was number one.

Next up was Paris–Roubaix, but two days before Tom had a contract to ride in the Good Friday meeting at Herne Hill. There he competed in three ten-mile, Derny-paced races against Barry Hoban, who was racing as an independent in France by then, two Belgian pacing specialists, De Paepe and Proost, Australian six-day rider, Reg Arnold, and the charismatic British time triallist, Alf Engers, They put on a great show and thrilled the packed stadium with three fast races, each one decided on the very last lap.

Tom's form had a little dip in Paris–Roubaix, though not much. His team-mates, Wolfshohl and Daems, were both going better on the day; in fact Daems won, so Tom worked for them, finishing 'only' eighth at Roubaix. Not much of a dip – a lot of pros would give money to finish in the top ten in this race.

Paris–Brussels is no longer regarded as a major classic. Traffic problems have affected its route and its place in the calendar has been chopped and changed about. In 1963 it was still firmly in place as one of the spring classics: 288 kilometres long, with a few nasty stings in the tail including the cobbled Alsemberg climb, and a history full of incidents and big-name winners.

It had been said of this race that no one who attacked before the Belgian border had ever won it. Well, Tom wanted to change that. Also, he reasoned that, because of this legend, perhaps the others wouldn't chase so hard and he could build up a winning lead. So, he attacked well before the border, taking a group that included Vin Denson and Jean Stablinski with him. Interestingly, and ironically in the end, the Frenchman had joined the move for a reason totally unconnected with winning the race.

Stablinski was scheduled to start the Tour of Spain next day and, deciding that he needed a quick work-out with the boys, had arranged for his wife to meet him on the race route near to the border, which was close to where they lived. Then he planned to nip home, get a quick shower, some food, and off to sunny Spain. Getting this break going would increase the race speed, and he would get his training session over more quickly, It made sense; but he never expected the break to be 13 minutes clear and for him to still have an excellent chance of victory by the border, and he shot past his surprised wife with, understandably, no time to explain what was going on. She had to go home and find out for herself on the TV.

The route north crosses several stretches of undulating country, little conks of hills which, along with stretches of cobbles, steadily reduced the break until just Tom and Stablinski were left to fight it out over the last 50 kilometres.

Jean Stablinski was a tough customer. The son of a Polish mineworker who died when Jean was quite young, he saw cycling as the only way of getting himself, his mother and the rest of his family out of the poverty surrounding him in the pit villages of the region around Valenciennes. A similar background to Tom's, in fact, although there was always employment and enough to eat in the Simpson family. In 1963, Jean was the reigning World Champion, and he was just the sort of rider you could do without, coming into the finish of a big race, especially with the rainbow jersey on his back. He was a tough and intelligent rider, and if he had a sniff of victory he was very difficult to beat.

Tom attacked twice. Both times Jean tenaciously hauled him back, then settled behind him, recovering, watching, waiting. Coming into Brussels the riders had to negotiate the cobbled ascent of the Alsemberg hill, and it was here that bad luck struck Tom once more. Forcing the pace, with Stablinski hanging on desperately, his gears slipped and he was forced to ease to allow them to mesh again, It was the chance Stablinski had been waiting for, and he took it. Tom couldn't close the gap before the finish line, so had to make do with another second place.

He might have been only second in that race, but, by virtue of it, he became number one in the world because he went into the lead of the season-long Super Prestige Pemod competition, which awarded points in major races and served in those days as a world ranking of riders. It was yet another landmark in British cycling history that has yet to be repeated.

The following week the circus moved on to the Belgian Ardennes for the two classics held there every year. Tom started off well with tenth place in the Flèche Wallonne race. Then he took part in Liège–Bastogne–Liège, the oldest classic on the books and one of the five super races – the five 'monuments' of the sport.

Like them all, it's hard, it's long, but it's also very, very hilly. The Ardennes abound with steep wooded hillsides, overlaid by narrow roads which have a tendency to be built along British lines – straight up and very steep. On top of this, the Ardennes in April are not famous for good weather. There are many tales of races run off through snowstorms, and rain is a regular feature.

It is ideal terrain for a strong attacking rider who can climb and give his all in bad conditions. It was an ideal race for Tom, but he gave just a little bit too much. Desperate now to land a big one, he did everything you would expect of a rider leading the world rankings, except win. He dominated the race and was on his own in the lead for 100 out of the last 105 kilometres. Alas, those last five proved his undoing. He had run out of steam and was battling into a terrific head wind; his lead disappeared like snow in the sunshine, and he was caught and passed, eventually finishing a lowly thirty-third. Although he had easily won the King of the Mountains competition, it was no consolation.

The big races of the first part of the season were nearly over, Tom had been up there in every one, but he couldn't win. Sometimes it was bad luck that defeated him; sometimes it was his own ambition. Tom was sure of one thing, though: it couldn't go on. He was bound to win soon, if only because of the law of averages. So he entered the Bordeaux–Paris.

I've said before that in many ways cycling hasn't changed much. Riders and sponsors come and go, training methods and attitudes change but, by and large, the big races just go on getting bigger, capturing more of the public's imagination. So a young bike fan in 2000 would have no difficulty understanding what faced the riders in the Paris–Roubaix in 1900. What he would have difficulty understanding, though, was the Bordeaux–Paris. For a start, they don't run it any more.

Even in 1963 it was something of an anachronism, the only race of its kind, an outlier from a previous age, when distance was the big thing in cycling and riders covered hundreds of miles in races like the Paris–Brest–Paris which, by 1963, had, in fact, disappeared.

Bordeaux–Paris, though, escaped the problems that had caused the demise of these marathons and was still going strong in the sixties. It was a race that every great rider would try to add, at least once, to his list of victories, although due to its somewhat specialist nature it did require a degree of special training. This tended to keep the number of participants down, but ensured that most of the ones who took part did so with realistic hopes of victory. It wasn't until the seventies that public and rider interest began to dwindle, and the eighties saw the final edition of this historic event.

Part of its popularity was due to its length – 365 miles to be covered in one go – and part was due to the way those miles were covered, since the last 180 plus miles were ridden behind Drny pacing motorbikes. This was where the race was decided, and the sight of groups of riders thundering towards Paris, each tucked in behind their pacer, with a spare riding alongside in case of mechanical breakdowns, and each with an attendant team car, must have been something to behold. And it *was* popular, too: over two million people lined the race route, and 30,000 spectators paid at the Parc des Princes track to see the riders finish the 'Derby of the Road' as the race was known. The prize money was good – over £1,000 going to the winner. In 1963 that was more than most people earned in a year.

This really was a step into the unknown for Tom. He'd never ridden this far before – how many people have? However, he was good behind the Dernys, as he'd found out on the winter tracks where Derny races are a regular feature, and they are also used a lot in training on the road in Belgium. His form, of course, was special. It would have to be because he hadn't planned on riding this race and, due to various contractual obligations arising from his good performances in the spring, his special training for it had been limited to just the week before the race.

What a difficult week that had been, though a lot more so for Helen because that was the week their second child, Joanne, was born, but at least the proud father got a chance to see her before he had to leave for Bordeaux.

On the weekend before the big one Tom rode two races. Each was 250 kilometres long, with the last part of the second being run off behind Dernys – a sort of mini Bordeaux–Paris. On the Tuesday and Wednesday he rode 50 very fast kilometres behind the Derny, then, on the Thursday, he tested himself out in a 114-kilometre criterium, which he won. From then on all he did was rest. It was said that Bordeaux–Paris was won in bed, so Tom spent Friday and Saturday there, just eating and sleeping, and getting his mind right for the battle ahead.

During the week he had also been getting his stomach used to some of the concentrated foods he would be using during the race.

Always on the look-out for scientific advantages, he'd heard about astronauts living off this stuff and somehow had got hold of some for the race, hoping that it would be easier to digest on the go. You can imagine that fuel is an important consideration over 365 miles, and anything you can do to improve its absorption will help. Today everyone is using this kind of stuff in races, but in the sixties riders depended on water, tea, various sandwiches, tarts and cakes for their in-flight refuelling.

The race was due to start at two o'clock on Sunday morning. Tom emerged from his bed at nine on Saturday night, stood up, and promptly fainted – a great start! He thought that he might have overdone the bed-rest because once he came round and got to his feet, his legs felt so heavy that he wondered whether he would even be able to get to Paris, never mind win the race.

After a final meal of vegetable soup, raw grated carrots, a big steak and rice, and two yoghurts, he joined the small band of other contestants, including two past winners of it in De Roo and Van Est, for the start of their marathon adventure. Even at this early hour there were a good few die-hard bike fans about to watch the riders sign on, all wrapped up in their long-sleeved tops, leg-warmers, and woolly hats to combat the chilly night air. It was an unreal gathering for the start of a big European bike race.

Tom was very relaxed, chatting happily with Jock Wadley who had decided to cover the race from start to finish for his *Sporting Cyclist* magazine. He must have known Tom was going to do something really special. Tom himself spoke about his family and especially the new addition. He was thinking of their future and said to Jock, 'One day I'd like to settle in Australia. Before that I want to ride a couple of their six-days with John Tressider and ride the Sun Tour on the road.' Tom always got on well with Australians because he appreciated their attitude and toughness, travelling thousands of miles for their sport; he also fitted in well with their easygoing nature, and would have enjoyed living there, I think.

It never happened, but the Bordeaux–Paris did. At two o'clock someone from the organisation blew a whistle in the darkness, the small group of riders assembled themselves into an orderly huddle, then set off northwards and into the night. It was a very subdued, casual group compared to the usual adrenaline-charged start of a big classic.

The first 161 miles were covered without pace and initially the group moved along very steadily, lit from the back by the headlights of the following cars. The riders had some strange sights to see, too, as families in their dressing-gowns cheered them by their lonely farms, or leaned out of upstairs windows in villages and towns. As the sky grew lighter, though, the pace increased, and gradually the happily chattering bunch grew silent, to face the more serious work that lay ahead.

Just before dawn, the riders stopped to take off their extra clothing. Up until this point no one had attacked. There was nothing in the rules to prevent them, but a gentlemen's agreement ensured that these first miles could be completed with the minimum of fuss. Now, though, in racing kit and in daylight, the tension and the pace increased as the Derny pick-up point, the town of Chatellerault, approached.

Here, a huge crowd was waiting for the riders and round it there went a real buzz of excitement as the Dernys coughed and spluttered into action amid a haze of blue smoke. Once they'd cajoled them into life the pacers rode their little machines up and down the main street to make sure that they were well warmed up. What a sight they were: never the slimmest of people – there's extra shelter behind a person of, shall we say, more than ample build – they rode their bikes sitting bolt upright with their knees sticking out, each one of them wearing the team kit of their own particular rider.

Soon the riders burst on to the scene and, after the obligatory handshake with the man that would take them to Paris, battle commenced. Tom's pacer was Fernand Wambst, one of the best in the business, who was tragically killed in an accident on the Blois track in 1969 when pacing Eddy Merckx in a race there. Merckx himself was so badly injured in that crash that it affected him for the rest of his career, though you wouldn't have guessed it if you'd been one of his rivals.

The attacks started straight after the pick-up point, but Wambst held Tom back – it's hard to be impetuous when somebody else is racing with your legs. He wanted to watch the other race favourites, Peter Post and Jo De Roo. Post was fantastic behind a Derny and of course De Roo had won the race last year, so it wasn't a bad plan.

These three let the race play out in front of them until Post punctured, whereupon Tom and De Roo picked up the pace. It took

Post 26 miles of determined chasing to get back to them. At this point these three were with a group of 12 riders, something like 13 minutes behind the leading group of three, with about 100 miles to go. Wambst then turned to Tom and asked him if he was OK. Tom just nodded in reply and Wambst began gradually to increase the speed.

He slowly turned the screw on the others and Tom was soon clear. Only De Roo held on, but as the speed climbed above the level he could handle, he lost contact with his pacer. They wouldn't see Tom again until the finish in Paris.

It took him just over 26 miles to close the 13-minute gap and catch the three leaders. Once with them, Wambst eased a little to let him recover. When he got the news that Post and De Roo had closed to within two minutes of them, Wambst led Tom to the front of the group. Then, climbing out of the Chevreuse Valley on the Côte de St Cyr, Wambst opened the throttle again and Tom was away on his own, in the lead. From that point on he flew towards Paris, gaining one minute on his pursuers every six miles.

The crowds towards the end of the race were absolutely huge: police estimated that over one and a half million lined the last 50 miles and, as I've said earlier, the Parc des Princes stadium was full to the roof. Tom was really enjoying himself now. He knew that he was going to win, long before the finish, and the release of all the pent-up emotions from the near misses he'd had over the last two years meant that he hardly felt the pedals as he sped through the historic streets of the French capital. He was in a state of grace.

There was a special prize for the fastest lap of the track at the end of the race, so, as they approached the stadium, Tom rode up alongside his pacer and asked him to go for it as he wanted to give it him as a bonus. Wambst replied: 'No, Tom, we're not sprinting. You've done quite enough today. I wouldn't ask it of you.' It was only the second time they'd spoken all day!

They entered the stadium to a huge roar from the waiting crowd and, despite Wambst's protestations, they flew around that last timed lap of the famous cycle track; only Peter Post went faster, minutes later, and then only by one-tenth of a second. Tom crossed the line grinning from ear to ear and with his right arm raised in victory. He was almost six minutes clear of the second-placed rider, Piet Rentmeester. He had won another classic at last.

At the finish, the fatigue of 348 miles just melted away. What a week! A second child and now a run of eight second places in big races had been ended by one of the greatest victories the French press said they had ever seen in the Bordeaux–Paris. Tom was both delighted and vengeful when he said to the newspaper *L'Equipe*: 'It's wonderful. I'm going back to Belgium with victory flowers for my second daughter. I feel that I've revenged myself on everybody. I had the idea that everybody was riding to cut me out, which is why victory is so sweet now.' *L'Equipe* couldn't say enough about him. They called him 'Mr Tom', and the name stuck – this was the sixties, remember, and the French were fascinated by us then. In fact, they still are fascinated by us then, if you see what I mean.

The magazine *Le Mirroir des Sports* was even more effusive. Their account of his victory reflects again a fascination with all things English, and is written in a style of journalism the French have made their own. This is one small passage describing Tom climbing the Dourdan Hill quite close to the end of the race:

> The fans witnessed Tom riding with a miraculous elegance considering he had ridden 500 kilometres. So impeccable was his style that he put us in mind of the Horse Guards of her Gracious Majesty, those ornaments outside Buckingham Palace.

The report goes on to say that when he spoke to the reporters at the finish he did so 'with his charming smile, and distinguished expression, reminding us so much of a student at Oxford'. However, they couldn't resist a barbed comment about Tom's tactical ability in general when they said: 'After seeing him on Sunday perhaps he should be radio-controlled in future. He races with such generosity which often goes wrong for him, whereas in Bordeaux–Paris he only had to follow Wambst, who decided all the tactics.'

There was a huge amount of publicity about this victory for Tom, but the bowler hat had gone for ever. Everyone knew he was English, anyway, and he had no need of gimmicks now as this win meant that he led Anquetil in the Super Prestige Pernod Trophy by 16 points. More importantly, though, Helen had put her foot down just before the race and suggested that perhaps Tom didn't look quite as good in it as he thought. So, stung by this criticism from one so close, he threw it in the wardrobe, and there it stayed because straight away he won Bordeaux–Paris, the first race he'd gone to without that hat.

Once again it was time to cash in with contract races, and Tom was keen to take as many as possible because he announced after Bordeaux–Paris that he did not want to ride the Tour de France. Instead, he wanted to concentrate on the World Championships which were to be held that year on the roads he knew around Renaix in Belgium, just south of the Tour of Flanders hills.

Given Tom's ambitions in the Tour wasn't this rather an odd decision? No, a British World Champion would be in even more demand than a British classic winner, and although he believed that he could win the Tour one day, he was sure that he could win the Worlds now. So it was a very level-headed decision: cash in on the classic win first, recharge your batteries while the Tour is on, then build up the training and racing for a victory in the Worlds. Whereas, if he rode a hard Tour – which he didn't really believe he could win, yet – and then found himself having to ride a load of criteriums, he wouldn't have had any form for the Worlds.

One of his contracts was to ride the Manx Premier and he was determined to give British bike fans a performance to remember. They would see a different Tom Simpson from the one they'd seen last year. This Tom Simpson had worn the yellow jersey, won another classic and was leading the world rankings – all since the previous year's race; this Tom Simpson was allowed to bring four team mates with him from Peugeot-BP, and shared top billing with Rik Van Looy.

The only thing that hadn't changed, in fact, was the weather: it was terrible – gale-force winds with rain and hail. It was so bad that only 16 of the 70 riders finished the race. Van Looy must have taken one look at this and decided he didn't really need to add this race to his huge list of wins: he showed his face for 60 or so miles before heading off to the changing rooms for a quick dose of Radox.

With him out of the way, Tom took over control of the race and attacked with the Frenchman and Peugeot team mate, Hamon, and a Spaniard, Manzano. They set off in pursuit of the lone leader of the race, a big, strong, barn-door of a Dutchman called Herbertus Zilverberg. They had to put in a hell of an effort to get up to him, too. Well, Tom and Hamon did. Manzano sat behind them and didn't do a tap.

They finally caught Zilverberg at 92 miles, by which time they had a four-minute lead over the nearest of the rest. Manzano still wasn't working, though. Tom thought that it was about time he had a quiet word with him. He knew the Spaniard just happened to be quite a good sprinter, so pointed out to him that it might not be good for his health if he planned on doing no work for the rest of the race and using his sprint at the end.

I don't know whether Manzano thought discretion was the better part of valour, but when Tom attacked the group inside the last mile he still did not come to the front; he did so only in the final 50 metres to take second place. Tom rode away from the others in that last rain-soaked mile to win, cheered home by many thousands of British bike fans who'd braved the atrocious weather conditions to see him.

After the race, an enormous crowd welcomed Tom at the award ceremony in the Villa Marina. Their applause lifted the roof. He thanked them for braving the awful weather to cheer him on, and was full of praise for the performance of the British riders in the race. He told the assembled journalists – and there were a lot there to see Tom race, even from non-cycling publications, including the celebrated Eamon Andrews who did a television interview with him after the race – that a British sponsor could be confident there was enough talent available to put a team on the continent. He was really trying to push this idea now, and he was right. There was enough talent around then and, because of Tom, these British riders were beginning to believe in themselves like never before or, with one or two notable exceptions, since. In fact, observers on the continent fully expected more British riders would emulate Tom's performances over the coming years. No one has ... yet.

That day on the Isle of Man had been a great one for British cycling: the number-one man had put on a masterful show, dominated the race, and won. All this was against world-class opposition, but he had suffered to do it. He told the crowds at the finish that winning had been harder than Bordeaux–Paris; that is hard enough, but Tom had actually damaged himself to win. If you look at pictures of him after that race you will see that even the joy of victory couldn't remove the fatigue from his face, and he would feel the effects of it for a long time after. It was a very brave ride, and one that he would pay for later in the year.

As the Tour de France started Tom went home to Ghent and took a short holiday. It was nice to be there with his family in the summer, something most of us take for granted, but something which he rarely experienced. The in-laws came to stay and Tom took Frank Sherburn to see the Tour while it was passing through Belgium. History was again being made in that race, for now an Irishman, Shay Elliott, was wearing the yellow jersey – a first for his country.

Tom only rode one race during the Tour, and that was a track meeting at his old stamping ground of Fallowfield where he won the pro omnium against some stiff British and European opposition. He put on a great show for the Manchester crowd including catching every rider on the track except John Geddes in a six-station pursuit.

By the end of the Tour de France Tom felt fit and ready to start training for the Worlds. The break had done him good mentally, but physically he was a bit below par. In his first races he suffered a bit, but he was soon race-fit again. Then, about a fortnight before the big race, he had three crashes and fell ill, losing a lot of weight in a short time. Three days rest saw him apparently OK, but in the back of his mind he knew all wasn't well, and he knew why. It had been the desire to win that Isle of Man race at all costs, coming as it did so close after the Bordeaux–Paris; he'd pushed his already tired body beyond its limit, and now he was paying for it. It was not a perfect build up to the race for which he'd missed the Tour.

There were two big favourites for the World Championships in Renaix: a real Belgian, Rik Van Looy; and an honorary one, Tom Simpson. By now, Tom had truly become an adopted son of Flanders. Albert Buerick had organised a thriving supporters' club for him in Ghent, and these and many other of the thousands of fans around the hilly cobble-strewn circuit were there to cheer for the Englishman who'd made their home his home. Like they do at cycling events they'd painted his name all over the roads and were carrying banners bearing his name, and the rainbow bands of the World Champion. But this mad, Buerick-inspired lot had gone further than that. The first thing Tom saw when he looked out from his bedroom window on race day were the words 'Tom Simpson World Champion' painted in huge white letters in the street outside his house.

Before the race, all the top riders named Simpson and Van Looy as their equal favourites, but in one respect they were far from equal. Van Looy, going for his third consecutive victory in this race, started with a team of ten top riders, all of them familiar with the pace and distance of this kind of racing, and all, except perhaps one, dedicated to a victory for the 'Emperor'. Tom, on the other hand, had just three riders in the Great Britain team used to competition at this level –Michael Wright, Vin Denson and Alan Ramsbottom – and, of them, Ramsbottom said that he wanted to try and have a go himself.

On top of this, it was common knowledge that Van Looy would pay each of his men £350 if he won, which was a lot of money at the time. This was just in case national pride wasn't sufficient to ensure their loyalty, and it probably wasn't in every case. Tom offered to match this for the British team if he won, but they were still a bit cagey and wouldn't commit themselves. Perhaps they didn't believe in him, despite the fact that all the continentals did. Tom would have to find help from somewhere else, because not even he could ride against the might of the Belgian, French and Italian national teams.

You see, even the greatest rider needs team, or other, support to win a big bike race. Energy must be saved for when the big decisions are made. A rider who has to do all his own chasing, close every gap, fetch drinks from the team car, get back to the front after a problem, is constantly tiring himself. Also, when a top rider gets in a breakaway group, it is much better for him if he has a team mate to work hard and get a lead established for him, rather than having to do it all by himself. This was the problem Tom was facing in 1963. Two years later there was enough committed firepower in the British team to help, and look what they managed to do then.

The Belgians blocked everything. They wanted to control the race so it would end in a sprint where Van Looy could use his devastating turn of speed to administer the *coup de grâce* and take his third rainbow jersey. The only break of any note they allowed clear was one containing Henri Anglade and Shay Elliott, a Frenchman and an Irishman. They were away in the last part of the race for over 40 miles, and though they weren't gaining they weren't coming back either. The whole race was in *status quo*.

The Belgians were just going to let this pair dangle out in front, then mop them up towards the end and hand the race to Van Looy. Someone had to do something. The other favourites were sitting tight, so Tom attacked. At first the Belgians countered every move he made, but eventually they cracked under his relentless pressure, and he was away, soon catching Anglade and Elliott.

Now there was panic in the bunch. Van Looy could see the title slipping from his grasp and he had the whole Belgian team working at the front to bring Tom under control. At the head of the race Tom was flying. As soon as he caught the two leaders he started to work with them. This injection of pace was too much for Anglade and he was left behind.

Then, surprisingly, Elliott stopped working – he just sat in Tom's slipstream and refused to take his turn at the front. Why? Elliott was the best of the two Irish riders in the race, so why not work with Tom and go for the title? He was no mean sprinter after all. The reason was that Elliott rode for the St Raphaël trade team, the same one as Anquetil and Stablinski, the team that paid his wages for the rest of the year. If he worked with Tom then he would have to be absolutely sure of winning the title, and he wasn't. The recriminations of failure and handing the title to the Englishman would do far more harm to his pocket than the good a silver medal could ever do.

Tom was getting desperate now. He was managing to hold off all the pursuers for the time being, but he couldn't keep this up to the finish. If Elliott didn't start to work then surely they would be caught. So he got to work on Shay, trying to get him to believe that if they stayed away then one of them must surely be World Champion, and that he had as much chance as Tom.

It was no good, so he decided simply to pay Elliott to work with him. They proceeded to have a conversation that was to cause quite a scandal two years later when they both had articles in the *People* newspaper which for the time were quite sensational, lifting the lid off a side of professional cycling that most British fans knew nothing about.

According to Tom's account the conversation went like this: Tom to Shay: 'Come on, work with me and I'll pay you.' Elliott says nothing and just looks at him. Tom again: 'I'll give you 5,000 francs [£350].' Shay replies: 'No, Tom.' Then Tom doubles his previous offer, but Shay still declines. Now, seeing the title slipping from his grasp because the Belgians were catching them, Tom says to Elliott, 'All right, 15,000 francs [£1,000].'

Elliott started to work a bit, but his heart wasn't in it. He was tempted, but eventually he looked across at Tom and said, 'No, Tom. I can't. I've given my word. I've got to support my team leaders.' And with that the race slipped from Tom's grasp and, ironically, from

Anquetil's and Stablinski's because once Tom and Shay were caught no one could get away from the Belgians.

Do you think what Tom suggested to Elliott was wrong? Well, let me tell you he was just a choirboy compared to some of the tricks perpetrated by the contenders in the final sprint for victory.

It started about 400 metres from the line with a Frenchman, Guy Ingolin, leading from the 30 riders still left in with a shout. His effort ended with 200 metres to go and Tom shot past him with a number of good sprinters on his left. Then Van Looy reached over and pulled him backwards, gaining a slingshot effect from doing so. Just as Tom got going from this, Jan Janssen came alongside and did the same thing, consigning him to the back of the group and twenty-sixth place.

And this was nothing compared to what was going on at the front. Van Looy was making his own sprint – he had asked the ultra-rapid Benoni Beheyt to lead him out, but Beheyt had told him he was shattered. Unknown to Van Looy, Beheyt was that single Belgian not committed to his victory that I hinted about earlier. He latched on to the wheel of the 'Emperor' and let Van Looy unknowingly lead the sprint out for him. About 25 metres from the line Van Looy was clear of everyone except Beheyt, but he'd run out of steam. Sensing his chance, the crafty Beheyt went for it. Both riders veered across the road, and Beheyt, who was going past his leader, put out his right arm and grabbed hold of Van Looy's jersey – and that is how they crossed the line: Beheyt first and Van Looy second. Did he pull Van Looy backwards? Rik said yes; Benoni said no, he was just fending him off. Van Looy had switched across the road in those dying metres, it's true, but it looked like a pull to me.

The whole of Belgium was divided into those who supported Van Looy, and what amounted to little more than Beheyt's friends and immediate family, and even some of those didn't believe him. Beheyt was branded a traitor. It speaks volumes about the almost feudal system that existed in pro cycling in those days that his victory brought him little joy. Although he managed to win the Tour of Belgium and a stage in the Tour de France after his World Championship, he won little else, despite some spirited efforts, and he was by no means as poor a rider as he's been painted since. But you would have had to have been a hell of a bike rider to turn on the 'Emperor' and get away with it.

After the race there was no doubt in a lot of people's minds that if Elliott had worked, then Tom would have been World Champion at Renaix: the £1,000 he offered Elliott would have been a good investment. He was quite open about this in an interview after the race. He had it all worked out when he said, 'A British World Champion would be special. I could ride on my laurels for three years and it would be worth about £40,000 to me in the year I was Champion, so the percentage returns are good.'

Never mind, there'd be other years. For now, Tom needed some good performances in the autumn classics to secure second place in the Prestige Pernod rankings – he'd lost the lead to Anquetil after he'd won his fourth Tour de France in the summer. Capitalising on his good form, Tom started his autumn campaign by taking second place to Anquetil in the Criterium des As, a Derny-paced race around 27 laps of the Bois de Boulogne in Paris. This used to be the biggest criterium of the year, with only a handful of the best contracted to ride, and every one of those had to have been a race winner in that same year.

A mixture of fast criteriums in which he scored a run of six second places, and good training rides, saw Tom in top form for the sprinters' classic, the Paris–Tours. He sprinted well, but not quite well enough. The Dutchman, Jo De Roo, won the sprint from Tom and a group of seven others who had detached themselves from the heaving pack.

Before this race, Tom had led Raymond Poulidor by only one point in the Super Prestige Pernod; now his lead on him was ten points, but he couldn't catch Anquetil's total with only one event remaining, the Tour of Lombardy. Tom Simpson, the man who loved to attack, was going to have to defend in this race and to follow Poulidor wherever he went. Wherever Poulidor finished Tom was at least sure of out-sprinting him because that was one thing Raymond could not do.

De Roo won again with Tom in tenth place and Raymond Poulidor back in thirteenth. Tom was second in the Prestige Pernod, and therefore the number-two pro rider in the world. Earlier in the race, the number one, Anquetil, had helped him when Poulidor attacked. Tom was making a big effort to bring him back, but Jacques, a master tactician, rode up alongside Tom and told him to go easy because he knew Poulidor would not be able to sustain his effort. Tom listened and Jacques was right: they soon caught Poulidor and he was quiet for the rest of the race. Why did Jacques do this? Well, he and Poulidor, his biggest challenger in the Tour de France were arch-enemies and, to keep him at a psychological disadvantage, Anquetil would have anybody do well if it was at Poulidor's expense.

The Super Prestige Pernod wasn't the only season-long ranking system in pro cycling. The newspaper L'Equipe ran a Classics World Cup based on the results of the eleven single-day classics, like today's World Cup. The Pernod Trophy was based on these, plus the big Tours and other fairly big races just as the UCI World Rankings are today. Tom won the 'World Cup' by three points from Poulidor. He also ended the season in third place in the French road-race organisers' classification. And his fame had even filtered through to Britain where he was voted third in the Sportswriters', and fifth in the Daily Express Sportsman of the Year competitions.

It had been a heck of a year. Tom had now broken into the elite of world cycling. Continental journalists couldn't say enough good things about him. René de Latour echoed all their thoughts when he wrote, 'This Simpson is capable of winning no matter what one-day classic; he has the class to do it.' These same journalists were predicting a flood of riders from this side of the channel, a flood that would dominate European cycling for years to come, and you can see why. Before the late fifties they'd never even heard of British cycling, then Brian Robinson came over and won a stage in their biggest race. Now, three years into the sixties, Tom Simpson was arguably the second-best rider in the world. Yet the flood never came. Why? Well, after writing this book and studying the man, I think that Tom was quite simply a one-off: a mix of talent, guts, intelligence, and application that you find in perhaps one in a million people. But, then, maybe that means that there are at least 54 people like him in Britain today.

A short rest at the end of the road season, then it was back to the indoor tracks, and first of all back to Madrid where he'd ridden so well with the Australian, John Tressider, the previous year. This time Tom was paired with another Australian, the rough, tough scourge of professional sprinting in the sixties, Ron Baensch. This was a match made in heaven; they were made for each other, riding together over the coming years as often as the promoters would allow. Many of those in the know believe that, if it had not been for Tom's death, these two would have been the number one team in six-days by the late sixties, though at first Ron wasn't too keen.

I met Ron in 1997 on Mont Ventoux in France where Tom's daughter, Joanne, in an effort to get to know the father she can hardly remember, actually cycled up the mountain on which he met his death. Ron and I arranged to meet the following evening, Bastille night, and while around us the French celebrated their revolution, Ron remembered his:

I was just a lazy bastard. I was a sprinter, a natural talent. I'd ridden a few sixes before I got paired with Tom and I could put on a show in the sprints – even beat Pfenninger, who was the best. Then Tom came along. Everyone thought he was just a road rider, but soon he was sprinting, even with the specialists. The crowd used to encourage him: the more they screamed the faster he went, drawing strength from them. I never knew anyone who could push himself like Tom. He really thought that if he was hurting then they were, and all he'd got to do was push a bit harder and he'd have them. It worked, but eventually it killed him.

Ron paused for a moment, as if to emphasise that point, then he went on:

Like I said, I could sprint in the sixes, but I didn't want to know about the long chases, the Madisons, they were too hard. In the chases the big guys decided the race; I didn't want to rock the boat. The sixes were all tied up in those days and I just wanted to go along with it. Then I got paired with Tom and his attitude just rubbed off on me. He wanted to win so much. All of a sudden I could chase. Tom wanted to take them all on and convinced me we could be the best team. He used to say, 'We're not having this, we're not asking them if we can take a lap. We can be the best and they will have to come to us and ask if they can win something.' And eventually we did it – we took them on, raced hard, even when they wanted to take it easy. I was fast: I could take half a lap and soon Tom could do the same, he was a natural, so fast. We showed those assholes and they had to let us in. If Tom hadn't died then in one, maybe two, years we'd have run the sixes.

I asked Ron if he remembered anything about their first race together in Madrid and he said: 'One night a guy was firing an air pistol at balloons in the roof, then Tom got hold of the gun and shot someone's tyres out. He was a mad bastard.'

Ron fell quiet once more, smiling at the recollection, then he looked up into the starry sky and said, 'I bet you're looking down now and laughing at me, aren't you, Tom?' With that he got up and said his goodbyes. I wished him a happy holiday, and he replied: 'All my life's been a holiday, Chris.' It might well have been, but it has been a working one.

A good ride in Madrid meant contracts for Brussels and Ghent. Then an offer came out of the blue which was also out of this world – well, our particular half of it. Tom, along with some of the big names from the road scene – Anquetil, Anglade, Baldini, De Roo and Elliott – were invited to compete in a number of meetings on the Pacific island of New Caledonia. A lot of Europeans lived there and some big businessmen who were missing their cycling, had clubbed together to bring the stars over to race for them.

Well, as you can imagine, they all had a fantastic time, skin-diving, fishing, sunbathing, eating all manner of exotic food, relaxing and, unfortunately, racing. There was nothing too strenuous, although Tom did establish a track record in Noumea of 1 minute 12 seconds for the kilometre, and it was a rough cinder track at that. He also beat the great Italian former Olympic and World Champion, Ercole Baldini, to win the final of a pursuit in a time of 4 minutes and 56 seconds for 4,000 metres, on another very slow track.

It was a chance for these top riders to get to know each other. Tom and Anquetil got on particularly well and, afterwards, Jacques always said that he enjoyed being with Tom because he could talk about things other than his bike. Jacques liked that because he found his chosen profession hard work and enjoyed anything that broke the monotony of it. Anquetil, though, received tragic news while he was on the island when he learned of his father's death, so he flew home before the others.

The next meeting between Tom and Jacques was, surprisingly, via the BBC. Tom returned fit and tanned to celebrate Christmas in England. Just before this he was a guest at the BBC's Sports Personality of the Year awards where Jacques Anquetil was voted their top International Personality! Yes, I know it's hard to believe, given the

BBC's less than warm attitude towards cycling over the last 30 years, but even more amazing things would happen in two years time. Tom was asked to make the presentation to Jacques in a studio in Paris, and to translate his acceptance speech, during which he expressed surprise at the level of interest in cycling in England, although privately he told Tom that he'd been bored having to sit through all the cricket highlights. Tom created that interest; a personality can, and still could.

At the end of 1963, Tom was interviewed about his year, and it was obvious that the Tour de France was still his prime ambition:

> In two years time Anquetil will have retired. When Jacques is out of the way I will be 27 or 28, the ideal age for a Tour rider. At the moment Jacques has us all beat because he can go through a three-week race without a bad day; I can't do that – not yet. Bobet had a similar weakness for years, I have read.

René de Latour, who was conducting this interview with Tom, said that in his opinion Tom had more class than Bobet. Now that's a compliment. Tom carried on with his thoughts for the future because this interview, like most with Tom, was about the future rather than the past.

> All this doesn't mean that I won't try next year to win the Tour. Now that I've spent time with Anquetil I've learnt things about him. For instance, he takes things quieter in the winter, so I'm going to do the same. He has a social side to his life; cycling is so hard that it would be unbearable if you couldn't enjoy life now and again, like any other human being.

And enjoying it he was. After Christmas, instead of getting straight on with the training like lesser mortals, Tom, Helen and the children went to St Gervais in the French Alps for the annual cyclists' skiing championships. All the top men, past and present, used to be invited to this event which, in these more serious times, is no longer with us. It was a time for the press to speak to the riders in a less-pressurised atmosphere than the races, and it was a time when old and new champions could meet and compare notes. It was all a great public-relations exercise, but some work was done. Tom found time to put in a few laps of the circuit for the Worlds which were to be held that year in nearby Sallanches. He'd done a lot, but he still had a lot more to do.

Mainly, though, it was a glamorous occasion for a few of the top riders to bask in their success – and why not? – whilst also engaging in a bit of light exercise and posing for every sponsor-pleasing photo opportunity. Tom, of course, had bought all the latest kit, even though he'd never been skiing before. Well, you can't ski down Harworth pit tip. I know – I've tried.

10

TOMMI SIMPSONI

The serious stuff came round soon enough and Tom moved to the Peugeot training camp in the Nice area, soon making it known that his intention was to ride every race on the Côte d'Azure in order to prepare for the first classic of the year, the Milan–San Remo.

Despite his newly professed, relaxed approach he had raced until mid-December, then had a good rest, and was back on his bike by mid-January. He had hardly let himself go, but the mental break had done him good, and he was soon in the thick of the action. The Grand Prix Aix en Provence was his best showing. There he was up with the leaders until a puncture in the last ten kilometres ended his chances.

While at the training camp he told *Cycling* magazine that he intended to race four times in Britain during 1964, and he confirmed that the Manx Premier had been his hardest victory of 1963; indeed, he had felt its effects until November of that year. The Belgian press had even blamed this race for losing him the Worlds, but that was because he was riding virtually on his own. Look at Lance Armstrong in 1998: he had a weakened team as some of the other good Americans couldn't ride. He did everything right, but against the might of Belgium, Italy and Holland in the finale he just didn't have enough left, whereas the winner even had the luxury of a team mate with him in the final selection.

After training in the south, the professional cycling circus of the sixties moved north, only to travel back by bike in the Paris–Nice. Before this, the riders who had serious ambitions for the spring classics could test out their legs in the weekend of racing which opens the Belgian calendar. Tom rode the Kuurne–Brussels–Kuurne in extremely cold conditions. So cold, in fact, that when he saw a friend by the roadside watching the race, he decided to pack it in. Some friend – he refused to give Tom a lift to the finish and told him to get on with it. So, to keep warm he attacked and eventually came second in the race!

The friend was probably a member of Tom's supporters' club, and as such wouldn't want to see his money going to waste with him packing. Supporters' clubs are a phenomenon in all Flemish sport. The customers of a café, what would be a pub in Britain, club together to support a local sports star, be he an athlete, swimmer or, most likely, a cyclist. And they really do support him or her, not just by being at races, but by subscriptions and collections within the club which, after administration costs, go directly to the athlete.

Albert Beurick had organised a big club for Tom, based at his Café den Engel. By early 1964, in the nine months the club had been in existence, they had raised £250 for Tom, and the club grew and grew with his victories over the following years, organising dances, races and merchandising, all of which helped keep body and soul together.

The President of the club was Tom's doctor, Dr Vandenweghe, who, until 1962, looked after his colds and minor injuries. Then he looked after Tom's preparation for the 1962 Tour de France, so you can see why he had faith in him. He was full of praise for Tom as an athlete, but saw the problems he was up against: 'If he was French or Flemish he would be World Champion by now, and when in peak condition he is practically unbeatable. He is best in a long, single-day race, but he is a great all-rounder. If he is to win the Tour de France, though, he would have to be backed by a British team.'

Paris–Nice saw Tom on the attack early. On the second stage he was third, but punctured on the fourth and lost five minutes in atrocious weather conditions – cold and snow often affects this race, and it is common to see pictures of the riders racing through a wintry landscape. He used the rest of the race as training and protected the interests of better-placed team mates, doing them favours he hoped would be returned later. From the start of the year his target had been Milan–San Remo, which started two days after Paris–Nice, so he retired early on the last stage to give himself an extra day's rest before the big one.

Milan–San Remo, 'La Primavera', 1964, had its usual huge field: 230 starters including, and I quote Tom here, 'some of the most hopeless load of cowboys you could ever meet'. But all of the best riders in the world were there, and in the eyes of many of them Tom was the prime favourite. René de Latour, who had really taken to the Englishman, and who was, of course, a great Anglophile and friend of British cycling. was convinced Tom could win this one; so much so that even though he was supposed to be, in the best traditions of objective journalism, neutral, he couldn't help himself giving Tom a little tactical pep talk at the start in Milan's Sforza Park. He told him not to do anything foolish like he had in this race four years before, and attack from a long way out. 'If you feel good then keep it for the last hour of the race,' he told him. He needn't have worried: this was to be one of Tom's most mature and confident performances ever.

Although still not enjoying riding in this huge bunch – they were so closely packed that he had four bent spokes in his front wheel by the finish caused by contact with someone's pedal – he sat tight and waited until the Capo Berta climb before making his first move when there were 'only' 177 riders left in contention. He meant this move only as a test to see who was going well. There was still a fair number of the 288 kilometres left to cover, but when he saw that only Poulidor, Blocklandt and Mecco were able to follow what had been just a half-hearted prod to see if the bunch was awake, he decided to persist, and the race was on.

When they got down to it, Tom found that Poulidor was going well, but Blocklandt and Mecco were not so strong. The old Tom would have attacked and got rid of them, but now he saw the sense in keeping them, as their teams, particularly Blocklandt's Flandrias, were very strong and would be blocking behind, which was a lot better than them chasing. Anyway, the Poggio would take care of them.

It did. As soon as the road began to climb, Poulidor attacked, and Mecco and Blocklandt were gone. Now it was a duel between Poulidor and Simpson – pistols at dawn on the Poggio. That first attack had in fact distanced Tom as well as the others, but slowly and surely he clawed his way on to Raymond's back wheel. Poulidor was a fantastic climber and, as such, capable of brutal accelerations uphill. Again he went, gaining lengths on Tom, but slowly the Englishman raised his game and came back to the Frenchman.

At first sight it didn't look like it, but Tom was in command. He was playing a tactical game. Those violent changes of pace were tiring Poulidor; Tom, on the other hand, was making a much smoother, even effort – and every engineer knows that an engine works much better like that. Maybe he could have matched Poulidor pedal stroke for pedal stroke, but this was more efficient. Plus, it must have had a devastating effect on Raymond's morale: when your opponent soaks up your best shots and comes back for more it's time to go on to Plan B, and Poulidor didn't have one.

Three more times he tried, and three more times Tom came back at him. They crossed the summit of the Poggio and descended together. It was going to be a sprint between them. On paper, the ex-track rider, Tom, was favourite, but he left nothing to chance. His sprint was a tactical masterpiece, just like the one against Defilippis, but executed differently. This time, Tom led out with 500 metres to go, close to his right-hand crowd barrier, putting his opponent on the windy side of the road. He led out, but not flat-out. Poulidor started to come past on Tom's left and, as he did so, Tom just kept steadily accelerating. keeping Poulidor in the wind, keeping him thinking he could get past, and slowly increasing his pace until Poulidor simply fried and had no sprint left. It worked: 50 metres before the line Poulidor blew and Tom had won the Milan–San Remo by four lengths in what was then a record average speed of 27.1 miles per hour.

Tom had been so tactically cool that day. The pundits were right: if he was on form, and sure of it, he was unbeatable. When he was confident, he could ride with tactical brilliance, but then when you win your tactics are brilliant. No one can criticise, because they worked. After the race, René de Latour commented that he'd never seen a rider finish as fresh. Tom surprised everyone when he said he had felt so good that he had only eaten a couple of honey rolls and had drunk nothing in the race. He was very, very good that day.

A second monument for the Englishman was big news all over the continent, and his home town of Ghent was *en fête*. When he got home to Helen the house was full of flowers from well-wishers, and full of the well-wishers themselves. Albert had organised a big reception at his café where, for reasons best known to themselves, the local brass band played 'It's a Long Way to Tipperary' to welcome him home. Perhaps they thought it was the National Anthem –though if they were as good as some European brass bands I've heard, they probably were playing the National Anthem and it sounded like 'Tipperary'.

Back to work in the five-day Circuit de Provençal, and Tom was a bit below par in the first few days because of an intestinal problem that was to recur and rob him of his form later in the season. By the fourth stage, he had recovered sufficiently to take second place to the

Belgian, Henri De Wolf, in a sprint disputed by a group of five that had gained eight minutes over the rest.

After that stage, he swore revenge, and, good as his word, didn't leave the finish to the sprinters: while they were looking at each other, he attacked and won the stage by two lengths from the ultra-rapid André Darrigade.

With a free week before Paris–Roubaix some training had to be done. Remember Tom's mad ride from Harworth to London in 1956? Well, he surpassed that by riding the 600 miles between Marseille and Paris, split up into stages, of course, along with the Belgian Ferdi Bracke, as preparation for another battle in the 'Hell of the North'. Tom's riding had made him a serious favourite for Paris–Roubaix, along with Van Looy, who was going through an unaccustomed lean time in the first few months of 1964. This was especially galling for the 'Emperor' as he had sworn to avenge himself on the treacherous Beheyt. Rik would be a dangerous and determined man on Sunday.

There were three Britons in the race: Tom, and, making their debuts, Barry Hoban and Michael Wright. Wright was really an Englishman in name only. Born in Bishop's Stortford, he moved with his family to Belgium when he was four, and grew up in the Liège area speaking French, and not English. Barry Hoban was very much the real thing, born and brought up in the mining area north of Wakefield, the son of a mineworker, and an international pursuiter as an amateur. He'd moved to France in 1962 and raced very successfully there as an independent rider, based in the home-from-home northern French coalfield. Now he was a fully fledged pro with Raymond Poulidor's Mercier team.

It was a usual Paris–Roubaix menu with one addition, and that had a profound effect on the outcome of the race: a strong tail-wind was blowing the riders towards Roubaix. Because of this there had been lots of activity even before the gates of Hell had been reached. The result was that a split had occurred, and Van Looy had missed it. The front group wasn't exactly full of his fan club either, as it comprised a number of riders who'd had a recent falling out with the 'Emperor'. These included Peter Post, his former six-day partner, who was now his arch-enemy due to an incident in the previous year's race when a certain amount of money which should have changed hands, hadn't. Also, there were two rather disgruntled former team mates, Planckaert and Fore, as well as public enemy number one, Benoni Beheyt.

Among the other riders making up this front group were all three Englishmen, and with the wind on their backs they weren't coming back. They had a lead of one and a half minutes by the first stretch of *pavé*, but almost as soon as they hit it the group started to split, as riders were bounced out of the back.

The *pavé* was wet and slippery that year, liberally coated with what, in future years, American riders would christen 'Flemish toothpaste', a mixture of mud and manure which sprays up from the wheel in front, directly into your gritted teeth. Barry and Tom were brought down fairly early on, but Tom fought his way back to the front of the race.

Just as he got there, Joseph Groussard fell and knocked him off. He was straight back up and closed a 300-metre gap to the front group in a flash. Then a TV motorcyclist, his machine slipping and slithering around the centre camber of the road, lost control and brought Tom down again. Once more he had to chase, now on a damaged bike with twisted handlebars. He inched back to the front, passing riders all the time. The selection was on and four riders were now clear of the others: Post, Molenaers, Blocklandt, and Beheyt. Van Looy, several minutes back in Hell, was chewing his handlebars and spitting out nails.

It was four against one, but Tom was gaining on the leaders and was in amongst their following cars. This, however, was as far as he got. Several times he was balked by one of his rivals' team cars, each time losing vital seconds, each second costing him more strength to gain back. Inevitably, his strength ran out, and he slipped inexorably back to the chasing group, finishing with them in tenth place on the Roubaix track.

Peter Post won this epic Paris–Roubaix in a record average speed of 28 miles per hour which still stands today. Beheyt was second, so you can see what I meant when I said he was never as bad a rider as history has made him out to be. It was Tom, though, who received the lion's share of the praise in after-race reports. All the times he'd fallen, only to get up and fight back to the front, hadn't won him the race, but it had won him more fans.

His next target was the Tour de France, so the following two months were spent training and racing to get the necessary form to achieve his ambitions for that race. These were not for winning. much as he would have liked to, for he still felt Anquetil was too strong and his team too good. No, Tom thought he could get a first-five placing and in doing so take forward his ambition of eventual victory.

His final race before the Tour was, as usual, the Manx Premier. This time, though, he didn't try to win it at all cost. He had bigger fish to fry, and finished a respectable eighth to the winner, Rudi Altig.

This was Tom's second appearance that year in the British Isles. The first had been at Herne Hill on Good Friday, where he'd come across the king of all 'More than my Jobs Worths' on the gate, checking tickets. Tom was the star attraction and wanted to get in, but the bloke on the gate wouldn't let him because he didn't have a ticket. Their conversation went a bit like this:

Jobs Worth: 'Who are you?'
Tom: 'I'm Tom Simpson and I'm riding here today.'
Jobs Worth: 'Well, I've never heard of you, mate. That'll be two bob.'

What's that about prophets in their own country?

Tom's Tour started with a bang, or rather a punch. Rumours had been circulating in the bunch and in the press that one of the riders in the Pelforth team, Alan Ramsbottom, who was, of course, English, would be riding the Tour to support Tom, and not his team leader, Henri Anglade. So the Pelforth management had left Alan out of their team for the Tour. This was obviously going to hit his pocket hard, and, what's more, it wasn't true, even though perhaps Tom wished it had been.

Now, it's fair to say that Tom was no particular admirer of Anglade, so he thought he would have it out with him –right there on the start line of the first stage. He started off quite calmly, and eloquently pointed out – in French, remember – the injustice of the situation. All very polite, but Tom was a bit taken aback by Anglade's reply which was: 'What's it got to do with you? Are you sorry you've lost a team mate?' It was a sort of dressed-up 'get stuffed', really.

They exchanged a few more pleasantries along similar lines and things went very rapidly downhill, both riders questioning the other's parentage, plus the fact that Tom was losing his by now sound grip on the French language. So he thought, 'Blow this for a game of soldiers, I'll hit him.' He swung a punch at Anglade, but they had by now attracted quite a crowd and they were pulled apart before Tom's blow landed.

It didn't end there. The stage started, and out on the road the two continued their squabble all day, and seemed quite capable of going on for the rest of the Tour had not René de Latour given them both a good talking to and got them to shake hands at the start of the next stage – the spoil sport.

Everything settled down. At the end of the first week, after the first mountain stage, Tom was lying in tenth place overall. It could have been a bit higher, but he'd punctured on the final descent of that first mountain day between Thonon-les-Bains and Briançon. And with this puncture came his first big problem with his team. He was in second place on the road, descending fast, pulling away from the chasers and set to take time out of them. Then came the puncture and his team car, following another rider further back, was nowhere to be seen. Tom lost 90 seconds waiting for them; he was furious with his team manager, with whom, it's fair to say, he hadn't really seen eye to eye since he joined Peugeot.

The next stage went over Europe's highest mountain pass, the Col de Restefond, all 9,088 feet of it. Bahamontes was first over the top, with Tom just a few seconds behind. There followed a long descent, then the short climb of La Turbie before the finish on the cinder track at Monaco which nestles prettily beneath the Royal Palace.

Tom attacked on the last climb and got clear, but 22 men came back together almost in sight of the track. There was no time to hesitate so he kept up his effort on to the track where they would cross the finish line once, then ride one complete lap. Poulidor forgot this and went straight for the line, followed by Anquetil, followed by Tom, then daylight between them and the rest. First time over the line poor Raymond eased, thinking he'd won the stage and the two on his wheel shot past. It's hard to win a sprint on a flat track from behind: Tom made his move down the back straight, but had to go the long way round the outside on the last bend. All the way up the finishing straight he was gaining on Anquetil, but was just half a wheel off winning his first Tour stage on the line. Nevertheless, he moved up to eighth place overall at 5 minutes and 40 seconds.

That was as good as it got. Next day he couldn't get going in the time trial. Anquetil won, but all Tom could manage was twentieth place. He hadn't been his normal self, either physically or mentally, so far in this Tour. Those who knew him well had noticed. Jock Wadley thought he wasn't as relaxed as usual – the argument with Anglade and his problems with the team had affected him where normally, Jock thought, he would have just shrugged off these incidents. Physically, he seemed OK, but his form wasn't there when he needed it and that was made glaringly obvious in the time trial.

Four days later, by the rest day in Andorra, Tom was in tenth place at 5 minutes and 30 seconds, still in with a fighting chance of a first-five placing, but all was not well. He knew something was physically wrong and he felt isolated within his own team which, by that stage, only consisted of three other riders from the ten who had started. On top of all this, he had been unable to talk to Helen. When you feel like Tom did at that point, it is important to have access to someone you trust, but due to telecommunication difficulties in Andorra – the tiny country didn't even have television in those days and the few phones available were being monopolised by the journalists – neither of them had been able to get in touch.

Things got worse. Late on the night of the rest day Tom got a telegram from Helen which said, 'Telephone. Very urgent. Helen.' Well, that was it. He just couldn't sleep; everything got out of proportion and he was sure something had happened to either her, or Jane, or Joanne. Next morning he tried desperately to get a phone line, and was dashing backwards and forwards between the start and the post office like a mad thing. Eventually, he had to start the race, but there was no way he could concentrate.

He was miserable. Everything seemed to be going against him, then the Peugeot team car came alongside and told him that, via the race radio, they had managed to get a phone line to Helen and everything was fine; there was no need to worry. She had sent the message simply because she hadn't heard from him. The relief was tremendous, and Tom's faith in Peugeot had been restored. It wouldn't last for long.

On the climb of the Envalira he wasn't going well, but at least the good news meant that he had the morale to hang in there, so he crossed the summit not far behind the leaders. Anquetil, on the other hand, was having a terrible time on the climb. No wonder. He hadn't spent the rest day like all the other riders: a lie-in, food, a short ride, more food, more rest, food and an early night. No, he was Jacques Anquetil and always did things his way, so he left his bike alone and went to one of the big receptions put on by the organisation where he enjoyed plenty of the things cyclists shouldn't eat, and even more of the things they shouldn't drink – well, only in moderation. Jacques could do this – there are many stories of him partying into the small hours, then being as strong as two men the following day. On this day, though, it had backfired on him: his stomach was upset and it took all his legendary will-power to limit his losses.

On the descent Tom was making up time, then punctured, and once more there was no Peugeot team car near to him. He had to wait two and a half minutes before a team mate, Mastrotto, arrived on the scene. They swapped wheels because there was still no sign of the car. This hit him like a hammer and his morale plunged again. He felt as though he was having to fight everything and everybody. He vented his frustration at the stage finish and gave the Peugeot team a very hard time in the press. They defended themselves, saying that the fog on the descent had made it very hard to keep up, but the truth was that other leading riders' cars had managed it. The atmosphere in the team hotel that night was not good.

A combination of the problems with Peugeot, not being on-song physically – for a reason he discovered only after the Tour and all the little niggles that had happened in the race so far, meant that Tom had a terrible time on the biggest stage of the Tour: a giant stage that climbed four cols – the Aspin, Peyresourde, Tourmalet and Aubisque. He started off all right, staying up with the leaders over the Aspin. Then on the next climb he felt his strength just ebb away. A breakneck descent got him up to the leaders again, but he had nothing left for the Tourmalet; his body was empty. Those last two massive climbs were a nightmare, as rider after rider caught and dropped him, and only sheer bloodymindedness got him to the stage finish at Pau.

Overall, he fell to seventeenth place. His lack of strength was put down to sunstroke, but later he discovered he had ridden the whole Tour with a tapeworm. No wonder he felt empty, and no wonder that all through the race there had been nothing there when he really needed it. For the remainder of the race he rode on courage and was able to gain back a few places to finish fourteenth overall in Paris – very depressed, ten places back from where he'd intended to finish, but a few days later he discovered what had been wrong with him. I'll not go into the details of how he discovered it – some of you may be eating. Those of you who know anything about tapeworms will know what I mean, though.

The 1964 Tour was a thrilling one. Anquetil overcame his bad day, but the cracks were showing. He'd already won the Tour of Italy that year but had to fight hard to do it. There had even been rumours that he wouldn't ride the Tour de France, that he was too tired. His arch-rival, Raymond Poulidor, was in great form, pushing him hard every day, particularly in the final week when it looked like Anquetil could crumble. Two days before the final time trial into Paris was a stage that finished on top of an almost vertical climb up an extinct volcano, the Puy de Dome. Here Poulidor intended to crack the man he'd never been able to beat, but, in the end, he failed. Side by side they fought up the climb, each time Poulidor attacked, Anquetil countered, then rode up alongside him in an act of sheer defiance, suffering. white-faced, hollow-cheeked, but proud, refusing to give way. Finally, he had to let Poulidor go, but there were only 800 metres left by then, not enough for Poulidor to gain significantly. Two days later Jacques, the master against the clock, won the time trial and the Tour by just 55 seconds, the narrowest margin ever, up till that time.

Tom had now to look at the World Championships to get himself back in the limelight. First, he got rid of the tapeworm, then mixed in some long training rides with appearances at criteriums, one of which was actually in England. The soft-drinks company Corona was putting a lot of money into cycle racing in the sixties. Their publicity manager was David Saunders, the man destined to become the cycling correspondent of the *Daily Telegraph* and the first 'voice of cycling', doing TV commentaries on the ITV's *World of Sport* programme. This was the man who taught Phil Liggett how to do it. Sadly, David was killed in a car crash in 1977. David and Tom were close friends, and, in 1965, David co-wrote Tom's autobiography, *Cycling is my Life*, with him. Anyway, in 1964 David had persuaded Corona to sponsor a criterium on the Crystal Palace circuit in south London and to bring over a number of continental riders including Tom, Alan Ramsbottom, and Shay Elliott.

It was these three who dominated the race, with Tom winning. They attacked early, got away together, stayed there and proceeded to lap all but one of Britain's best home-based pro riders. That one was Billy Holmes – there was no way he was going to let his Olympic room-mate do that to him.

Sallanches, a small town in the French Alps, not far from Mont Blanc, in fact, was the venue for the 1964 World Road Race Championships.

The pro race was to cover 174 miles: twenty-four laps of a circuit which basically comprised a stiff three-mile climb to the village of Passy, a tricky descent, then a flat bit through the finish.

The day before, the amateurs had their championships on the same circuit, and the world at large got its first glimpse of the rider who was to go on to become the greatest of them all. Nineteen-year-old Belgian Eddy Merckx won the race with a masterful performance which saw him win alone. I wonder how many people watching him that day predicted he would go on to grace the top spot on the podium more than 400 times as a professional, and win nearly every major race on the calendar.

Incidentally, Tom had already met Merckx and predicted a bright future for him. He used to visit the *soigneur* Gus Naessens at his home in Brussels, which is where Merckx comes from, to receive treatment. As you'd expect in a house devoted to cycling, plenty of young hopefuls would drop in on the off-chance of meeting some of the stars that Gus treated. One who always seemed to be there was a young Eddy Merckx, only he wasn't like all the others, content to just meet their heroes; he constantly fired questions at them, probing for every bit of information about his future chosen profession. Tom recognised this – he'd been just like it himself.

Tom was not a favourite for the title in 1964. His professed objective for the year had been a good overall position in the Tour de France and in that he had failed. So the pundits had no form or expressed ambitions on which to base a prediction. Privately, though, he fancied his chances. He'd ridden well in those criteriums where he could get a ride. He wasn't popular again with the promoters in 1964 because his riding was ruffling more than a few feathers, by now. He was in danger of eclipsing some of the established stars. Whatever journalists thought about his current form, Tom was a threat in the Worlds and he suspected Van Looy, among others, of blocking contracts for him. It was a different story from the generous Van Looy after his 1962 Tour of Flanders victory; Tom was a big name now and seriously affecting the popularity of the 'Emperor' in his own country.

To round off his preparation, a few days before the championships he moved to a small hotel up in the mountains to get himself ready and to get some rest. On the eve of the race he felt good. The circuit suited him: it was just hard enough to prevent the Belgians controlling it. Indeed, in the race, Van Looy's all-powerful team was to be totally eclipsed, their best-placed rider being defending champion, Benoni Beheyt, in eleventh place, which in some small way proved a point about his victory in 1963.

The race didn't start well for Tom: on the third lap he crashed on the tricky descent, made worse by the wet conditions which prevailed throughout the race. He wasn't too badly hurt – a few bumps and grazes – but he had bent one of his pedals, and this may have led to the problems with cramp he was to experience on the last couple of laps.

Meanwhile, the early aggressor was Frenchman, Henri Anglade. He attacked after just 28 kilometres and was at the front, with different groups of riders, for almost the whole of the race. It was an uncharacteristic, but nevertheless classy, performance.

Tom quickly caught the bunch after his crash, then stayed put and watched. The other favourites were giving Anglade free reign – too much free reign in Tom's opinion. Anglade now had some strong riders with him – his team mate, Foucher, the Swiss Bingelli, and a good Italian, Vito Taccone. He had to get up to them, but not take any passengers with him.

He had read the race perfectly, and realised that the other big stars were content to see Anglade as World Champion. Anglade had made few enemies in his career, he'd paid his dues, not upset the system, so everyone knew that he would not dictate to promoters who could, and who could not, ride the criteriums – unlike Van Looy. So it served the ends of most of the riders for Anglade to be champion rather than Van Looy; except Tom: he just wanted to win no matter what the cost or repercussions, but the problem was that Tom would be chased – cycling still wasn't able to accept a British World Champion.

A typical daring descent saw him clear of the bunch. At the start of the finishing straight he swung over and saw that he only had Van Looy for company. That would do Tom: he wasn't as afraid of Van Looy as Van Looy was of him, so he gestured him to the front, but Rik wasn't having it. He obviously didn't relish the long hard pursuit, so sat up to wait for the others and take his chances with them. Tom, though, was impatient to get on with it. He stuck it in top gear, put his head down, and began an incredible 42-mile lone pursuit of the leaders.

His commitment was absolute, eyes focused on his objective over six minutes up the road, head characteristically to one side, legs turning smoothly, his face a mask of concentration. Minute by minute the lone figure in the Great Britain blue top with red sleeves ate into the lead of the four in front, a symbol that riders from this country could perform at this level.

At last he made it, but with only two laps remaining and with only the two Frenchmen left at the front, and both of them were shattered. Others were now gaining, so Tom couldn't rest. He hit the front, dragging the two Frenchmen with him. Near the top of the penultimate climb they were caught by Vittorio Adorni and Jan Janssen. Immediately, Adorni attacked. It was too much for Anglade and Foucher who blew wide apart, almost ridden to a standstill. Tom, too, was distanced, but he fought to limit his losses and another Dan Dare descent saw him back in contention with just one lap remaining.

Behind, the bunch were closing, but splitting to pieces under the power of the stronger riders. The strongest was Poulidor: he alone caught the three leaders as they started the climb for the final time.

Poulidor, Adorni and Janssen were full of fight; they had gambled that the bunch would get close enough to the leaders for them to make a big, but short effort to get across, and it had worked. Tom's gamble hadn't: he was hurting now, his legs cramping on the climb, possibly due to the bent pedal. Once more he couldn't hold them, but a last, and by now desperate, effort down the other side saw him get to within a few metres of their back wheels with just 300 metres to go.

There was no point in finessing. All he could possibly hope for was to catch them by surprise, so he lifted his tired body once more from the saddle and stamped down hard on the pedals in one defiant final effort to win. There was nothing there – he couldn't even get level with the other three. He'd emptied his body of every last gram of energy and crossed the line still in fourth position, absolutely shattered.

Again the press said that Tom was the moral victor; they'd said that in 1959 and in 1963, but it doesn't pay many bills. Jan Janssen won, becoming only the second Dutchman to win the title, and he was the one who could look forward to the big pay-days. Adorni was second, and the 'eternal second', Raymond Poulidor, third.

The World Championships would have to come Tom's way: he was too good not to win it – 1963 and 1964 had proved that. Meanwhile, there was plenty still to go for in 1964. He'd won the first classic of the season, now Tom wanted to win the last, the Tour of Lombardy, and with good reason. He was attracting a lot of interest from Italian sponsors, including the Ignis squad owned by the very rich Signor Borghi. As well as being a successful businessman Borghi was a passionate *tifosi* – a big bike fan. A big bike fan with a big cheque book. For example, when he wanted to sign Ercole Baldini, who looked likely to become the next Italian 'Campionissimo' in the late fifties, Signor Borghi gave him his full salary, £40,000, up front, just for his signature on the contract.

There is no doubt that Tom would have ridden for Borghi. He was very unhappy with Peugeot, but they had a hold on him. Every year they insisted that he sign a contract with them for the following year before the Tour de France, with the threat that if he didn't sign then, there would be no place for him in their Tour team, and Tom needed to ride the Tour. It was an impasse only broken in 1967 when the Tour reverted to national teams. Tom would be the automatic leader of the British team and he took the opportunity to sign for an Italian team for 1968. What a team it would have been, too. He was to have been joint leader with Felice Gimondi, and there would have been good Italian and English support, putting him in an enviable position to build on his list of wins. Tragically, it was never to happen.

A few days after the Worlds Tom got his revenge of sorts by beating the first three placed riders when he won a criterium at Nantes. Then he trained hard for Lombardy, using the Paris–Tours, which preceded it by a week, as final preparation.

The 'Race of the Falling Leaves' is Italy's oldest classic, a 'monument' along with Milan–San Remo. You can use a single word to encapsulate the impression or the feeling of these races: the Tour of Flanders is 'brutal', for example, and Paris–Roubaix, 'treacherous'. The only possible single word to describe the Tour of Lombardy is 'beautiful', as it winds its way through the Italian Lake District clothed in autumn colours, over alarmingly steep, hair-pinned climbs, on pretty pink-paved roads and into the heart of Italian cycling history. A chapel dedicated entirely to cyclists is on its route, on the Ghissalo climb. Inside, there is a picture in memory of every cyclist killed on Italian roads, regardless of their status in the sport, and you can see bikes ridden by some of the 'greats' when winning this race, including one of Coppi's, some of whose greatest exploits were on these roads.

His five victories in the race included an amazing four in a row from 1946 to 1949.

The 1964 race started in Milan and finished in Como. Tom was confident of victory and rode so strongly in the race that only one rider could stay with him – the young Italian, Gianni Motta, for whom great things were being predicted. Tom didn't win, but neither did Motta beat him; his own team did that.

At the start, Tom was careful to tell Gaston Plaud, the Peugeot team manager, exactly what he wanted in the way of food and drink to be handed to him at the half-way point. When he got his musette during the race there was nothing in it he had ordered, only stuff that he couldn't digest, so he threw it away in disgust. Despite this set-back, Tom attacked so strongly on the climb from Lake Maggiore that he reduced the front runners to just five. Then, on the next climb, Motta made a further selection when he put the hammer down and only Tom could follow.

That was it: the others would not see Motta again, but Tom was now suffering from lack of food – remember these classics are over 150 miles long. Motta very sportingly gave him some of his and, for the time being, it kept him going. Then, on the last climb, the pair got the news that a group containing Adorni, Poulidor and Janssen, the men very much in form, had closed to within 50 seconds.

Tom was determined to hold them off and, perhaps a bit rashly, went at such a pace on the last climb that Motta was unable to share the lead; it was all he could do to hang on. It worked. At the summit they had over three minutes on the Poulidor group, but Tom had completely emptied the tank: he was shattered. It was an effort fuelled by his frustration with Peugeot as much as his huge will to win, for he must have realised that he was getting into an impossible situation in the race.

On the final ten-mile flat run into Como, Motta was able just to ride away from Tom, who could hardly focus his eyes on the road ahead. In cycling terms, he had been 'hit by the man with the hammer', meaning that he'd used up all the sugar, the fuel, in his tired body. He struggled along the road to Como where he was caught and passed by over 20 riders. At the finish he hardly knew where he was. The journalist, Roger St Pierre, had to untie his shoes for him. He was in a terrible state, shaking like a leaf, a symptom of glycogen depletion; but half an hour later he'd recovered, laughing and joking with everybody and trying to get St Pierre, who was on holiday, to extend his trip and go with him to a race in central Italy.

Another headline performance, another time when Tom had thrashed his body to a standstill, and another time when forces outside his control had conspired against him, and the result? More fans, more respect, but another blank on his win list. At least he would only have to wait one more year to fill it.

His riding in Lombardy earned him a contract for the two-man time trial, the Barrachi Trophy, where he was to ride with Rudi Altig. A very, very strong rider, ex-World Pursuit Champion, Altig was a bit of a nightmare to ride with in these events. A team needs to be smooth, play to each other's strengths, keep the pace high, but steady. A couple of years before, Altig had ridden with Anquetil in this event and had nearly killed him. Jacques complained that once he'd done a turn at the front the German would come through too fast, and the changes of pace had reduced him to his knees. Although they won, Jacques was so far gone at the finish that he forgot to apply his brakes, and crashed into the wall at the end of the home straight.

Tom wouldn't normally have had a problem with this. Like Altig, he was an ex-track rider and accustomed to changes of pace; he was also, probably, basically faster than Anquetil. Still, due possibly to the damage he'd inflicted on himself during the Tour of Lombardy, he had a terrible experience and suffered more than he ever had in his life, so much so that he confided to his friend Vin Denson that at one point he was sure he was about to die on the bike:

Tom told me that he was suffering so badly, digging deeper and deeper to hold Altig. He was in a bad way and at the point when he thought he couldn't stay with Altig any longer. Then he said that the objects around him faded from view, it was like he was in a tunnel and there was a feeling of peace. He said it was as though he was outside himself, looking at himself. He was sure he was dying. Tom told me that after that experience he was no longer afraid to die.

Vin will never forget that, and he remembers clearly the eerie feeling that came over him as Tom recounted this story: 'And he was serious. I began to worry that he was prepared to push too hard to win after he told me that,' Vin added. It was a worry that was to grow over the coming years.

He was right to worry, too. Despite this terrible experience Tom and Altig finished third, only 1 minute 10 seconds behind the winners, Motta and Fornoni. This race was a typical, chilling example of how much Tom needed to win, just how far he was prepared to go, even when he was far from being 100 per cent physically fit. It is something very few people have in them.

The road season was now over and it was time to go indoors and on to the track. Tom's first six-day race of the winter was at Brussels where he was paired with the Dane, Freddy Eugen. They were to have a difficult time as Eugen had just recovered from pneumonia, and this race saw a big battle going on between Willy Vannitsen, a very fast sprinter, and Rik Van Steenbergen, still very much the king of the sixes then.

Ron Baensch was riding with his compatriot Bobby Ryan, and he remembers the battle between the two Belgian stars and the effect it had on the other teams in the race:

> During a hard chase, Vannitsen wanted to call a truce because he was hungry, but Van Steenbergen wouldn't have it, in fact he increased the pace. Then, when the race was neutralised at four in the morning, Vannitsen attacked. I went for a meal just before this and the race was calm. When I came back all hell had broken loose and we'd lost another two laps.

The battle raged throughout the event. Coming into the final two hours, Vannitsen/Scrayen were one lap ahead of Van Steenbergen/Lykke, and the team of Pfenninger and Peter Post – the man to whom Van Steenbergen, who was 40 years old by then, (his partner, Lykke, was actually his son-in-law) – was gradually handing over his crown.

Those final two hours were amazing. The last five teams in the race were withdrawn, leaving only the top eight to fight it out in a derny-paced Madison. Tom and Eugen had survived well all week, given the battle that had been going on, and they made the cut, but the technique in this last, high-speed race proved very difficult to master. Still, they did well, considering that they were relative novices in what turned out to be a 120-minute inferno of a race, with laps being gained and lost, and reputations made and destroyed. Two of the eight top teams retired. Vannitsen/Scrayen were run into the ground and simply threw in the towel, losing ten laps. The establishment had put down the uprising – Post/Pfenninger ran out winners from Van Steenbergen/Lykke. Tom had survived one of the hardest six-days ever. He and Eugen ended the race in fourth place overall, and earned loads of respect from the masters of this branch of the sport. Soon he would be beating them at their own game.

Next came the Zurich six, with Baensch as his partner. This race had a very unusual start as the first hour was a scratch race for all the riders, any lost laps being combined when the riders joined to ride as two-man teams for the rest of the race. The top riders rode very hard to establish their superiority and a pecking order from the word go. It was a tough start to what is still regarded as the hardest six on the calendar.

This was the race in which Tom and Ron were accepted by what was known as the 'Blue Train', the elite group of riders who controlled the races and got the biggest cut of the primes and gate money. The pair was asked not to contest a sprint series too hard so that the local man, Fritz Pfenninger, a big winner and very much part of the train, could look good. They refused, and won the series. The big boys could see that they weren't going to be able to deal with these two like they had with Vannitsen and just ride the legs off them, so they let them in. They had to: Ron and Tom had forced their character on to the racing, and the crowds loved their attacking style of riding; the only thing the 'train' *could* do was let them in.

In establishing themselves they'd been guided by the man who was looking after them at Zurich, the vastly experienced ex-rider, Fred Strom. One time when it was getting a bit physical and Palle Lykke had cut in on Tom at speed, Fred told Tom to go straight up to the Dane, act annoyed and threaten him. He did and it worked, just like Strom told him: 'If you jump on 'em right away, then they know you're not to be messed about.'

Tom also learnt about the lighter side of indoor racing, and how entertaining the crowd, either with spectacular riding or just playing to the gallery, would get them behind you. With the crowd behind you it is easier to take a lap because their cheering spurs you on – well, it worked for Tom.

Despite the hard work he had enjoyed the Zurich six, particularly an incident when a woman, suspecting that her husband was at the track with another female, used the stadium public address system to donate huge sums of money from the family bank account as primes for the riders. She soon found him or, rather, he found her.

Tom came away from Zurich with contracts for Milan and Antwerp, and a favourable impression of the other riders, now they'd accepted him, who were, he said, 'much more pleasant to work with than the road riders'.

Tom following his pacer, Fernand Wambst, into the Parc des Princes stadium at the end of the Bordeaux–Paris, 1963. After this race he was leading the Super Prestige Pernod rankings. (*Presse Sports*)

Milan–San Remo, 1964: five times Poulidor attacked on the Poggio; each time Tom brought him back, and then outsprinted him to win by four lengths in a record average speed of 43.42 k.p.h. (*Cycling Weekly*)

World Professional Road Race Championships, San Sebastián, 1965: Tom following Rudi Altig with one lap to go. 'Look at Tom's eyes, and you'll see that there was no way Rudi was going to beat him that day.' (*Presse Sports*)

Rainbow jersey. (*Presse Sports*)

Tour of Lombardy, 1965: Tom, in the rainbow jersey, has ridden everybody off his wheel to win alone on the Como track by three minutes – 'an exploit in the tradition of Fausto Coppi'. (*Presse Sports*)

'There is nothing at all to prevent him starting the stage, but everything to prevent him finishing. He will be riding virtually one-handed.' Under the watchful gaze of Dr Dumas and a posse of photographers, Tom struggles towards retirement on the Col de Montgenevre during stage 17 of the 1966 Tour de France. (*Presse Sports*)

Manx Premier, June 1967 – Tom's last race in Britain and his last victory – a virtuoso performance in storm-force winds and torrential rain. (*Manx Press*)

Marseilles, 13th July 1967: Tom before the start of
stage 13 of the Tour de France. (*Cycling Weekly*)

11

'I HOPE THAT ONE DAY, MR PRIME MINISTER'

After a short Christmas break back in England, Tom, Helen, and the kids headed for St Gervais, and a different kind of break. Their annual ski trip was great fun for two weeks, then Tom fell, sustaining a fractured foot, sprained ankle and a twisted knee – not as bad as it could have been, but still bad enough to put his participation in the Milan six in jeopardy as the start was only two weeks away.

There was no way Tom wanted to miss this race – it was a big pay-day. The Milan six had lots of sponsorship and good contracts were paid, though the event was criticised by some six-day die-hards as being a bit soft. It was understandable. The Italians, unlike the northern Europeans, did not have the same history or appreciation of the finer points of indoor racing; all they wanted to see was their top road stars looking good. These were paired with the best regular six-day riders to make up for any lack of track-craft, and the race was eventually won by Gianni Motta, riding with Van Steenbergen, so everybody went home happy.

Tom had enjoyed himself immensely. The injured leg held out well, considering that the plaster was removed from his foot only four days before the race started. The racing, though fast – the average speed in the chases was 32 miles per hour – hadn't been as gruelling as usual in a six-day and the heat in the stadium had helped the healing process. There had been plenty of diversions, and Tom had the crowd in his hand playing referee in the elimination races where the last rider over the line each lap has to drop out.

With his leg well run-in he returned to Belgium looking forward to a good performance in the Antwerp Six. In preparation, each day he covered at least 50 miles on the road in the morning followed by two hours on the Antwerp track in the afternoon. This was to maintain the speed in his legs he'd got from Milan and to get used to Antwerp – at 250 metres, it was the biggest of the indoor tracks. He'd picked up a slight cold in Milan, but otherwise everything was on target for the six and the 1965 road season, which was just around the corner.

As well as being on a big track the Antwerp Six was unusual in that it was contested by three-man teams instead of the usual two. The reason behind this was that the race contained a lot of Derny-paced racing and each team included a specialist at this kind of event. Tom rode with Ron Baensch and the Belgian, Paul de Paepe, but his cold worsened during the week, and he was forced to pull out of the race with two days to go.

He didn't want to compromise his road season and thought a couple of days at home would do him good. It didn't: two days later he only managed about 50 kilometres of the Genoa–Rome. The infection had spread to his chest and he couldn't breath.

The problem persisted through most of March and Tom had to abandon in both Milan–San Remo and Ghent–Wevelgem. Only in the last few days of the month did any sign of recovery come when he finished fifth in the Antwerp–Harelbeke and sixth in the Circuit of Eleven Towns, both tough Belgian semi-classics.

Gradually, he was starting to get where he always wanted to be, up with the best. In the Circuit Provençal he finished third overall, giving the winner, Bahamontes, a terrible time on the last stage. Tom got in a break with Janssen and Anglade which quickly gained time on Bahamontes, but it wasn't enough. So he attacked and left them, taking with him two Belgians, one of whom was a team mate of Van Looy who refused to do anything to help Tom. He did not need that. Undeterred, though, he flogged on, gaining sufficient time at one point to be leader on the road.

Unfortunately, in the latter part of the stage they turned into the terrible Mistral wind and Bahamontes made a huge effort to get back on terms, so much so that after the race he said, 'I've never suffered so much in my life, and if I had to start again I'm not sure that I would.' By now the two Belgians were no help whatsoever and the result was that Tom ended up towing them to the finish where they both beat him. So, he was third on the stage, and in third place overall. Maybe once more his tactics were flawed, but at least he knew his legs were on song, ready for the most important spring classics.

He rode the Tour of Belgium to prepare for Paris–Roubaix, but somehow contrived to close a car door on his own foot. It became very painful and saw him retire from this tough stage race which used to be famous for its terrible weather.

As ever, Tom was one of the first to attack in Paris–Roubaix. On the Doullens Hill he was away with Poulidor, and the pair worked well together through the 'Hell of the North' until Tom crashed and smashed his back wheel to pieces. Back up, and on the road again, he forced his way across to the winning break, but then his problems really started as Van Looy was there with an incredibly strong, young team mate, his protégé, Ward Sels. They controlled the break and Sels went after every attacker like a terrier dog, bringing each and every one back for the benefit of his master who attacked close to the finish, and won on his own. Tom finished in seventh place.

Tom's position was made even more difficult when, in the last ten kilometres, his pedal started to unscrew and he couldn't make a single attack because he was afraid that it would come away from the crank completely. From being so strong in the race to being so passive in the finale, Tom attracted criticism from his team manager, Gaston Plaud, who practically accused him of selling the race to Van Looy.

However, he had more pressing problems than what Plaud thought had happened. Next day Tom could hardly walk because his foot hurt so much. He had to have injections into a tendon and more time off the bike. In addition, he had to miss the Tour of Flanders, but his morale was soon restored by a win in the Grand Prix of Berlin on Easter Monday.

Two days later was the Flèche Wallonne, a major classic in its own right in those days and, with its now more famous sister race, Liège–Bastogne–Liège, the first part of what used to be called the 'Weekend Ardennaise'. In fact, 1965 was probably the first year of the Flèche's demise as a big classic, as it was the first year that there wasn't an official classification for the 'Weekend Ardennaise'. It was a pity that, because, typical of the luck of the Simpsons, Tom would have won it with his high placings in both races.

The Flèche was run off, as it often is, on a day of glacial rain and strong winds. Tom dominated the race. He won the 'King of the Mountains' prize and he won the most aggressive rider prize, but he didn't win the race. Too generous by far with his efforts, he was eventually out-manoeuvred by his final co-escapees, the two Italians, Roberto Poggialli, and a man destined for greatness, Felice Gimondi, who was in his first year as a pro.

Tom opened up the race by winning the Sarthe Hill prime after 50 kilometres. From this point he decided to press on, expecting reinforcements to join him. They did, but they weren't the ones he wanted; they weren't top riders. Still, he pressed on, working with them, but eventually they were caught by the bunch which, with about 120 kilometres to go, was only 36 strong. The weather was so bad by then that one of the survivors, Michael Wright, was riding wearing an anorak – not a racing cape, an anorak, complete with hood, and furry bits round the collar and cuffs.

Shortly after Tom had dropped back, Gimondi attacked, and Poggiali and Tom went with him. They worked well together, soon building up a lead of three minutes. Of course, Tom worked the hardest. On the climbs he was flying. Whenever he hit the front the speed went up. At times the Italians were hanging on for dear life; in the last 25 kilometres Gimondi did nothing. With the lead growing all the time and the bunch dwindling, don't ask me why Tom was going so hard. That was Tom: he felt good, so he rode hard. It was his instinct. Sometimes, though, it was almost self-destructive.

On the last climb, Poggiali attacked. Tom held him to five lengths for ages, then had to let him go. As he sat down Gimondi attacked. It was all over. Poggiali won, Gimondi was second, and Tom third. Everyone said Tom should have won. They all asked why he had raced like he had. Plaud was furious. Publicly, he said, 'Tom was the strongest, but he wasted his strength. He should never have worked so hard in that early break – the riders in it weren't good enough to stay away. Panache is all well and good, but it brings nothing in. If Tom had used more common sense he would have won.'

Privately, he was even more convinced that Tom was selling races and his thoughts were gaining credence. Articles started to appear in the press and Tom was forced to defend himself against accusations which, as he said, 'If they were true and I hadn't sold the races they say I have, and gone on to win them, I would be the greatest rider ever. The accusations are quite fantastic.' No, Tom didn't sell races, not by 1965, and definitely not races as big as Flèche Wallonne. This, of course, was a race he hadn't won before, and it was one that he needed because it is a race that all the greats have won.

There should be no suggestion, though, that he had always been above this kind of thing. In his early years, he was over there to break in and make money, any way he could. I believe that he sold the 1962

Tour of Flanders to Van Looy, but he had to. In 1962 he needed money, acceptance and criterium contracts. He'd not received any of those by winning that race in 1961. But, by 1965, Tom was just too big to sell a race like the Flèche. He was part of the establishment, a star, and accepted by riders and promoters as such. It was simple economics: he would have made far more from winning Flèche Wallonne than anyone could have paid him for losing it.

Why did he race like this, then? Why did he seem to want to smash everyone to pieces? I think the reason was revealed in an interview he did for Belgian television shortly after he'd won the World Championships, when he said:

> Plaud doesn't understand when he sees what he thinks is me throwing away a race, but I like to fight in a race. I give so much because I want to win by minutes, not in a sprint. The great riders, Coppi and Kubler, they all won their races by minutes, and I want to be like them.

This was Tom's driving force; he'd already gone further than any British rider either before or since, but it wasn't enough. He wasn't content. He wanted more. He wanted to be one of the greats. It was no more complicated than that.

Tom didn't have time to worry about what Plaud thought – it was just another nail in the coffin of their worsening relationship. He now set his sights on winning Liège–Bastogne–Liège. Perhaps stung by all the criticism over Flèche Wallonne, Tom decided to change his tactics and bide his time in the bunch until an early break, containing Vin Denson and Alan Ramsbottom, was caught.

Still, he was the first of the big names to attack, and did so just as the break was being caught, coming out of the town of Spa with about 50 kilometres left to race. It was a big attack: Gimondi, now a lot more confident, went with Tom and the pair worked really hard for 25 kilometres. At this point, Gimondi's confidence deserted him and, as they only had 20 seconds on the furiously chasing bunch to show for half an hour of intense, killing effort, he sat up, and waited.

Tom would never sit up, even if he had just a one-second lead, so he put his head down and went for home. He was flat-out but not gaining, but neither was he being caught. After the race he said, 'I was hoping all the time that some strong boys would get up to me.' This proved his undoing as, while he was looking round to check on what was happening behind him, he rode straight into a patch of oil on the wet road and fell.

He slithered to a halt, badly grazing his left arm and side, but his bike was OK, so with the finish now so close he was up and after the first few riders that had passed him. There had been a split and Tom was now at the head of the bunch that was chasing. Straightaway he attacked, taking five other riders with him, including the eventual winner, Carmine Preziozi. None of them could work with him – his instinct had taken over now and he wasn't thinking. The gap was closed in double-quick time – too quick: the race was now on the last climb and Tom was shattered, suffering really badly. His arm was killing him and affecting his climbing. He couldn't survive the last attacks and at the finish crossed the line in ninth place – another maybe. But for the fall, he had the legs to win that day – there's no doubt about that; everybody said so.

This year, 1965, was starting to look like 1963 – lots of effort, lots of pain, lots of bad luck, lots of near misses, but not a win; well, not a big one. Bordeaux–Paris had been Tom's salvation then, so he decided to enter it now. Furthermore, he heard that Anquetil had entered, and Jacques certainly wasn't going to ride all that way just for second place. He would try to win and Tom fancied his chances of beating him head to head. It would be the first time. Anquetil had never really been serious in the classics. Sharp businessman that he was, he asked why should he add classics to his list of wins when the promoters could hardly afford the price the five-times Tour winner charged now? It wouldn't increase his market value as the market couldn't support an increase. But now Jacques Anquetil would really try to win the Bordeaux–Paris in 1965 because, if he did, his sponsors would let him off riding the Tour, and he really didn't want to ride the Tour that year. So Tom was going to try and beat him in a race they were both going for; to do so would be another brick in the wall of his Tour de France ambitions.

It was going to be one hell of a battle, but before it Tom had some light preparatory work lined up by taking part in the longest unpaced road race in the world then, the London–Holyhead, here in Britain. He was looking forward to racing on the open roads of the mainland for the first time as a pro, even though it would mean 275 miles of open road.

Corona sponsored the race and had paid for the 'continental' British to ride – Tom, Vin Denson, Barry Hoban, Shay Elliott and Keith Butler. They had also brought two foreigners with them: a Belgian, Van Meenen; and the Dane, Soni Kari – a good little team, for there is no doubt that, though they were officially all from different trade teams on the continent, they were riding for one thing in this race: a victory for Tom. This has caused a good deal of ill feeling over the ensuing years, with accusations about the race being fixed and any opposition to Tom being discouraged by the continentals once the winning break was established. Maybe so, but do those same people think that the result would have been any different in a free for all? One of the continentals would have won, whichever way the race went.

Tom did win in a close sprint finish from Shay Elliott and the British-based Albert Hitchen, with all the continentals, apart from Soni Kari who crashed, showing well. It has been said by some people that Bill Bradley, a very good British-based pro in the winning break, was leaned on by the continentals not to make it too hard. Maybe he was. So what? Are the same people saying that given free reign Bradley would have won? He wouldn't. He was a very good rider, I'm not saying he wasn't. In fact, after the race Vin Denson said that Bradley, along with Bill Holmes, should have gone to the continent where he was sure they would have made it, but he was based in Britain and, therefore, didn't have the depth of racing, and if he hadn't toed the line, the continentals would have worked him over and the race would still have ended in a Simpson victory, but with everybody shattered. Tom didn't need that a matter of days before Bordeaux–Paris. There was a definite hierarchy in pro cycling in those days, and in some races the stars expected a certain degree of deference from the others. It made sense – they raced a lot more than they do now, for a start.

After the race, Tom was very complimentary about the homebased riders. There was good media coverage and Britain's best had won in front of them, giving him another opportunity to hammer home the point in which he believed so completely: that there was talent enough in this country to take on the best if only a sponsor could be attracted with enough money to put a full-time, all-British team on the continent.

The 1965 Bordeaux–Paris was to be the second part of one of the most amazing – although before it, most were saying foolhardy – doubles the sport of cycling has ever seen. Anquetil did not want to ride the 1965 Tour de France: he'd suffered a lot to win his fifth Tour in 1964 and, though the chance of a history-making sixth win was tempting, I think the chance of a defeat at the hands of Poulidor was more than enough to remove that temptation. But, he was still Jacques Anquetil: the whole of France expected something from him every year, and he had a responsibility to his sponsors, Ford, and the other riders they employed. How could he avoid the pressure of a three-week fight to the death with Poulidor, whilst still saving face and keeping the whole team in employment?

His team manager, Raphaël Geminiani, came up with the idea of one great and grand exploit that had never been done, and would capture people's imagination perhaps even more than a sixth Tour win, which they probably expected in any case. Anquetil would ride the 365-mile Bordeaux-Paris and win. So what? Well, before it, he would ride, and win, the eight-day, very tough, Dauphiné Libéré stage race, which finished on Saturday afternoon with the Bordeaux–Paris starting in the early hours of Sunday morning. If Jacques did this he would be a superman, the whole of France would be amazed, and Ford would let him off the Tour.

He did win the Dauphiné, not only beating Poulidor whilst winning two tough and wet mountain stages, but by comprehensively taking him apart in Friday's time trial. So that was the ghost of Poulidor laid to rest: Jacques didn't need to beat him in the Tour now. In fact, if Jacques could complete the second half of his exploit, Poulidor could win the Tour for all he cared; it would have proved nothing, except that he won a Tour de France without Anquetil. Alas, even that was beyond Poulidor, but that's another story.

At five o'clock on Saturday afternoon, the last stage of the Dauphiné ended in Avignon, a city in the southern Rhône Valley. Within 40 minutes Jacques had visited the victory podium, done his post-race interviews, showered, grabbed a quick meal and was on the road to the airport at Nîmes along with a police escort to clear the way. Twenty minutes after their arrival there they were off in a business jet bound for Bordeaux, landing at 7.45 p.m.

Another quick sprint in a car to join his Ford team mates, Jean Stablinski and Vin Denson, and straight into a four-course meal, saying that he wasn't tired, but was very hungry. During the meal he gave interviews to all and sundry, and, at 10 p.m., he finally got some time to himself. He needed it – the race started just four hours later. During the interviews he said that he feared two things: the early, unpaced section, and Tom Simpson.

At the 2 a.m. start there were still over 5,000 spectators in the old Bordeaux velodrome, such was the way in which Anquetil's exploit had captured France. Next day, nearly the whole country listened to the blow-by-blow, live radio broadcast from the race, all following the fortunes of Anquetil who, by exposing himself to the possibility of failure, had fired people's imaginations far more than he ever had when handing out his yearly beatings of their favourite rider, the country boy, Poulidor.

Up until now Anquetil's morale had been buoyed by all the excitement of the day, but once on the road, and in a cold wet night, the reality of it all hit him, big time. He was feeling very uncomfortable and visibly struggling. Ten times he went to his team car and asked Geminiani to let him stop, but the answer was 'no'. Eventually, towards morning, he began to recover; he even said to a journalist: 'I'm racing up near the Belgian border tomorrow. Do you think I'll be ridden-in by then?' He *should* have been racing there; in fact, he would be at home, ill and in bed.

Once the Derny pacers were picked up the race began. The first attacker was Vin Denson, sent ahead on the instructions of Geminiani to make Anquetil's rivals work to fetch him back, but, in fact, the attack only caused Anquetil problems: the exploit was looking threatened.

Denson eased and was caught, only to be replaced by François Mahe who led the race for the next 200 kilometres. In chasing him the bunch began to split, and Tom soon found himself riding with only Stablinski and the slowly recovering Anquetil for company.

This is where Tom's problems started. Several times he attacked, but each time his pacer's motor broke down. He had a spare pacer, but wasn't as comfortable behind him as he was with Wambst, the man who'd led him to victory in 1963, so he was finding it difficult to put Anquetil under pressure while he was struggling and looking as though he'd left his legs back in the Dauphiné.

It was an opportunity missed, because, with about 100 miles to go, Anquetil amazingly began to feel stronger. It was time for the last stage of Geminiani's plan. Stablinski was sent off on the attack and Tom had to chase, distancing Anquetil, but then he hesitated. Anquetil caught up, then Tom attacked on the Dourdan Hill. The whole of France was stunned by the news coming over the radio: 'Simpson seul en tete.'

Once more Anquetil chased him down, now on the roads he was so familiar with; the roads over which the Grand Prix des Nations, the time-trial classic, used to be run; the roads over which Anquetil had triumphed seven times already in that race. Finally, he caught Tom with 18 miles to go, and they both flew past the hapless Mahe.

Then they both eased and Stablinski caught up once more, and immediately he attacked. Tom brought him back. Then Anquetil attacked; Tom chased him down once more. Stablinski went again. How many times had this happened? Tom was the meat in a very uncomfortable sandwich. The two team mates were beginning to wear him down.

Eventually, Anquetil put everything into one last, desperate attack. Tom chased, but the gap stuck. It wasn't much, but it was enough to enable Anquetil to enter the Parc des Princes alone and win to a huge ovation. It was incredible. Less than a minute later Tom appeared with Stablinski glued to his back wheel. Tom had nothing left and Stablinski easily won the sprint for second place.

With the joy of success, the fatigue just fell away from Anquetil. This truly was one of the greatest exploits in cycling, and writing about it all these years later it seems unbelievable that anybody could do this. It seemed unbelievable to many at the time, and once again the accusations started.

They said that Anquetil paid Tom, that Tom's break on the Dourdan Hill was just a bit of stage management to build up the tension. They refused to believe that Anquetil could possibly have recovered from the Dauphiné in time to beat Tom fairly.

I don't know about this one, I'm sure. I do know that Anquetil could suffer, and he went very deep to win this race – next day he was ill. I also know that Helen was at the finish in the Pare des Princes and that she had never seen Tom win a big race. Why then would he make sure she was there to see one that he'd sold to Anquetil? Also, if Tom had agreed to let Anquetil win, is it likely that it was part of the deal for Stablinski to take second? So was his outsprinting Tom evidence that he was indeed shattered and beaten fairly? Fair point, but on the other hand I recently met a Belgian who claims to have won a packet of money after talking to Tom before the race by betting on Anquetil. I'll let you decide. Whatever happened it was an incredible ride by Anquetil; he was an incredible man and maybe this victory, along with the other occasions in his career when his pride forced his body to go beyond the red line, cost him more than he knew: he was only 53 when he died.

The rumours had done nothing to improve Tom's relationship with Gaston Plaud. Once again he made him sign a contract with Peugeot-BP for 1966 and '67 before he would give him a place in the Tour de France. Then, once he'd secured this, Plaud made it a further condition that he ride the Midi Libre stage race before the Tour. Tom didn't need this. It wasn't going to improve his form – he already had good form. What he needed now was rest. After all, he'd just completed the two longest single-day races in the world, winning one and coming third in the other, and they say that just riding one of these can leave you dead for the year.

On the last day of the Midi Libre Tom's young team mate, Roger Pingeon, was leading the race. Tom was marking Stablinski as he had the idea that the crafty son of a Polish miner was not happy with a young rider like Pingeon winning. He was right, and Stablinski attacked. Tom followed him. A group formed without Pingeon and gained a big lead. Tom was soon leader on the road and only had to finish with this group to win the Midi Libre. Then, on the final bend, he punctured, his back tyre rolled off the rim and he fell. There were only 100 metres left, but by the time Tom had got sorted out and crossed the line he had lost too much time, and ended the race in third place overall.

So to the 1965 Tour de France, an open Tour for the first time since 1960 now that Anquetil wasn't riding. But an open Tour often means a hard one, with several riders all believing absolutely in their chances of winning and, just like 1960, slugging it out from the start, rather than basing their race on an obvious favourite.

On the face of it, Poulidor, through a right of accession for having pushed Anquetil so hard the previous year, would take over the role as marginal favourite. But he hadn't the presence and stature of his rival to dominate men like Adorni, who had already won the Tour of Italy that year; Wolfshohl, the Tour of Spain winner; Janssen; and

Tom. All these were listed as favourites by the press in the run-up to the Tour. *L'Equipe* said of Tom, in one of their previews of the Tour which, by the way, start about two months before the race: 'He now has an indefinable aura surrounding him. He stands out in the bunch; he has the mark of a man whose personality is imprinted on any race he rides.'

At the start Tom was optimistic. That doesn't mean that he was confident – he knew that he hadn't much in reserve for this Tour. He'd had a hard classics campaign, trying at great length to win every one he rode. Then there had been the differences he'd had with his team. He had no confidence in either the riders or the manager: in every race he seemed to be on his own, riding against teams with men dedicated to helping their leader – his rivals. Bordeaux–Paris was a prime example of that. While Stablinski and Denson rode their legs off in support of Anquetil, Tom only had two weak riders, entered by Peugeot just as a token gesture, to help him. Neither of them lasted five minutes when war broke out at the Derny pick-up point. It had been the same all year long, and having to follow up the two marathon one-day races with the Midi Libre had helped neither his physical nor mental condition.

Just in case you think I'm exaggerating the importance of team support then mark the words of Rik Van Looy when talking about his team soon after his retirement: 'Without them I would have won nothing, and I owe them everything.' This, remember, is the man who won everything – well, every classic. His words, I think, more than any other, put into context Tom's victories, most of which he owed to no one but himself.

He would give it his best shot, of course, to win the Tour. He was still absolutely sure that he could win, though he knew now that he would have to have a different start to his season, and a different team.

Sometimes the Tour de France starts in another country: in 1998 it started in Ireland, for example. Well, in 1965 it started in Cologne, not too far from the Belgian border with Germany, and Tom had a problem right away. Just before the start somebody stole his bike! A replacement was found in time, and guess who was off up the road as the first attacker of the race? Yes, it was Tom, but it was just a bit of bravado, really, and the first stage ended in a predictable bunch sprint in the Belgian city of Liège, with a predictable winner in Rik Van Looy.

Next day was a team time trial in which the Peugeot team were placed second. Not a bad start, but, unknown to Tom and the rest of the field, by the time the race reached Roubaix on the next stage it would be virtually over. In the Hell of the North, not a place traditionally loved by the Italians, Felice Gimondi dragged two Belgians clear of the rest and gave the world a demonstration of sheer class that took him to within striking distance of the yellow jersey.

Seizing his opportunity, next day Gimondi went for it again, and again the bunch dithered. Surely a young, first-year professional in his first Tour de France couldn't hold out until the finish? And, if he did, then maybe he'd wear the jersey for a few days, but surely he couldn't hold out to the end?

He could and he did: he took the stage into Rouen and the jersey; then he lost it for a few days, but won it back with a dogged display in the Pyrenees, then clinched it with a superb victory in the mountain time trial up Mont Revard. At the finish, in Paris, Poulidor was second again, now to an unknown Italian. He couldn't win the Tour either with or without Anquetil, and the writing really was on the wall for the 'Eternal Second'. In fact, he never did win the Tour de France, despite riding it until he was over 40 years old.

Tom tried valiantly to play what cards he had left. By the time the race reached the Pyrenees he was in seventh place overall, but he fell on the descent of the Aubisque and damaged his hand. It seemed nothing at the time, but the injury was to have very serious consequences later on in the race.

A couple of days later, he tried to make a move on the stage from Montpellier to the top of the infamous 'Giant of Provence', Mont Ventoux. He was never really happy in this area – he didn't like racing in the oppressive heat. Even the sound of the cigalles, the insects which sing in every bush in Provence, used to get on his nerves. 'I hate those little bastards,' he once told Vin Denson. So why chose the Ventoux to make a move? Remember what Ron Baensch said, that if Tom was suffering then he knew the others were, so all he had to do was push a little harder and he could beat them? That's why. He knew that he would be suffering on the Ventoux, so they all would, and if he pushed a little harder then ... maybe he would win.

On the climb he tried hard to shake them off, but physically he was starting to come apart. His hand was troubling him, his health was failing and his morale had not really been there since Cologne. He put up a solid performance to finish ninth on the stage and conserve his ninth overall place, but he could not pick it up and put the others under real pressure.

Two years later he would try the same thing on the Ventoux, this time believing he was making an attempt to win the 1967 Tour, and the consequences would be disastrous. It was just not his mountain. It is now, though. Go there: you can feel him all around you.

Two days later, on the stage from Gap to Briançon, Tom cracked completely. Overnight he'd contracted bronchitis and he lost nearly 19 minutes on the stage. He should have stopped there and then. He was in a terrible state: his hand had now gone septic and was poisoning his entire system.

Next day he lost more time, being dropped on every climb, but, like a boxer who doesn't know when he's had enough, he kept getting up off the floor and catching them on the descents. He fell to thirtieth overall. There was no point in going on, but still he was there next day for the Mont Revard time trial. Eventually, a day later, at the end of the stage from Aix-les-Bains to Lyon, the Tour doctor stepped in and refused to allow Tom to continue. His condition was serious, and the doctor was very worried.

He was immediately taken to hospital where they were surprised he could even stand, let alone ride a bike. For a while it was even thought that he would lose his hand – it was that bad. They operated that night, drains were inserted into the hand and powerful antibiotics used to fight the blood poisoning that had infected his entire body. He'd been like that for days – only Tom Simpson could have contemplated trying to get through the Tour de France in that condition. What did John Geddes say about Tom being mad, about doing things that no one else would even think of?

People will talk about drugs and Tom's death for ever, saying that one was the only cause of the other, but, as Harry Hall, the mechanic on the 1967 Tour and a close friend of Tom, has said: 'He was his own drug.' It sounds trite, a bit like a friend making excuses, but there is an element of truth in what he says. People who talk about his death only in the context of drugs simply cannot understand just how anyone could push like Tom. I think that the 1965 Tour shows just how far he was prepared to go, and this without even the chance of victory. Just think how committed he was when he thought that he could win, when he had to win. And, as we shall see, he had to win the Tour in 1967. If you can understand this, you can understand Tom, and why he was such a success, and also why it all ended in tragedy for him.

That tragedy was two years away yet; Tom was beaten now, but not defeated. The Tour had been beyond him again, but the World Road Championships weren't. So, while he regained his health, he sat at home in Ghent and plotted: plotted his comeback campaign to take the title in San Sebastian.

Tom had ten days off the bike. Ten days at home, another unplanned but welcome time to play with Jane and Joanne under a summer sun. At the end of July he had to honour a contract at Crystal Palace, the event which he had dominated only 12 months before. This time he was content to sit in the bunch and finish in sixth place – not the usual show he liked to put on in Britain. The race was won by Michael Wright, who was making a really big impression that year, having already won a stage in the Tour de France a few weeks earlier.

Two more contracts in after-Tour criteriums were all Tom had to show for his efforts in France. Once they were out of the way, though, he had the chance to go home and prepare specifically for the Worlds, which was something he'd never before been able to do.

He started putting in the miles on the road, building up the distance and intensity every day. Then he started to compete in the infamous Flemish kermesse races. These were tough – they were the mainstay of racing in Flanders – and were probably why the Belgians were such a force in world cycling. Run off on six- to ten-mile circuits, always including the main street of the village in which they were held, the kermesses supported a whole band of tough Flemish pros who rode nothing else. They lived by what they could win from lap prizes and the overall prize list always went down to thirtieth, so everything was fought for. If these characters didn't win lap prizes, or finish in the first 30, they didn't eat!

The big stars didn't need to win money in kermesses, but they still rode them because they were hard and fast, and therefore excellent training. In fact, the classic Belgian method of preparing for a big race, particularly the Worlds, used to be to ride these races and, Flanders not being a big place, ride to them from home, then back again. This is what Tom did, often riding 50 kilometres to the race, then the race of perhaps 160 kilometres, then riding home. That way, he was building up speed and super strength, strength that was the key to performing in the closing stages of the Worlds when it just gets harder and faster as the best pile on the pressure.

Jean Stablinski was also riding these races with the very same objective. Brilliant at analysing other riders he remembers Tom in these events:

> I noticed Tom would turn up in his training kit, or sometimes behind a car, then change quietly. In the race you could feel the force he was pedalling with, but he was careful not to show too much. Then, after the race, he would leave for more training. I knew that he had great form, but that he was trying to hide it.

Just before the Worlds, Tom rode a criterium at Mende. Here, he decided to really test himself. In the first half of the race six riders got away and lapped the field. Then, towards the end, he went off the front and lapped the field on his own in very quick time. This put him on the same lap as the six and he still managed to finish third in the race.

His final preparation was in the Paris–Luxembourg stage race. Most of the big riders were there, but Tom tried to stay out of the limelight, while still trying to work hard. He played the role of *super domestique* in the Peugeot team, frequently dropping back to pace puncture victims to the front of the race. He made several hard efforts each day doing this, building up his form still more, but without attracting the attention of the press.

Anquetil was the big favourite. He'd shown fantastic form in the run up to the championships, winning a number of tough races, including one which, according to legend, he'd started with a hangover. Jacques was certainly fond of a drink and, apparently, the night before the race things had got a bit out of control. He felt too ill to start the race, but Raphaël Geminiani said that as it was a nice day, a good sweat would do him good. It did. He got stronger and stronger throughout the race, eventually winning on his own.

At the finish, Geminiani, expecting Jacques to be thankful to him for making him ride, and perhaps to be a little contrite for the state he'd got into the previous night, rushed up to him and asked, 'Now have you anything to say to me?' Jacques replied, 'Yes: go and put the champagne on ice.' They don't make 'em like that any more, do they?

Anyway, Jacques was the favourite and Tom wasn't, not even in *Cycling* magazine, who, in its pre-race forecast and to its eternal shame, said: 'Tom Simpson will be there again to keep our colours flying, but the best chance could be with Michael Wright.'

What they didn't know was that Tom was ready for this race like never before. He was absolutely sure of his ability to win it. For about a week beforehand, he'd been feeling, 'I couldn't lose'. He'd spent that last week travelling to Spain by car with the Australian rider, Nev Veale, and training with the other British riders at the team's hotel near the Lasarte circuit. On the journey down, Tom was so confident that he and Veale had even planned what they were going to do to celebrate when he was World Champion.

The British team were just as focused as Tom. For the first time they were committed to just one objective: a Simpson victory. They were going to take on the world's best and beat them; they all shared that dream. They also knew that, if he won, Tom would pay them well. He quickly got them in order, as Vin Denson remembers:

Tom had us all round at the hotel at eight o'clock on the first morning to go training, and you knew you had to be there at eight. The weather was awful, the rain bucketing down. On parts of the course, great big boulders had been washed down on to the roads, but Tom wanted to see the circuit. It was important that he saw the circuit, so we went and did a few laps, then off for a loop in the mountains. And you could see that he was very fit, very strong, and that he thought he could win. But, there again, he always thought he could win if it was a big race.

It wasn't all hard work. Just to bring a bit of light relief, Tom got Vin to dress up in a striped T-shirt with a bag marked 'swag' over his shoulder, and chased him through the hotel foyer wearing a British Policeman's helmet and furiously blowing a whistle, both of them on their bikes. Out through the door and off up the street they went, much to the delight of the fans and the press gathered outside the riders' hotels.

The Worlds circuit was quite hilly, just under 12 miles long, and had to be covered 14 times; and it was still raining. Ninety-six of the world's best professional cyclists lined up for the start, all the leading nations confident that they would be able to launch their best rider on to the top step of the victory podium. They had just one problem: for the only time in the history of cycling, the British team believed that they could do the same.

And it was only due to the spirit of the riders. Unlike the other teams, who were there with mechanics, doctors, masseurs and, most importantly, money, the British only had their spirit; and, of course, Tom Simpson. Norman Sheil was the manager that day, and he remembers it well:

> In San Sebastian we had nothing for the riders from the B.C.F. – no bottles, no race food, nothing. Me and Albert Buerick had to get everything to feed the riders during the race, and we stole everything we gave them. As soon as we got the riders started, me and Albert took a walk down the pits. Albert would get the team personnel talking – he knew everybody – and I'd nick their bottles and fill my pockets with food – peaches, bananas, anything I could get hold of.

As soon as the race got underway the Spanish riders attacked. The atmosphere was incredible because San Sebastian is in the Basque country, the heart of bike racing in Spain. Four Spaniards got into the first break which, by the end of the first lap, also contained Post and Den Hartog from Holland, Balmamion and Mealli from Italy, Bingelli from Switzerland, Kunde from Germany, Swerts from Belgium, and Britain's Barry Hoban. It was early in the race, but it was a good group with strong riders from each of the strong nations, apart from the French. When Tom learned that they had gained one minute in just 12 miles he decided that he had to get across to them.

The Tom Simpson of the last few years would have just attacked until he got away, but he knew that today was his big chance, and that, to take it, he must curb his impetuousness. And he knew that, for once, he had a team totally committed to him, so he had to use them. He had a quick word with Ramsbottom and Denson, and they led him to the front of the bunch at such a pace that when they moved over, Tom was dear with only two riders strong enough to hang on to him – the Spaniard, Elzorra and the German, Rudi Altig. They quickly bridged the gap up to the leaders.

Now this group was seriously strong. The Spanish crowd, with five of their riders there, went crazy, as did the riders themselves, working like mad. Most of the others were working, too, at this early stage, and by half-way they had three minutes on the bunch, but a small group containing Sels and a lone, desperate Frenchman, Stablinski, was chasing in between.

By the eighth lap they had closed to two minutes. The Spaniards were still working, but getting tired, so were some of the others. Post and Den Hertog were starting to fox a bit and miss turns, and Swerts and Balmamion had done very little after the break had got established. Tom and Altig were working, and Barry Hoban was doing more than any of them to make sure the break wasn't caught. In fact, Tom, appreciating how much Barry was doing and how much he was committing himself, said to him, 'Barry, if you get tired and feel like falling off, then fall off in front of Balmamion.'

Barry's hard work saw off the threat from behind, but Tom was getting very worried now about how fresh the non-workers would be if they towed them to the finish. With four laps to go he knew he would have to attack to get rid of some of them, and to see if Post, whom he feared most, was foxing or actually tired. For the time being, though, he knew that he had to wait: it was too early. At this stage, once he made a move, he would be committed; he would have played his hand. So, he waited; waited for the right moment.

It wasn't for long: with two and a half laps to go, on the big climb, the Hernani Hill, Tom shifted to his biggest gear (54 x 14) and went – all the way to the top without once looking behind, without once changing gear. At the top he moved over in the road and saw that the only one who could follow him was Rudi Altig. Tom had confirmed to himself now that he was going to win, no matter who was in his way, so he said to him, 'Come on, Rudi, remember the Barracchi.' Altig just nodded, and probably started to feel quite confident since he'd nearly killed Tom in that race the previous year.

His confidence didn't last long. Next time up the Hernani climb he had to ask Tom to ease – he was going too hard for him. Tom did because he needed Rudi's power on the flat, but it helped his confidence no end. He was going to need all that confidence to beat Rudi, who everyone reckoned was the better sprinter. But was he? Look how many races Tom had won in a similar two-man sprint. Both men started life on the track as pursuiters. They both rode in the six-days. Sure, Rudi was fast, but what about Tom's beating of Reg Harris's track records, and there's Ron Baensch's stories of Tom mixing it with the specialists in track sprints. No, they were both fast, both of them had the sprinting ability to win, but Tom *needed* to win, needed so much that you could feel it, and see it. If you see a picture of them in that final break, look at Tom's eyes, and you will know what I mean, and you'll see that there was no way Rudi was going to beat him that day.

He did win. With about one kilometre to go they came alongside each other. Tom started his sprint first, and Rudi never got near him. Tom Simpson was Champion of the World; but even in victory his detractors started: 'Surely he couldn't have beaten Altig fairly,' they said. Now the people who had accused him of selling races were accusing him of buying one.

He didn't buy that title. I know that for an absolute, 100-percent certainty, because I know what was said between them when they were alone on that last lap. Altig leaned over to Tom and said, 'How much would it take for you to lose this title, Tom?' Tom looked long and hard into the German's eyes and said, 'How much would it take for you to lose?' Nothing more was said, but Rudi remembers, 'From that moment I knew I was beaten.' Tom Simpson won the World title fair and square, and of that I'll take no argument.

Neither will big Albert Beurick. He was the first to get to Tom, moving at surprising speed given his bulk. He picked Tom up like a child's toy and held him in the air, bike and all. Albert's friend was World Champion and he was filled with so much joy he didn't know his own strength. Norman Sheil got to him next, still trying to be a team manager, wiping his boy's face, but overcome with emotion. Despite his detractors, Tom was one of the most popular World Champions ever. Even Gaston Plaud, with whom he'd had so many disputes, could not restrain his tears. A British World Champion – the cycling world could not believe it. It was unbelievable.

That is the phrase everybody uses to describe their feelings when Tom won that day. Vin Denson uses it. He heard Tom had won over the race radio, just before he finished the race. 'I could not believe it. It was unbelievable,' he recalled, 32 years later. Back home in Ghent, Helen was so excited, watching with neighbours on the TV, that she jumped up in the air, fell back down, and broke the sofa. She uses the same phrase as Vin when she remembers her feelings. So do many others, so much so that I nearly used it for the title of this book. It was unbelievable, and it seems even more unbelievable now when it is a rarity for a British rider even to finish this race.

There was hardly time to savour the moment – the new World Champion had to race in France the following afternoon. A quick glass of champagne with the team and a look at the fireworks display which brought the championships to a close, and Tom had to be off. Vin remembers them both having a laugh at two elderly English ladies, there on holiday. They were watching the fireworks when one said to the other, 'What's all this about, then?' Her friend replied, 'Apparently, some boy from Doncaster has won a prize for the best fireworks in the show.' Tom liked that.

He also appreciated the congratulations he got from fellow professionals: not one of them had a bad word to say about his victory. That night he shared a room with Jean Stablinski who told him, 'It does me good to see you as World Champion.' This was in spite of Tom giving him a sleepless night. 'He kept getting up to look at himself in the mirror in the rainbow jersey, he was so excited about wearing it. Eventually, I told him to just keep it on and go to sleep. So that night he slept in the jersey,' recalls Jean.

Everybody wanted to talk to him and the newspapers and the television were full of the British World Champion. Everybody wanted to know how he did it. In a Flemish programme he was asked what was different in his life now he was champion. His reply shows his typical mixture of flippancy and seriousness: 'Well, as you can see, I don't have to buy fresh flowers! I race much more now and I get paid more, but I must race harder to show the jersey.'

And he really did show it. The contracts came pouring in and Tom tried to give the crowd what they wanted at every one. He was riding on the crest of a wave. At a track meeting in Antwerp he was given a huge standing ovation, and had to ride lap after lap of honour. He appeared in Britain at Heme Hill where, though the meeting was rained off, he was stood on a rostrum wearing the rainbow jersey, in a mock victory ceremony for the crowd and the press. His character and athletic performances were even capturing people's imaginations in this country, and not just cyclists. He was now one of the country's most popular sportsmen. Just how popular we would soon see.

And how he loved it. Everything seemed possible for Britain in the sixties – the Beatles, fashion, football and now cycling. The world was fascinated with us. So you can imagine that, in Europe, where cycling was their number-one sport, this British World Champion was something very special indeed. And a British Tour de France winner would be even more special. Even in the midst of all the celebrations this thought was in the back of Tom's mind. If he won that race, he really would be the next great British success story. There was no time to rest on his laurels – that was still very much his ultimate target.

But there were races to be won before that, races to be won wearing the rainbow jersey, something every World Champion wants to do; something that is the seal of approval on anybody wearing it, because the rainbow jersey is marked in every race, and the only way to win is to ride everybody off your wheel. That was the next target: to win a classic wearing the jersey.

First was Paris–Tours. In an effort to bring an additional dimension to this race, which often ends in a bunch sprint, the organisers banned the use of derailleur gears. If the riders wanted to change they had to jump off, undo the back wheel, slip the chain on to another sprocket and get back into the race.

Despite this, the race still ended in a bunch sprint, with Dutchman Gerben Karstens winning in a record average speed of 28 miles per hour for 153 miles. Tom, however, was the man of the race, the author of two lone efforts: the first at 120 miles which lasted about ten miles; the second lasted from almost the moment he was caught to just over two miles from the finish. It was a real champion's performance, and the day after *L'Equipe* carried the headline, 'Karstens a good winner; Simpson a superb loser.'

Paris–Tours was always going to be a tough one for Tom to win – the race profile did him few favours. It favoured a sprinter with a strong team who could hide in the bunch and keep his legs fresh for a final burst of power up the wide Boulevard finish in Tours. The Tour of Lombardy, however, was something completely different.

The profile of the 'Race of the Falling Leaves' is like an upturned saw. In 1965, no less than five mountain passes were to be climbed in the Italian Lake District. It was probably Tom's finest hour. He set such a pace on the climbs that only the previous year's winner, Motta, who had finished third in the Tour de France that year, could live with him.

Soon he, too, was dropped, and Tom simply rode away from people like Poulidor, Motta, Gimondi and Anquetil, all of whom were in the group chasing behind, to win alone on the Como track by more than three minutes from Gerben Karstens.

It was masterful – 'An exploit in the tradition of Fausto Coppi,' the Italian papers said. They couldn't know just how much of a compliment they'd paid Tom by saying that. But it was true: the young lad from Harworth could now hold his head up with the greats. He was the first rider to win this race wearing the rainbow jersey since Alfredo Binda in 1927. Only Merckx in 1971, Gimondi in '73, Saronni in '82, and Oscar Camendzind in 1998 have done it since. He had now won both of the Italian classics, and not many riders have done that, either. The Italians loved him.

After the race, he said: 'I've learned the secret of climbing fast is to use a gear ten inches higher than everybody else. I dined with Cino Cinelli, who won this race in 1938, in the week, and he told me about this. So I restricted myself to 53 by 15 on the flat and as a result I could turn 42 by 17, when others were down on the 21, 22, or 23.'

Offers from Italian teams came pouring in, but, of course, Tom had signed for Peugeot for 1966 and 1967 before the Tour de France. It was a shame because he was getting offers of much bigger money from these teams. Gaston Plaud had been very shrewd.

Although they had their differences he was full of admiration for Tom and after the Worlds he spoke about their relationship: 'Tom will carry out some real exploits to honour his title. We have had our conflicts. Tom is a man of deep contrasts, he can be the best of companions and the worst, depending on his mood.'

He was right there, and he went on to speak about their differences in the '64 tour and how things came to a head at the end of that year: 'We cleared the air, I think, at the beginning of this year. I know Tom well enough to know that you must be hard on him for his own good.' On a more personal note, he added: 'I know that he is filled with self-interest to the point of being an egotist, but his charm and pleasant spirit make full amends for this. In my opinion, no one can touch him in a classic. He has one weakness, though: he is too generous.'

Yes, he'd analysed him well, but in the end he knew that he had a low-priced winner with Tom and exploited that by making him sign contracts before each Tour. As soon as Tom could, he would be off to another team.

The last word on the Tour of Lombardy has to come from one of the guys chasing him, someone with whom Tom had had his differences in the past, Henri Anglade, who, at the finish, simply said: 'Simpson was fantastic, just fantastic.' You can't get a finer tribute than that.

Tom intended to cash in as much as possible as World Champion. He confided to friends that he expected the title would bring him more than £36,000 over the coming year, a massive amount for a sportsman in those days. In the three weeks following the Worlds, Tom travelled the equivalent of half-way around the world to honour contracts.

Always, he tried to put on a show – like the Golden Wheel Race on the Cipale track in Paris where, in front of 15,000 spectators, he and Anquetil lapped the field, with Tom taking the final sprint.

There was only one blot on the horizon. Cashing in on his new found fame in Britain, he'd put his name to a series of articles in *The People* newspaper that lifted the lid off some of the greyer areas of professional cycling. There was nothing very bad. He spoke about buying help from other riders when his team wasn't strong enough, and stuff like that. Stuff that Tom quickly learned was part and parcel of the game when he first arrived in France. However, the public had rather more Corinthian ideas about sport in those days, and the articles caused quite a stir, both at home and abroad. To be fair to Tom, it was more the article's headlines than their content which caused the stir, but some put the worst possible interpretations on what was said. These included the boss of Peugeot, M. Dommage, who claimed that he had commissioned an advertising campaign based on 'Gentleman Tom', and that now he couldn't use it.

It all blew over quickly. Tom issued a statement clarifying what he had said. His public image had been little affected and Dommage had over-reacted, especially in the light of Peugeot being lucky to have him. Offers were still coming in from other teams. The Romeo team, for example, offered to pay him a whole years salary up front, but he just couldn't get out of his contract with Peugeot.

The first part of the winter was a time for more honours and more victories. First, Tom won the Brussels six-day, the first British winner of a modern six. He was teamed with Peter Post and said of his partner at the end of the race, 'Peter was so strong, this was a pedalling holiday.' I don't think it was that easy – just look at whom they beat.

Going into the last Derny-paced hour of the race, Tom and Peter were in second place, on the same lap as the six-day dream team of Patrick Sercu and Eddy Merckx. The Belgians were in front by virtue of a bigger points total, so Tom and Peter would have to gain a lap on them to win the race. Right from the start they made that last hour brutal. Merckx was struggling to hold his pacer, and that hour of racing finally made up the mind of the great Rik Van Steenbergen that, at the age of 42, it really was time to call it a day and hand the crown of the 'King of the Sixes' to Post. He announced his retirement at the end of the race. It was that hard.

Brussels was a big track and the Anglo-Dutch pair had almost gained their lap when Tom crashed during a changeover, which was a very tricky manoeuvre behind a Derny. He was quickly up and the pair resumed their attack, eventually gaining that vital lap with just six minutes of the race remaining. Tom went straight to the front of the bunch and handed over to Post who rubbed it in by pedalling away from the rest. Only the fastest man who has ever graced a six-day track, Patrick Sercu, was able to get past for a consolation sprint victory, Simpson and Post having won the race outright.

Whilst Tom was riding in Brussels, the first of the honours ceremonies took place. For the second time in his career, he won the *L'Equipe* World Cup and, also for the second time, he was ranked second in the Super Prestige Pernod competition, to Anquetil again. History was made on this occasion when Helen, who was deputising for her husband, became the first woman in history to mount the Pernod podium. In fact, the organisers were a bit upset by Tom not being able to appear at this most prestigious occasion, but he had signed a contract for Brussels long before he'd clinched his place in the rankings. And money came first: Pernod had to give him the £740 he'd won, so he wasn't going to give up the money the Brussels promoters were giving him for racing there.

Talking of money, the BBC Grandstand programme sent a team over to Brussels to film Tom in the six-day. Their presenter asked him straight out what the World title meant to him in terms of money. His reply was a masterpiece in playing it close to his chest, whilst revealing just what a success he'd become, when he said: 'Well, £1,000 a week in a good week, but it's not 52 weeks of the year.'

In Britain, Tom won the *Daily Express* Sportsman of the Year award, the first leg of a unique awards treble in his own country.

Once more, Helen had to deputise, this time assisted by Tom's mum, Alice, who thoroughly enjoyed the glittering occasion. She loved her son's success.

All the family were together for the next ceremony when Tom was given the freedom of his Belgian home town of St Amandsberg. Tom, Helen, his mother and father, and Jane and Joanne were driven through the streets in an open carriage from Albert Buerick's café to the Town Hall. They were preceded by a cavalcade of police motorbikes and dignitaries' cars, and thousands turned out to line the route and cheer their adopted son of Flanders with his family.

All this star treatment hardly had time to sink in before he was back to work, this time on the newly finished Ghent track (the old one burned down, remember) in the first six-day to be held at the stadium where his statue now stands. It was also one of the first trips to Ghent in what is now an annual pilgrimage for many British fans.

They weren't disappointed. The Six boiled down to another ding-dong battle between Merckx/Sercu and the team they'd all come to see, Simpson and Post, with the rest hanging on to their shirt-tails for grim life. Coming into the final hour it was just like Brussels: the Belgians led on points with Tom and Peter in the same lap. And just like Brussels they had to gain a lap in that last hour to win the race.

This time they couldn't do it. Attack followed attack, but the young Belgian team fought back every time and they ran out the eventual winners. The pace was so high that the track record for a 50-kilometre Madison was shattered: the new time of 58 minutes and 4 seconds stood for many years. There aren't many Madisons run off at a faster pace than that, even now.

Post was full of praise for Tom. When asked how he rated him as a six-day rider, he said, 'Tommy? If I get a mate as good as him every time, I will have a pretty easy life until I ride my last six.' This was really something coming from one of the toughest six-day riders of all time, and a man not renowned for having a high opinion of his fellow competitors.

Back in Britain for his winter break, the honours continued to roll in. He won two cycling awards, the Bidlake, and the B.C.F.'s Personality of the Year. Then it was announced that he'd been voted the 'Sportswriters' Personality of the Year', an award given by all sports journalists, not just cycling scribes. This was a reflection of the terrific impact Tom had made on sport in general in this country, and on the nation's consciousness – an impact that no other cyclist has come close to making since.

The presentation ceremony took place at the Europa Hotel in London, and Tom was presented with the trophy by none other than the then Prime Minister, Harold Wilson, and it was Tom who stole the show.

For a start he caused the Prime Minister to change his speech just as he was embarking on his favourite subject, that of the successes of famous fellow Yorkshire men; he thought Tom was one, and Tom raised the roof when he politely pointed out that he was actually from Durham. He enjoyed that moment. Then, in his speech, he thanked the Prime Minister, cracked a joke with him – 'We are both in the saddle, but I hope your bottom doesn't hurt as much as mine' – and proceeded to try and promote British cycling by giving the great man a quick lecture on how to speed up Britain's entry into the Common Market. Tom told him: 'I hope one day, Mr Prime Minister, that British commerce and industry will wake up to the fact that the sponsorship of a British team on the continent could be useful to them and useful to the country as a 'whole in gaining acceptance and entry into the Common Market.' His eloquent speech greatly impressed the PM and greatly impressed the mainstream British media. It was even featured and discussed on the BBC Today programme, such was its impact and topicality. How far had the Durham miner's son come now?

A very long way indeed. The personality that had helped him break down the prejudices of another country's sport was now doing the same in his own land. Tom was now more than just a talented bike rider: he was a personality. He impressed everyone he met with his charm and wit, and it is because of this, because he was more than just a cyclist, that he is still remembered so fondly by them now.

Just how much he'd impressed people over here can be judged by the next award he won, the BBC's Sports Personality of the Year. This is the number-one sporting popularity poll in Britain. It is quite unbelievable, today, that a cyclist actually became famous enough to win this award when we remember that cycling, despite having had several World Champions over the years since Tom's death (though none in the pro road race), hardly gets a mention on the programme. But Tom was famous now, more famous than the rest of the sporting personalities in the frame to win. Just look at the great names he beat: Jim Clark and Graham Hill from Formula One, the footballer Sir Bobby Moore, athletes, cricketers, jockeys, all of them from sports that have produced regular winners over the years, all of them from sports that have big media coverage in this country. Tom beat them all, and this despite the fact that there was little coverage of cycling in this country even then. He had just forced his personality on people, and captured their hearts by what he'd done.

And what had he done that meant so much here? I'll tell you. Something that everyone could approve of: he'd gone over there and beaten the continentals at their own game, in their own back yard. It was Agincourt all over again; it was like a reliving of the Battle of Britain, and didn't we love reliving it? On top of all this, Tom looked the part. Tall, slim and elegantly English, he could have passed for the hero in any one of those black-and-white films made just after the war, when everything still seemed black and white, and England wasn't the confused little island it is now.

The three victories Tom achieved in the sporting popularity polls were a unique achievement for a cyclist – that almost goes without saying – but what I always find amazing is that it was a unique achievement amongst all sportsmen. In the history of these awards the only other person to achieve what Tom did – winning all three – was Princess Anne, and look what she has behind her. There can be no better yardstick to measure Tom's success and impact in the sixties than that.

So how come young cyclists in this country know very little about him today? I think it is simply because it has served the ends of the cycling establishment, and certain individuals, to play down his achievements and let his name be dragged, undefended, through the mud of doping in sport. That way, Tom doesn't make them look so bad.

By now it was Christmas. In *Cycling* magazine he said that his ideal present would be 'the same support from British cyclists, and indeed everyone at home, that I received this year. Apart from that, a really warm track suit.' It was his way of saying thank you.

12

AFTER THE RAINBOW

After the holidays came two more accolades: the Prix Orange, awarded by the continental press for the 'Rider most affable towards them'; then he received the absolute seal of English establishment approval when he was invited on to the BBC's Desert Island Discs radio programme. Among his records was 'Help' by the Beatles, his luxury item was a set of golf clubs and the book he chose was *The Complete Works of Dickens*, which I think was more a value-for-money choice rather than evidence of any intellectual aspirations.

It had been a wonderful time, but now Tom had to look to his future. He'd done a lot, but there was a lot left to do. To win the Tour he was going to have to get the best team he possibly could around him, and in Tom's view the best meant British, because he felt that he could rely on their loyalty and he would be able to mould them into a top team under his influence. Tom never saw being British as a handicap to a rider. Indeed, he felt that the Brits had a better standard of living than riders from the continent, a better start in life, which meant that they were stronger. All they had to do was go to the continent, race, listen and learn. He also knew that he could get more from himself, more from his body. He was 28, approaching his peak, and was constantly adapting his training and preparation to new methods and new ways of thinking.

That is how he found himself, one cold January morning, in the Loughborough laboratory of Dr Vaughan Thomas, who had developed one of the first ergonometer tests to evaluate the fitness of cyclists. Tom was the first World Champion Dr Thomas had tested in his study of hundreds of cyclists. Not surprisingly, he produced the highest maintainable power output, which is an absolute measure of endurance-cycling ability, of all the subjects Dr Thomas had tested.

So much for those who say that Tom was more guts than talent. He was the most talented rider this country has ever seen. He just happened to have the guts and intelligence to exploit that talent. If he had one chink in his armour, though, it was this: his talent was huge, but his body was frail. He wasn't like Eddy Merckx, for example, so robust that he could hammer for days on end, so robust that he could win the first and the last races of the year and two major tours in between.

While he was at Loughborough he picked up some of the new ideas that were circulating regarding training theory, and would start to use them in his quest to get more from himself. With this information he could get into the best possible form to win the Tour. Now, he only had to get the best possible team to support him and then he would have a real chance of winning.

Despite his efforts with the Prime Minister there had been no takers from British industry, at least not with the money to pay a British team and Tom. So, along with Albert Beurick, he started a plan to raise money by means of subscriptions and raffles to support a small all-British team on the continent. If successful, this would have provided a vehicle for more British talent to be blooded over there. A bigger percentage of Britons in European races would mean more opportunities for success – factors which could be used to attract the big sponsor Tom needed for a serious assault on the Tour. He was absolutely convinced that, at the head of ten Brits who had all raced full time on the continent, he would be able to make a serious attempt on overall victory.

He was right, and he wasn't the only one over there who thought so, too. They started a supporters' club for British cycling with subscriptions at ten shillings (50p) and Tom donated his World Championship-winning bike to be raffled off. The project was off the ground. Peter Clifford, a sportswriter, started a recruitment drive. British cycling had never felt better about itself. In 18 months the dream would all be over.

Before even then there was a set-back. Tom's team manager told him not to go skiing, but he was determined to enjoy his family holiday. He wanted the best for them, always. Anyway, lightning doesn't strike in the same place, twice.

It does. It did. On the very same day as the previous year, 25th January, Tom fell and injured his leg, only this time it was more serious. This time he had broken his right tibia, his whole leg was put in plaster, and any kind of cycling was completely out of the question. The cast would be in place until the end of February, so the first part of his season was totally destroyed, the part when he had hoped to win one of the spring classics – Paris–Roubaix, perhaps – wearing the rainbow jersey.

Do you believe in curses? Cycling does. They call it the 'Curse of the Rainbow Jersey'. Many times in the history of this sport the Worlds have been won by a rider at the height of his powers, who has dominated throughout the year in which he won the title, only to have a disastrous time wearing the jersey. In the last ten years it is possible to point to many examples: Laurent Brochard, Johan Museeuw, Luc Leblanc and Rudy Dhaenens, for instance. And, in 1998, on the track, Matt Gilmore – who is, coincidentally, the son of Tom's sister-in-law – won the World Madison Championships, only to have an horrific, freak crash on the Herning track, which wiped out his year as World Champion, and almost his entire career. Is there any wonder that the superstition exists?

On a more materialistic note, the crash was going to cost Tom a fortune in lost contracts. Ironically, he'd missed the Dortmund Six because everyone was snowed in at St Gervais when it was on. He shouldn't even have been there when he had his fall; now, he couldn't fulfil contracts at Antwerp and Milan, contracts that, for the reigning World Pro Road Champion, were big, because he was the big crowd-puller.

As soon as he could, he travelled to see his personal manager, Daniel Dousset, to see what could be salvaged. In the meantime, he'd had the good news that the bones were knitting together well: he would be available for anything going in March, so it wouldn't be too bad. I don't believe that the crash damaged him financially as much as some rumours that have sprung up since his death would have it. It was certainly not the reason why he was desperate to win the 1967 Tour de France, nor why he would go to any lengths to win it. He was desperate, yes, but for quite another reason.

One engagement he could honour, without having to ride a bike, was attending the first-ever Falcon Cycles training camp on the island of Mallorca. Nowadays, there are loads of these camps for British cyclists, giving them a chance to do some pre-season training away from the ice, cold and gloom of a British winter, just like the continentals do, but this was the first one, and the people who went on it still remember it as something special.

It was organised by Billy Holmes, then a Falcon pro, and Ernie Clements, the factory manager. Billy was one of the attending coaches, along with Brian Robinson and Tommy Godwin, but Tom was the star attraction. It would have been better if he could have ridden the bike with his fellow campers, but Billy remembers that his presence still dominated the camp: 'I can only describe the effect Tom had on all the riders and people there as being like the Pied Piper of Hamlyn. They hung on his every word. They followed him wherever he went. If Tom stood up, they stood up. If Tom sat down, they sat down.' This wasn't the same kid Billy had found crying in his room at Melbourne.

Billy was full of praise, but also full of envy: 'I envied Tom. I envied his personality. I envied his sense of humour. He had such a light way of looking at life and he could light up a whole room just by being there.' Don't get Billy wrong, though: this wasn't envy in its usual, bitter sense. There wasn't a trace of bitterness in Billy's voice when he told me this, only admiration. This speaks volumes, because these bike-riders have got big egos.

The camp consisted of supervised training sessions, racing, and talks, and demonstrations from the coaches. One novel idea that Billy Holmes came up with was typical of that era, when cycling was trying hard to capitalise on the inroads Tom had made on the nation's psyche. Every evening he picked on a few of the guests and asked them to give a two-minute talk on a subject totally unconnected with cycling, which he gave to them. No one was exempt, not even the coaches, who had their subjects picked by the journalists, David Saunders and Jock Wadley. And what stinkers they were, too – Tom had to speak for two minutes on 'the refraction and defraction of molecules'. He loved it, and proceeded to give an entertaining lecture on moles that lived in holes, or cules, as the moles called them.

Billy explained his thinking behind this idea when I spoke to him about this book: 'I started winning open events when I was 16, and I had to go to club dinners where I was expected to give a speech. Well, I was terrified, so I thought that it would be a good part of a prospective champion's training to get them used to talking in front of a crowd. It was important for them, and for the sport, that they could give a good account of themselves.'

Having done his bit for the future of British cycling, Tom now had his own future to take care of. He was optimistic: perhaps the inactivity would mean that he could start the Tour de France with all his reserves intact.

He started to ride his bike at the beginning of March and straightaway announced that 'I think I can win the Tour de France.' He wasn't alone in this belief, either. A number of team managers, journalists and riders thought so, too. Even Anquetil, who said: 'In certain circumstances Tom can win the Tour, but he will have to build his entire season around it.' Well, this period of forced inactivity wasn't quite what Jacques meant, but at least he would have an opportunity to prepare for the 1966 Tour without tiring himself out in the classics because there was no way Tom would be ready for them.

By the time the plaster came off, his left calf was only half the size it used to be. When he first started to ride his bike again, getting out of the saddle was impossible, so it is a tribute to his class that he was able to start racing after just two and a half weeks of riding.

His first event was a criterium in St Niklaas. The organiser had begged him to ride and he was presented with a gold medal at the start. He only lasted 20 miles in the race, but he was not the first to be dropped. Next he rode an international omnium on the Antwerp track with Vin Denson. They were last, but throughout the meeting Tom was progressing and, in the final event, a Madison, he and Vin actually beat the Italian pair, Gimondi and Adorni.

It wasn't all plain sailing. Bad weather had set in in Belgium, forcing Tom to ride on rollers rather than on the road, but physiotherapy and specialised exercises between these sessions saw him ready to put on a show in his rainbow jersey in front of a big crowd at the Herne Hill Good Friday meeting.

This was a great moment in British cycling history. Our only World Pro Road Race Champion appearing before his home crowd in his rainbow jersey. Tom only had a few hundred kilometres in his legs, but was determined to put on a show. No one went home disappointed.

He raced in the big event of the day, a series of three Derny-paced races over five, ten and fifteen miles against four British pro riders: Keith Butler, Roger Gray, Pete Gordon and Dave Bonner. And, in case you're thinking it, these guys were no pushovers. Butler had a lot of continental experience and was part of a cycling dynasty – his father, Stan, and son, Gethin, both being British cycling champions – and great things were being predicted for Dave Bonner, especially on the track.

Tom won the first race with Bonner taking the second. Then, in the final race, he left it late, letting Bonner build up a big lead, reeling him in with two laps to go, and just getting past to win. The crowd were delighted. The World Champion had won in front of his home supporters, just as he should do. He was on his way back.

He started Liège–Bastogne–Liège, but didn't finish. Then he raced over 100 kilometres for the first time since his injury when he got to the finish of a criterium at Vilvoorde. After the race he gave journalists an update on his progress: 'I'm getting out behind a moped most days. Last week I did 120 miles one day, then raced, then did 85. I can definitely feel it coming back.'

It *was* coming back. In early May he took twentieth overall in the Dunkirk Four-Days while working hard for his Peugeot team mate, Theo Mertens, the race winner. He'd tested his leg and it had come through well. Now it was time to give it some stick in a big, one-day race.

The spring classics were over, but there were still some big races about. The Grand Prix of Frankfurt was one of them, easily Germany's biggest race in those days. It was Tom who made the decisive attack of the day after 112 kilometres, being quickly joined by Barry Hoban. The pair worked together until they were joined by a number of others. At this point, Tom began to attack to try and split up the group, but lack of racing miles meant that he could not get a decisive gap. Barry could, however. He went away with 50 kilometres to go and rode alone to a superb victory.

It really was coming back quickly, now. He was beginning to feel like his old self again and every day saw improvements. Shortly after Frankfurt he was on the podium at a race for the first time that year when he took second place to Wilfred Peffgen in the Grand Prix D'Argovia. A good ride in the Tour looked more and more likely.

Before then, Tom met the Queen. She was on a Royal visit to Brussels and the Belgians thought it would be a nice idea to present the most famous Englishman in Belgium to her. She was, of course, pleased to hear of the success of one of her subjects, but wondered why he had to live in Belgium, and not England. Tom told her that it was because cycling was so popular there. To which she replied,

'I expect that is because it is so flat.' He resisted the temptation to correct Her Majesty on her theory, but commented afterwards that, 'She obviously hasn't seen the course for Flèche Wallonne.'

At the start of the Tour he was making confident noises, though privately he was worried and nervous. Only he knew how well he was going after coming back from his broken leg and the truth was that he was concerned about not having enough depth to his form. Also, although the press were building him up as one of the big favourites to win, he felt that the Peugeot team preferred to support the talented young Frenchman, Roger Pingeon. He could not trust them and this would work against him.

His build-up had not been ideal, and I think that though he was putting on a brave face, he really wasn't confident. This lack of confidence was going to affect the way he raced. He would make mistakes, the kind you can't afford to make if you're going to win. He would crash out of the race; but, before that, he would prove that, physically, he could win it. He would only need the confidence in himself that comes from having a perfect build-up to the race, and confidence in his team. He didn't have either of these in 1966.

He told journalists that he intended to ride himself in for the first few stages, but once on the road it was a completely different story. He was on the attack right from the start and after two stages he was in tenth place overall, the highest placed of the favourites.

Then, on the third day, he worked long and hard to force a break with Altig and Van Looy that ultimately failed, and brought forth the following comment from Tour Director, Felix Levitan: 'I would love to see Tom win the Tour. He can knock them for dead in a one-day classic, but he must learn to shadow and spar with the others to win this race. He dreams of getting into a paying break and stealing a packet of time from the others. He might have been able to do this in his early days, but now his reputation is too great for his rivals to allow this.'

He wasn't wrong. To win, people were telling him, he would have to follow, watch for an opening, and take it. At the moment, he was trying to shape the race on his own. It was how he won classics and it was how he was trying to win the Tour. An Italian journalist, bemused by the way he was racing, asked him this question: 'Why, when you can finish on the podium in this Tour, or in certain circumstances win it, are you riding such a race? You have no need to prove yourself, why not then take things quietly in the bunch and let your team mates chase down any breaks or take you up to them?'

Tom's answer was vague, he muttered something about him 'needing more work', but he knew that he had to make his own race – the Peugeot team wouldn't make it for him and because of his time off the bike he could not be sure of his form. These two things must have been playing on his mind and affecting the way he raced.

Despite all this, his riding was spectacular. For the next 1,000 miles his chances of a podium place were very much alive, but he was going to make those mistakes. One he would make with the rest of the favourites; the other he would make on his own – but it would be a glorious mistake, an attempt to win the Tour de France with one spectacular attack on the Galibier; an attack that gave us some of the most evocative pictures a British cycling fan could ever hope to see: a Briton alone in the lead of the Tour de France, set against the awesome backdrop of the Alps, and wearing the rainbow jersey. They should make every member of our national squad look at one of these photographs for ten minutes every day.

Meanwhile, back in the race, Tom dropped a few places after the third stage because Peugeot did a terrible team time trial, and he crashed on the fifth between Dieppe and Caen. He'd injured his right thigh and hip, but he was more worried about the 21 seconds he'd lost to Anquetil and Poulidor. These were the two he saw as his biggest rivals, the ones he was watching; but in the end he watched them too closely.

The race now passed into the hands of the sprinters as successive flat stages down the west coast brought wins for Ward Sels at Angers, Albert Van Vlierberghe at Royan, Willy Planckaert at Bordeaux, and Gerben Karstens at Bayonne. The race had arrived at the foot of the Pyrenees, and, as the French press are fond of putting it, 'the favourites must face their destiny'.

An interesting incident occurred on that last flat stage from Bordeaux to Bayonne. Just five kilometres from the start almost the entire field dismounted and walked alongside their bikes for 200 metres. They were doing this in protest against a new law on the French statute books which forbade the use of stimulants in sporting events and the methods that cycling officials were using to enforce it – the taking of urine samples. Not all of the riders supported the protest; ironically, in view of some of the outrageous stories that have circulated about him since ltis death, Tom refused to take his proffered place at the front of the group with the other stars, and, in fact, made a point of not getting off his bike. He was one of the few who actually rode those infamous 200 metres.

I'm not saying that Tom was white and the others black. I'm not saying that he hadn't taken drugs. He had, and was quite open about it. He took them because others did and he would not see himself disadvantaged, but he did support any move by the authorities to rid the sport of them. Tom didn't believe, as other riders at the time did, that you had to take them just to compete in a race as hard as the Tour. He knew, however, that he had been beaten by lesser riders who had taken them and, right or wrong, he wasn't going to fail because of that. He had come too far and tried too hard – it was as simple as that.

Does it not add to the tragedy of Tom Simpson that he was destined to become the most famous casualty of the problem of drugs in sport, and destined to leave this as his legacy? Because, in the light of recent revelations from cycling, athletics, football and many other sports, this does seem to have become his legacy. I feel that Tom is seen by the average sports fan as the man who started it all. This is just not true, and it has happened because he died. Dead men can't speak, and above all they can't sue. He has been an easy target.

The first mountain stage was from Bayonne to Pau, and it was here that Tom made his first mistake. He marked Anquetil and Poulidor too closely, not fully realising that Anquetil would rather anybody win the Tour, than Poulidor.

The drama unfolded even before the first mountain had been reached. Skirmishes along the switchback route across the Pyrenean foothills resulted in three distinct groups forming on the road. The first consisted of two opportunists out to gain as much glory as they could on the day: Tomasso De Pra, who went on to win the stage and take over the yellow jersey, and the man with the impossible name, Willy In'T Ven. These two rode really well, but they weren't the big problem. The favourites could have given them half an hour and it would not have affected the outcome of the Tour.

The big problem was the men in the next group on the road. They included Lucien Aimar, who eventually won the Tour, Jan Janssen, who was to win in 1968, and Jos Huysmans, who would become a *super-domestique* in the service of Eddy Merckx. Four riders from this group would finish in the first six in this Tour, and the favourites had let them gain seven minutes on this one day.

After the stage, two of the beaten riders had public excuses, but private hidden agendas for why they hadn't chased. Anquetil said that he couldn't chase as Aimar was in his team. Privately, though, Jacques, who had won five Tours by then, was worried that he was not strong enough to win this one, but was certain that Poulidor was. He simply could not bear to lose a Tour in which Poulidor was the winner. So, seeing Raymond trapped in the same group as himself, and making no inroads on those who'd escaped, he sat tight and watched the Tour ride away from both of them, happy that Raymond was losing a Tour he had possibly his best ever chance of winning.

Tom used the very same excuse. He had a team mate, the tiny German Karl-Heinz Kunde, in the Aimar group and he publicly claimed to be protecting his interests. This didn't hold water because a few days later, when he had returned to his attacking senses, he was instrumental in Kunde losing the race lead. No, the fact is Tom had made a mistake. Perhaps due to lack of confidence in his form, he had done something which was completely foreign to his nature: he'd sat tight, convinced that Anquetil would join forces with Poulidor in limiting their losses. For the first time in his life, probably, he had ridden conservatively and it hadn't worked.

He had all of the next day, a rest day, to mull over his mistake. Tactical riding had landed him with a huge deficit to make up, but he would probably end up with a place in the first six if he continued with those tactics. That was no good; he'd done that already. Tomorrow it would be back to plan A: attack, then attack, then attack again.

For the next few days he would shake the race till its teeth rattled in a brave effort to gain back the time he'd lost – though some observers said, rather uncharitably, that he went on to the offensive only because the after-Tour criterium promoters had joined the race. Whatever, he rode like crazy on the next stage between Luchon and Revel, eventually getting clear, towards the end of the stage, with his old sparring partner, Rudi Altig. It was a repeat of their dual at San Sebastian, only this time Rudi won. Tom was second, and he'd clawed back a few seconds. It wasn't much, but it was a start.

Next day, between Revel and Sete, he tried again. On this largely flat stage the bunch stayed together until there were just seven kilometres to go. Here, Tom really piled on the pressure, and despite the fact that everyone was chasing, he dragged clear Guido De Rosso and George Vandenberghe of Belgium. In those last few kilometres he buried himself, taking second again to the fast Belgian on the stage and gaining another handful of seconds from the riders who had gained time on him in the Pyrenees.

At the end of that stage, Kunde had the jersey and Tom was eighteenth overall, at 7 minutes 35 seconds. Anquetil and Poulidor, his two co-favourites, were lying fifteenth and sixteenth overall, just over 20 seconds ahead of him. It sounded a lot to make up on the current overall leader, but they were both still talking of overall victory.

Nothing changed much during the following morning's stage, but in the afternoon there was a time trial where Poulidor confirmed Anquetil's worst fears about his strength and beat him to win the test by seven seconds. Tom finished a very creditable fifth on this stage and moved up to sixteenth overall at 6 minutes and 44 seconds. He was still very much in touch with the two warring Frenchmen.

In the three stages since he'd let the race get out of his control Tom had pulled back only 53 seconds. There were only nine stages left and on some of them it would not be possible to gain much. He had to do something dramatic and, as the next few days were in the Alps, he had the material to work with. He decided to see how he was climbing on the next stage, then, if all was well, let them have it on the giant Galibier climb which would be crossed on the following day.

Stage 15 was from Vals des Bains to Bourg d'Oisans, the town at the foot of the Alp d'Huez climb. Overnight, the weather had gone mad. Torrential rain had caused a landslide on the Col d'Ornon, completely blocking the race route. Only frenzied work with bulldozers allowed the race to go ahead at all.

During the stage the weather continued to make the road conditions treacherous. Tom rode to his plan, riding well within himself to stay with the leaders. He even forced the pace a little on the Ornon, and his acceleration caused Anquetil to lose contact. It was a good sign.

He finished comfortably in a group along with Aimar and Janssen and, more importantly, was now convinced that he had the legs to do something special the following day. He had gained time on Anquetil and moved up one place overall. Poulidor gained the most, though. Sensing Anquetil was in trouble, he took some terrible risks on the treacherous descent of the Ornon and gained 30 seconds on

Tom, and even more on Anquetil; but at what cost to his nerves, only he knew.

The start next day was a complete contrast to the Wagnerian weather they'd ridden through to get there. Bourg D'Oisans was bathed in bright sunshine for the riders who faced the climbs of three big cols before the finish in Briançon. These were the cols de la Croix de Fer, Télégraphe, and the mighty Galibier, all of them woven into the fabric of Tour de France history. Tom was going to make his move today; one way or another, he would know in Briançon whether or not he could win this Tour. His attack, in the end, did shape the race and it virtually decided the final pecking order in Paris, though it would be others, and not Tom, who would benefit from it. Still, it showed all his class, guts and fighting spirit, right there on centre stage of the huge natural theatre the Alps provide for cycling.

After a quiet start the bunch reached the Croix de Fer. Here the pace began to hot up as the favourites started to test each other. This was going to be the big day of the Tour and already the favourites were applying pressure, probing for any signs of weakness in each other. The bunch began to stretch out under the strain, but this was nothing to the damage caused on the twisting, dangerous descent, where several riders, including Tom, crashed.

He wasn't hurt and quickly rejoined the front of the race. Once there, he attacked, just before the feeding station in St Jean de Maurienne. From this point there is an eight-mile flat stretch along the valley bottom to the foot of the Télégraphe and Galibier climbs. Tom was gambling that the confusion caused by the breakneck descent of the Croix de Fer would give rise to a lull while the teams sorted themselves out. He was right and his lead grew to just over one minute before the other top riders were in a position to take control of the race once again.

This was the lead with which he was able to start the Col du Télégraphe. Tom was in full flight now, climbing those early slopes with strength and style. He forced his lead up to 90 seconds on the now-splintering bunch where a big selection was taking place due to the efforts of the stars to bring him back under control.

Even with this battle raging between the favourites, the only rider who was able to make any inroads on Tom's lead was the Spanish climber, Julio Jiménez. This man was the climber of the latter half of the sixties. Small, thin, balding and never looking quite well, when the road started going upwards he sprouted wings on his feet and danced up the mountain passes, just like Marco Pantani does today.

Jiménez was of a different dimension that day: he pranced up to Tom by the time the summit of the Télégraphe was in sight, and it was here that Tom made his second big mistake of the race. He should have let Jiménez go by – he was still holding all the others off, and would have gained more time on the descent of the Galibier.

He didn't. As Jiménez went by, Tom latched on to his back wheel and in doing so was forced to climb at about two miles per hour faster than he had been doing. He even started to work with the Spaniard. Why? He was gambling; gambling that he would be able to hold Jiménez and in doing so the Spaniard would drag him to the top of the Galibier so far clear of his main rivals that his plunge down the mountainside to Briançon could also have been to victory in the Tour de France. He was on thin ice, though, running the grave risk of cracking wide apart by trying to match the pace of the Spanish super-climber; but this was a man who lived his whole life on thin ice.

At the top of the Télégraphe all was well. Jiménez won the prime and the pair began the short descent to Valloire, 95 seconds in front of the next riders on the road, a group of 15 including Anquetil, Poulidor, Aimar, Janssen, and Huysmans.

The Télégraphe is a stepping-stone to the Galibier climb, at 2,646 metres one of the highest cols featured regularly in the Tour, and it always provides a decisive moment in the race. Bernard Thévenet, who won the Tour in 1975 and '77, underlined its importance when he said, before the 1998 Tour: 'The first few to cross the summit are usually the ones found on the podium in Paris.'

Once on the climb, Jiménez hit the front again and really began to apply the pressure. Tom summoned up all his courage and, focusing only on the Spaniard's back wheel, he held on as the pair began to put real time into the others. If he could have hung on, the gamble would have been one of the most beautiful exploits in Tour history, but he couldn't. He didn't crack, but he just couldn't climb at the pace Jiménez set – no one could have that day. Bit by bit the gap between them grew, and bit by bit the fluency began to disappear from Tom's style. He didn't give in; if he got to the top in second place he would still be able to gain time on the descent, perhaps even get back up to Jiménez and take the stage into the bargain.

And maybe he would have, if Anquetil and Poulidor hadn't been acting out the final battle of their Tour de France rivalry, a rivalry that over the years had almost split the country. They were the only two gaining on Tom; the others – Aimar, Janssen and the rest – were still falling back. But the two Frenchmen were catching him. Riding side by side, each one too proud to look at the other, neither prepared to give an inch, they caught and passed a now-struggling Tom just before the summit of the Galibier.

At this point the time gaps were so great that if Tom could have kept his place on the descent and, as we know, he was a brilliant descender, he would have moved right up into the first ten overall. From there he had now shown that he had the form to make an assault on a podium place in Paris.

He was now mixed up with Aimar and Janssen, who were fighting it out for the top two positions overall and were descending like demons, but Tom was going even faster. Casting all caution to the wind, he was desperately trying to get back up to Anquetil and Poulidor, though they were well in front by now. He was, perhaps, trying too hard; if he'd been content to stay with the Janssen group, he would still have made it well into the first ten overall.

He never could think like that, though; he would never concede one metre on the road, no matter how much sense it made. It was essentially what made him so great, though, wasn't it? He didn't care if something made sense or not, he just went for it regardless, and it worked – but not today. Almost predictably, he crashed on the descent, although this time it was not his fault. He was knocked to the ground by a press motorcycle that took a bad line through one of the many hairpin bends.

The great escape was over. He remounted, but was really shaken and had suffered a deep laceration to his right arm. It was impossible to get going properly and he lost a lot more time to the Janssen and Aimar group. Yet so spread out had the race become by then that he still moved up to eleventh place overall, just over seven minutes behind the new race leader, Janssen, but he could have been very much nearer, especially if he had stayed clear of the Dutchman, as had looked likely.

What a stage. Tom's attack had exploded the race: it had provoked a virtuoso climbing performance from Jiménez, who won the stage; it provided the last glimpse the world would ever have of Anquetil at his uncompromising best when he stubbornly refused to let Poulidor get away on the Galibier and then outsprinted him for second place; and it saw the elimination of over a quarter of the field, including Van Looy and four of his team mates, who finished so far behind that they were outside the time limit.

At the finish, Tom was very distressed: his huge attack had shaped the Tour, but brought him nothing. During the evening it became obvious that his injuries were far worse than at first thought. After having five stitches inserted in his arm at the local hospital the race doctor, Dr Dumas, was asked if Tom would be able to start the next day. He replied: 'There is nothing at all to prevent him starting, but everything to prevent him finishing. He will be riding virtually one-handed.'

And so it proved. Next day the race went from Briançon, across the Italian border to Turin. Soon after the start there was the stiff climb of the Col de Montgenevre. They tackled this at no more than a moderate pace, but by the summit Tom was already three minutes behind the leaders. He could hardly even rest his right arm on the handlebars let alone pull on them, and if you can't pull on the handlebars you can't climb. The descent was even worse: Tom could not control his bike and continuing was just plain dangerous, given the exposure on these Alpine descents.

The Tour was eventually won by Aimar with Janssen second. Once he had made absolutely sure that Poulidor couldn't win, Anquetil retired on the nineteenth stage. Poulidor confirmed that he was indeed the strongest man in the race by moving up to third overall by the finish in Paris, his race ruined by the awe in which he held Anquetil. Tom was back at home, licking his wounds and thinking what might have been. Fourth? Fifth? Maybe he could even have overhauled Poulidor for third? Certainly he would have had a high place. For example, Van Springel who was 36 seconds behind him overall at Briançon, even after Tom's crash, eventually finished sixth, so a place in the first four or five was definitely on the cards. Tom had proved that he had it in him to make a real challenge; now all that was left was to try again next year – to try and take the one victory he wanted above all others. Only now he wanted it too much.

Tom's efforts on the Tour had not gone unrewarded. Every criterium organiser wants the World Champion in their race and his attacking riding in the Tour had only increased his popularity. It was time to put long-term objectives to one side again and cash in. Tom wanted success for himself, but he also wanted the good things in life for his family, and security for them. For these you need money. He was planning for the future, a future after cycling, and he shared many of these plans with his closest friend in the bunch, Vin Denson. Vin was a builder by trade and Tom wanted to involve him in his projects after they'd retired. He said to him: 'After we've finished with all this hell, we're not going to work for someone else. We'll have people working for us and we'll be able to relax.'

He had a run of six good victories in the criteriums, some of them memorable. For example, he lapped the entire field twice in winning the race at Felletin, something that had never been done before, and then won another one the following day.

Such was his form in these races that only two people were being talked about in the run-up to the Worlds at the old Nurburgring motor-racing circuit in Germany: Tom and Eddy Merckx. That was all well and good, but the Nurburgring was a tough course with constant ups and downs, and, anyway, like every World Championships, it required a period of specialised training, not riding 40 criteriums in the 44 days following the Tour, like Tom had. But with his starting price as World Champion being at least £250 per race – plus, as one of the star riders, a good share of the prize money – I'm sure you can work out why he wanted to ride every one of these races he could.

Tom was never there in his defence of the rainbow jersey. He was uncomfortable from the start and in the few pictures I've seen of the race he looked as though he didn't even want to be there. He was using a bottom gear of 42 by 21 while the others were using a 23 or 24 sprocket. Eventually, this took its toll on his legs and he blew wide apart on one of the steep climbs, and retired from the race. He was over-raced and unhappy with the whole day. Perhaps he even fitted the higher gear as his get-out clause. Remember what Norman Sheil said about him being defeated in his head? It could still happen in 1966, even though he was as hard a pro as any of the other top riders by then. It must have hurt, packing at the Worlds, especially as reigning champion, but it was a price he had to pay – a trade for all the money from those lucrative criteriums, and for the future he was trying to build.

In the end, the Championships were a victory for the home rider, Rudi Altig, from Anquetil, with Poulidor in third. All three medallists refused to take the by-now mandatory drug test after the race and, after a lot of huffing and puffing by officials, the result was allowed to stand. By and large, riders were refusing to accept efforts to control the substances that they used in their preparation, and officials, by fudging the issue, were condoning the situation. This was the prevailing background of cycling in the sixties and, as we have seen from the events of the 1998 Tour de France, it still prevails. And cycling as a whole still fudges it, laying the blame conveniently at the feet of the riders, branding them cheats instead of listening to them. No one has ever listened to the riders, yet all of us – fans, sponsors, managers, the media – expect them to perform like supermen and conduct themselves like angels – lonely angels in a corrupt and compromised world. I hope, one day soon, that this will change and something is worked out, that some common ground be found, because, in taking risks with their health, the truth is that the riders cheat no one but themselves.

Tom continued with the criteriums and track meetings after the championships, putting on more displays of speed around Europe, including taking second place to Anquetil in the Golden Wheel in Paris where, for the second year running, the pair of them dominated the assembled field of stars. He was still paying the price, though, and had a terrible time in the autumn classics. A combination of crashes and lack of strength saw him retire in both Paris–Tours and the Tour of Lombardy. He must have been glad when the road season ended.

It didn't mean that it was time to rest. Tom had a good six-day season that winter, though he didn't win one. Still, he finished fourteenth in the winter's rankings with a second, third and a fourth place from seven rides.

The promoters wouldn't yet give him a regular partner, but that would have changed, and Tom saw his future on the winter tracks. At Berlin, he told *Cycling* magazine's reporter: 'I will carry on on the road until I am 34, then I'll finish my career with a few years on the track. That way I can have my holidays with the kids in the summer. Post rides 15 of these in the winter and that's what I'll do.'

One of his best races was at Milan where he rode with his preferred partner, Ron Baensch. There he was visited by Hubert Starley, the Managing Director of Champion spark plugs, who was the chairman of the committee organising the return of six day racing to Britain in 1967. He'd come to get some idea of the flavour of a modern six, which Milan was, and the London Skol lager-sponsored event was going to be. Naturally, Tom was to be one of the main attractions at the race, planned to be held at Earls Court during the cycle show in the September of 1967. He was really looking forward to that.

Another piece of news which he welcomed was that the Tour de France was to return to the national team format. Some of his closest advisers had misgivings about this, wondering if a British set-up would be professional enough to support Tom in an all-out attempt to win the race, but he was very enthusiastic about it. The team might not be as strong as a trade one, but at least he could trust the riders in it.

It also released him from the pressure of having to sign for Peugeot before the Tour. He was guaranteed a place in the British team and, as his contract was in its final year, he had received more than ten offers from other teams, all of them prepared to pay more than Peugeot.

Eventually, he signed for the Italian kitchen manufacturer, Salvarani. He was to take Vin Denson with him and would be joint leader with Felice Gimondi. What a strong pair they would have been. Strong enough, perhaps, to check the rise, in 1968 at least, of a man who, in 1967, would still be with the Peugeot team, Eddy Merckx. He was being slowly groomed for stardom and although there would be friction between him and Tom in the coming year, Eddy has always paid tribute to the help Tom gave him at the start of his career, and spoken in admiration of him as a rider.

For their Christmas break, Tom, Helen and the children went to Corsica. They had bought some land there and were having a place built. He was full of it when he returned to Ghent, and told the journalist, Ken Evans, that he could see himself retiring there, perhaps buying a yacht and setting it up with a captain to charter out. He also planned to get Vin Denson to build some holiday homes there – Corsica featured large in his future plans.

So did England. About this time he bought a farmhouse in Tickhill, the next village to Harworth, and had it converted to smaller units. Not one to waste money, he didn't take the usual step of having an agent manage this property. Instead, he sent his mother on the bus every Friday to collect the rents, which, I must add, she enjoyed enormously: I think she liked the idea of being thought a woman of property.

13

'PUT ME BACK ON MY BIKE'

It was a time for thinking about the future, a time to plan and a time when he realised that time itself was running out. Tom was 29. His one unfulfilled ambition was victory in the Tour de France. He wasn't old, and did not accept yet that he was at his peak, though he knew definitely that he was close, and definitely that with a British team he had never had a better chance of victory than in 1967. So it was time to plan his whole season around the Tour, just like people had told him he would have to if he was going to have any chance of winning it.

That is what he decided to do. He planned to ride more stage races in preparation, and in preference to the spring classics. He planned to use races, rather than try to win every one. He planned to give himself every chance of winning the Tour which, he stated publicly, was his only objective, along with the world one-hour record.

The hour record? Yes, why not? His riding towards the end of the winter track season showed that even without any specialist training he had, if anything, improved as a pursuiter and that is essentially what you have to be to have a chance at the record. Also, as we shall see in Paris–Nice, his time trialling had improved enormously, and that helps with the hour record, and is an indispensable weapon for a Tour contender.

His best form of the winter came in one of the last meetings at Ghent when, in an omnium event, he won the 4,000-metre pursuit in a scintillating time of 4 minutes and 46 seconds – six seconds inside the world record. It didn't stand as a record because the pro distance was 5,000 metres in those days, but it was world class pursuiting. The only other rider around then who had been even close to that time was Ferdi Bracke, and he went on to become World Pro Pursuit Champion, and set a new hour record, so it was a hell of a ride.

In the same omnium, Tom did a flying kilometre in 1 minute 4.7 seconds, only one-tenth slower than the very, very rapid sprinter

Patrick Sercu. In another meeting he set a time of 6 minutes and 6 seconds for the 5,000-metres distance, and scored a stinging victory over the 'King of the Sixes', Peter Post, in his speciality, a Derny-paced race. This last race was doubly humiliating for Post, as the pace Tom set was so fast that Peter was dropped by his pacing machine on the last lap, and that was the sort of thing that he did to others.

So Tom started the 1967 road race season with the form of his life and a mind-set focused on the Tour de France. He was going to win and already he was saying that the key to his victory would be the day the race crossed the Mont Ventoux in Provence. He planned to move right up the classification there, then take overall victory on the final time-trial stage to Paris.

He didn't have to wait long for success on the road, either. In one of his first races, the Tour of Sardinia at the end of February, he won one stage and finished second on another. It was a good start, a start made in the manner of one of the bosses of the peloton, a man with a feeling of destiny, a feeling that this was going to be 'his' year, that this was 'his' time. You could feel it in the way he spoke in interviews. It's hard to put your finger on it, but there was a kind of sureness about Tom now. Something bigger than confidence.

Paris–Nice was his first target race. He needed to demonstrate, to himself as much as anyone, that he could take charge of a big stage race and win it in front of the best riders in the world. They were all there, past, present and future Tour winners: Anquetil, Poulidor, Gimondi, Aimar and perhaps the biggest threat to his ambitions, a man in his own team, Eddy Merckx.

This race was also Merckx's professed first target of the year, and he got in the first punch when he won the second stage to Château Chinon, taking over the race leadership. Eddy must have been feeling pleased with himself, but Tom wasn't pleased at all. He confided in Jock Wadley: 'I've based my whole early season on winning Paris–Nice. Now my own team mate is leading. What do you do in a situation like that?'

The answer is that you keep smiling with one face, and look for an opportunity with the other. Luckily, it came the very next day. Merckx was very strong, but not yet experienced enough to know how to defend a lead in a race like this. He went to sleep on the next stage and let a break of 16 riders get away on the Col du Grand Bois, a 2,000-foot climb out of St Etienne. Immediately, Tom realised that this was his chance. Seeing Merckx hesitate, he was quickly across to the break and once there could let the others do the work while, on the face of it, protecting Merckx's interests. It worked: by the finish at Tournon in the Rhône valley, the break had 20 minutes on the chasing group and Merckx had lost all chance of winning the Paris–Nice.

Eddy was furious and the accusations were flying round the Peugeot camp. But the truth of the matter was that it's a tough world. Tom knew what was happening – of that there's no doubt – and he took his opportunity, but Merckx should never have let such a group get away, because it was studded with star riders. Tom didn't work in the break, though it was to his benefit, so Eddy had nothing to reproach him for. Anyway, this must have been pointed out to the young Belgian that night, because he worked for Tom for the rest of the race. It was the right thing to do. Tom went on to prove that he was by far the stronger of the two by Nice.

The race was now between Tom, Wolfshohl, and the new French 'hope', Bernard Guyot. There was very little time between them, and one of them would have to take the initiative to win. It was Tom. On the stage to Hyeres, crossing Mont Faron, Merckx and Simpson simply rode away from the rest of the race.

The Peugeot tandem was a magnificent sight. Eddy attacked first and once he had a gap Tom sprinted away from the splitting bunch, joining his team mate just before the Faron climb. Behind them the race blew apart with Wolfshohl heading a frantic chase, but losing with every turn of his pedals.

On Mont Faron, Tom was fantastic: so powerful were his stints at making the pace that he distanced Merckx several times and had to wait for him. Afterwards, he told Jock Wadley that he could easily have ridden away from Eddy on the climb, but he waited because he needed his power on the flat to put as much time as they could into Wolfshohl and the rest.

And they did just that. At the finish, where Tom did not contest the sprint, allowing Merckx to win the stage, he had gained nearly 90 seconds on the German, even more on Guyot, and ten minutes on the bunch. Tom had taken over the race lead.

Next day, he defended masterfully, under repeated fire from all quarters as the teams of Wolfshohl and Guyot launched numerous serious attacks in an attempt to dislodge him from first place. It was a torrid 100 miles between Antibes and Nice, but at the end of it his lead was still intact, and he only had the next day's time trial to survive in order to win the race.

In that time trial Tom only had to lose no more than 1 minute 25 seconds to Wolfshohl, and two minutes to Guyot to ensure overall victory, but he had two points to prove: one, that he was the strongest in the race; and, two, that he could now time trial with the best.

He certainly did prove those two points. He did a fantastic ride, taking second place and losing just two seconds to Guyot, who, incidentally, admitted later in the year that he had been paced by his team car during his ride. On top of that, just look at who Tom beat in that time trial: Gimondi, Merckx, Bracke, Poulidor and the master himself, Jacques Anquetil. Tom had done more than just a good time trial, more than win the second most important stage race in France, he had shown that the last thing he needed to make a serious attempt to win the Tour de France was in place: he could beat the best in a time trial.

This was crucial to his Tour strategy. Accepting that a British team would not be strong enough for the task of defending the yellow jersey for days on end, he planned to work himself up through the classification, using some of the harder key stages like the Ventoux, then be in a position to take the jersey with a good time trial on the final day. Victory in the Tour was a real possibility in that spring of 1967.

The Peugeot pair continued their dominance in Milan–San Remo, the first classic of the year, coming straight after Paris–Nice. Here Tom was determined to pay Merckx back for his help in Paris–Nice, but to do it in a way that, if things hadn't gone to plan, then he and not Eddy would have been in a position to win.

He was flying again on that day. He attacked after three miles with Da Rugna, Preziozi, Lelangue and Vin Denson. It was a good group, especially with Tom in such fine form. They stayed away for 128 miles before the bunch realised that they were left with an awkward dilemma. Should they let them stay away, thus giving Tom the victory, or should they chase hard and catch the break, thereby giving Merckx an easy ride to the front? Either way, a Peugeot victory was almost certain.

They took the latter course of action, and it went exactly as Tom and Eddy had planned. Merckx won for the second year on the trot, the second of an amazing seven wins in this race during his career. Tom wasn't far behind at the finish, having had enough left in his legs to help Eddy once he'd been carried up to the front on an armchair by his rivals. Tom had been at the front of the race for all but three of its 180 miles. It was an amazing day.

The terrible twins continued to cut a swathe through pro cycling during the spring. While Tom had a bit of a breather and soft pedalled a bit to help with his Tour ambitions, Eddy was up there in the Tour of Flanders, and won Ghent–Wevelgem, before the pair were at full bore again in the GP Salvarani, a big race with a big prize list, run off in the Brussels area to replace Paris–Brussels.

Just as with Milan–San Remo, Tom attacked first, this time a bit later, after 27 miles. Every time a group formed around him, he attacked to break it up. He was once again at his devastatingly aggressive best. Finally, on the Alsemberg hill, Willy Monty and Adriano Durante managed to haul themselves up to Tom, towing along Eddy Merckx. Straightaway, Merckx attacked and stayed away for victory, Tom policing the two chasers, and eventually taking third place in what was a classic in all but name.

They followed this up with a one-two in the G.P. de Corriges. It was the last time they raced together. Eddy went off to ride the Ardennes classics, winning Flèche Wallonne, and Tom was to ride the three-week Tour of Spain, the first time he'd had the opportunity to ride a national tour other than the Tour de France.

Eddy would never see Tom again. The next time their paths crossed would be in the parish church in Harworth when he attended Tom's funeral. Eddy was deeply affected by Tom's death and, like most cyclists of his age, can vividly remember where he was when he heard the dreadful news, just like people say they can remember where they were when they heard of the assassination of President Kennedy. 'I remember I was driving home from a race in Belgium when I heard the news on the car radio. I burst into tears and had to stop by the roadside,' he recalled, some 30 years later.

Tom wanted to use the Tour of Spain to bring him the strength-in-depth he would need for the Tour de France. Preparations were going on at a pace for the whole British team by this time. Fyffes, the banana importers, had agreed to sponsor the team during the Tour and to pay for the selected British-based riders to race in Europe for a total of five weeks before the big one. Also, they agreed to pay for three *soigneurs* for the race. Tom was insistent about this: he welcomed the national team format, but he made it clear that he wanted no part of a team run on a shoestring. This was going to be the team that produced the winner, after all.

Still, it was going to be a tall order. The French, the Italians, Belgians and Spanish were going to have the pick of the very best riders in Europe: climbers, sprinters, and, most importantly, strong *domestiques* who could ride all day for their leaders. Plus, all these riders would be used to the pace of racing on the continent and very few of them would be riding their first Tour, which is what more than half of the British team would be doing. Still, if anybody could pull it off, Tom could.

In the spring of 1967, Ken Evans asked him if he was a gambler and Tom replied, 'Oh, absolutely. I love to see how far I can go, what risks I can get away with, which is why I always try the unexpected. But I'm never surprised when I win, I'm only surprised when I lose.' If you want to sum Tom up you couldn't have done better than use these, his own words.

In Spain, he soon lost any ambitions of a high overall placing, if he had any, when on a very hot second stage he crashed, and found himself trapped in the bunch with a number of other good riders when a break they had completely underestimated gained 13 minutes. His enthusiasm for the race waned after this, so much so that on the eve of the fifth stage, from Salamanca to Madrid, he saw the race doctor, and was planning to retire. Only the fact that it was easier to get a plane from the Spanish capital than from Salamanca made him start the next day.

Everything changed on the road to Madrid because he managed to get into a break, then drop his companions to take the stage alone. He decided to stay, and was second on stage seven to the ultra-rapid Gerben Karstens in a bunch finish. Then he won again on the sixteenth stage to San Sebastian, the scene of his World Championship victory. Both of his stage wins had come on difficult days, and just as importantly he came out of the race much stronger than he went in, so he'd achieved his main objective – that of preparation.

Tom was now going very well. In the Polymultipliée, an extremely hilly circuit race in France, he was the author of a solo break which lasted from the thirtieth to the eightieth mile. Only then did three of the best mountain men in the world get up to him: Jiménez, Poulidor and Paul Gutty. Despite his heavy day's work, they couldn't get rid of him; though, not surprisingly, he didn't have enough left to finish any better than fourth.

There was a more worrying side to this race. Three teams of British riders, all of them possibles for the Tour team, started the race and not one finished. There were less than three weeks to go before the start of the Tour. It didn't bode well: the fears of Tom's advisers – that the team would not be strong enough to support him – were starting to look very real.

There were only a few races left before the Tour and one very special weekend of racing was planned in Britain. A televised criterium was to be held on the Saturday at New Brighton in the Wirral, giving everyone in the country the chance to see our Tour de France team in live action just before the start of the big race. Then, next day – in theory – the whole show would move over the Pennines to contest the very tough Vaux Grand Prix, though without the TV this time.

It should have been a great day for British cycling, but due in part to bad luck, and in part to a tendency the sport in this country has always had for killing golden geese, it ended up being a disaster. David Saunders had done the work getting the TV there and the promoter, Alan Williams, had attracted a major league sponsor in the tobacco company, Players. A tremendous amount of work had been done behind the scenes and it almost came to nothing.

The bad luck hit when Tom and the other foreign-based Tour riders, Barry Hoban, Michael Wright and Albert Hitchen were delayed so long by 'red tape' at London Airport that they missed their connection to Manchester, only arriving in New Brighton when the day's main event was nearly over. On top of this, their bikes failed to arrive at all and they each had to borrow one from one of the many club racers in the crowd so that they could compete in a hastily arranged five-mile race, put on to keep the crowd happy, and to try to avoid losing another big-name sponsor from the sport.

In addition to that, most of the British-based Tour riders hadn't even turned up. It seems that some of the riders didn't like the fact that the prize list was small in order to pay contract fees to the 'foreigners', but, with the greatest respect to them, they weren't going to bring 50,000 people to New Brighton prom on a Saturday afternoon, like Tom did. Whatever the rights and wrongs of all this, at the very least it wasn't a good display of team spirit.

Incidentally, that crowd and the television audience were indicative of the huge buzz of expectation that was going on around this country in the run-up to the Tour that year. Every cyclist on the road was Tommy Simpson and club riders from that era were often cheered with cries of 'Come on, Tommy' on their day-to-day rides from passers-by in the street. England expected.

All was not lost by bad luck at New Brighton. Tom managed to send the huge crowd home with some wonderful memories. He apologised to them all over the public address, did the TV interviews, then gave a powerful display of riding in the special event, winning in splendid isolation, though he was doggedly chased by a gutsy rider from Nottingham, John Aslin. In a story full of sad ironies, Aslin was to become the first winner of the Tom Simpson Memorial Race the following year.

Tom had more problems. He desperately wanted to ride the Vaux race the following day, but due to a mix up with his agent he was contracted to ride a track meeting in Paris at the same time. He had been trying all sorts of ways to get out of this, but not appearing in Paris would have meant a fine and even ex-world champions didn't willingly upset the powerful French promoters of those days.

He had two reasons for wanting to ride the Vaux: one was practical – 'a race as tough as the Vaux would do us all good just before the Tour'; and the other was personal – 'my family have got together a bus trip to come and see me'. The Vaux race was held on the Durham Fells; he would have been racing a bike in his home county for the first time in his life.

Sadly, it couldn't happen, but, just a few days later, Tom did return to the British Isles, for the last time, to ride in the Manx Premier race on the Isle of Man, his last race before the Tour de France, and what a virtuoso performance he gave.

Once again the hilly Clypse circuit was lashed by the worst weather you can imagine for the end of June – storm-force winds and torrential rain. And, once again, the race organisers had assembled a star-studded field to do battle. Lucian Aimar, who had won the previous year's Tour, was there, so was Dino Zandegu, already a winner of the Tour of Flanders that year, plus a gaggle of good pro riders from both sides of the Channel; but Tom just hammered the lot of them.

Signs of his good form were there to see early on in the race when he punctured, got a very slow wheel change, but closed a two-minute gap on the bunch in just eight miles. Then, at halfway, he went clear with a small group of riders including Aimar, who eventually finished second.

Once he'd got this group established, and with the race splitting to pieces under the efforts being made by riders trying to get up to Tom's group, he attacked. No one could follow. In two miles he had a 40-second lead. With 60 miles covered he had stretched this by another minute. Four miles later he had 2 minutes and 20 seconds on the nearest chaser, and then he literally just rode away from everyone. He even began to lap riders towards the end of this 50-mile race – some going on a four-mile circuit. He was ready for the Tour de France.

So we come to the eve of the 1967 Tour de France and the final episode of my book: it's going to be a difficult one to write. So much has already been written about this race, even more said, and still more left unsaid, that I feel what really happened has, over the years, been obscured by layers of uncorrected opinion and half-truths.

For example, a picture has been painted of Tom as a desperate man prepared to go to any lengths to win a race that he ultimately couldn't. It has even been said that he was desperate to win because he needed the money to fund his extravagant lifestyle. Both are convenient explanations for what happened and both sound very plausible, but neither do him justice.

Tom was desperate, yes: victory in this race would set the seal on his career, for him probably more than any other rider in the race. If he won the Tour, Tom really would have become the next big British success story at a time when the eyes of the world seemed focused upon us. He'd tasted the fruits of fame in his own country when he became World Champion in 1965. Now England had won the World Cup. A victory in the Tour would top even that. He would again be the number-one sports personality in his own country. And this would be nothing compared to his fame on the continent. In the light of the influence Britain had on popular culture and fashion in those days there would never be a more opportune time than the sixties for an Englishman to win Europe's biggest sporting event. He would have been made for life.

So, yes, he was desperate; desperate because the stakes were so high. He had so much to gain by victory, more, perhaps, than it is possible to imagine now. And he could have won. I know that it's all ifs and buts now, and people will say that it's just wishful thinking on my part, but I really do believe that he had a very good chance of winning the 1967 Tour de France. I'm not alone in that opinion: the rider closest to Tom in the Great Britain team, Vin Denson, remembers the atmosphere of the time: 'We were all convinced Tom could finish in the first three that year, maybe better.' And there is very good evidence to support that belief. Just look at his performance in the 1962 race. Sixth overall and a day in 'yellow', and it could have been third, all at the age of 24 and in only his third Tour. If that isn't evidence of a potential winner then I'd like to know what is. Then, in 1966, tactically he'd been all over the place, but he'd shaken the race on flat stages, done a good time trial and blown it apart on the Galibier stage before his crash.

Yes, in other years the race had beaten him, crushed him even. But now, in 1967, after years of chasing the classics and arriving at the Tour start without the necessary reserves to challenge for victory, he had built his entire season around this one race. Plus, he was at his physical peak that year. Already, he had shown he could climb, he could time trial and he had the strength to last a three-week race. All year he'd been able to win as he pleased: Paris–Nice, a stage in the Tour of Sardinia, two stages of the Tour of Spain, the Manx Premier, but mostly he'd been patient, slowly building for the only race he now felt that he had to win.

The form and reserves would be there. He'd even sorted out his tactics. He'd had to, because there was only one way he'd be able to win, and that was to take the lead in the last few days and defend it himself in the final time trial to Paris. With the greatest respect to them, the British team would be one of the weakest in the race: only four of them had any kind of experience of racing at this level; six of the ten were riding their first Tour. Now that's not their fault, and it didn't particularly worry Tom. He knew that none of them would have loyalties elsewhere and that every one of them would do as much as he could to help him. It was more than could have been said for his Peugeot trade team and it was the best he was going to get as far as team support at that time; anyway, look what they'd managed at the Worlds in 1965. It was still going to be a problem, though. France, for example, had both national and regional teams in the race. Their A team read like a Who's Who of cycling, and the possibility of collusion between the teams in the name of national pride could certainly not be ruled out. There was no way the British team would be able to defend Tom against the French onslaught that would have occurred if he took the lead too early.

So he would have to ghost around the peleton in the early stages, follow on the first important days across the Hell of the North, and in the Vosges and the Alps. Then he planned to hit them where it hurt on the thirteenth stage which climbed the Ventoux. They would all be suffering on that day and the strongest team in the world couldn't save you if you were having a bad day on that brutal climb, and Tom planned to give them all a very bad day indeed. If it worked then he would be close enough to make his final move for victory in the time trial. It was a long shot, and it depended on everything going right for him, but he could have done it – he really could have done it.

The distinct chance of his success had captured the interest of a British media normally indifferent to cycling. *The Times*, for example, sent their now chief sports reporter, Rob Hughes, to follow Tom's every move and record his every thought. The idea was that after the Tour he would be able to write an exclusive fly-on-the-wall account of his triumphs, trials and tribulations. The American film company, Paramount, sent a film crew to follow him with a view to producing a film about the race with a million-pound budget.

So there was pressure. Tom must have felt the weight of hope and expectation on his shoulders; in fact, I know that he did. When things started to go wrong for him later in the race, and he was unwell, one of the few journalists who knew he was having problems, Sid Saltmarsh, worried that he was pushing too hard and tried to persuade him to abandon hopes of victory. Sid tried to tell him that there were still other things to go for that year, and that there would still be other years. Tom would have none of it. His back was against the wall and he said to Saltmarsh: 'I can't, Sid. Everybody expects me to win the Tour. I just can't let them down.'

This is how he sincerely felt. Now, I'm not blaming anybody; I accept that a lot of this pressure would have been of his own making. It was in his nature to put pressure on himself. By constantly raising the bar, putting himself into impossible situations, he was able to extend himself and achieve all that he did. This time, though, he would go too far.

I mention all this here because I just want to make a point about Tom's state of mind coming into and during this race. The pressure and his bravery would prove a lethal cocktail, and it's something that, in my opinion, has been little considered since his death. Sadly, I think it's easier to label someone simply as a cheat; then he is on his own, marginalised, and everything can go on as normal. This is what has happened to Tom.

But at the beginning, everything was hope and light. The British team that assembled for the prologue time trial in Angers consisted of Tom, his three fellow 'continentals' with previous Tour experience – Vin Denson, Barry Hoban and Michael Wright – three others who, though they were based abroad, were riding their first Tour – Albert Hitchen; the new pro, Peter Hill; and the Australian, Bill Lawrie – then the three home-based riders, Pete Chisman, Colin Lewis, and Arthur Metcalfe. They were the best Britain could field and they were a talented bunch, as, I think, any cycling historian will confirm.

They were going to ride 100 per-cent for Tom. Their team manager, Alec Taylor, had instilled into them that if they only got half-way and they had done all they could for Tom, then they would have done their job. Morale was good, the senior pros freely giving advice to the first timers, little things that would help them get through. In fact, the last words Tom said to Vin Denson before the Ventoux, just as he was going up the road to take his place in the battle with the leaders, was, 'Remember to tell the British boys about the state of the descent from the top of the Ventoux, and not to risk a crash just to gain a couple of minutes.'

This was the first year of the prologue time trial in the Tour de France, which was seen then as a handy way of introducing the riders to the public and establishing some kind of order for the first few days, but nothing more than that. Even some of the press referred to it as something of a novelty appendage to the race proper.

In the end it didn't prove much: it was won by a Spaniard, Errandonea, who couldn't get further than the third stage due to the most unpleasant injury that can befall a cyclist – boils on the bottom. The greatest talking point was the fact that the outcome of the event, being spread over a whole evening, was greatly affected by when a particular rider started. The last few had to start in pitch darkness, the 3.6-mile tricky circuit being lit by *Gaz* lanterns. All well and good, but one or two sharp bends were left unlit, and Tom felt that he was slowed by this in recording a time of 8 minutes and 2 seconds, which lost him 13 seconds on Poulidor, for example. Of course, the leader of the French National A team rode in total daylight, didn't he!

The first two stages, which took the riders from Angers via St Malo to Caen, were uneventful apart from the British team losing Hitchen and Chisman, who had both been doubtful about their form before the race. Most of the others were doing their bit for Tom and saving as much energy as they possibly could.

Most, but not all. Peter Hill, who was, coincidentally, from Doncaster and was famous for winning Britain's Best All-rounder time-trial award whilst still a teenager, had been one of the best amateurs in France in 1966, but was finding the step up to the pro ranks with Peugeot-BP a bit difficult. Why then did he expend valuable energy, working in a 90-mile break on the third stage between Caen and Amiens? Because the previous year he had been based in Normandy and the race passed through his adopted home town of Elbeuf where he wanted to look good in front of his supporters. He did look good, and finished fifth on the stage, but his moment of glory cost him dearly and two days later he was out of the Tour. Tom had lost another team mate before he should have done. Already, things were not going to plan. To win the Tour he would have to spend his energy like a miser does his cash, every kilometre a team mate could help him would take him a little closer to success in Paris.

The next stage was from Amiens to Roubaix, over the cobbled roads of the 'Hell of the North'. This was a day when the favourites would have to be on their mettle, perhaps not a day when one of them could win the Tour de France, but certainly a day when one could lose it. Tom did everything he should have and survived well in the leading 12-man break which forced its way clear across the *pavé*, and contained all the other race favourites: Poulidor, Aimar, Gimondi and Janssen.

All 12 arrived at the Roubaix velodrome together with Tom the last of the string and riding high around the top of the track bankings. From there he began his sprint down the back straight and, going like a train, got up to third place before a puncture on the final bend relegated him to seventh. After the stage, Tom was pleased with the way things were going and told reporters: 'I'm playing a waiting game. In the past I've always had to impose my supremacy on the team, now I don't have to do that.'

So far, not bad, but next day the favourites made a mistake that was to cost them all dearly. To be fair to them, though, they made it because there were just too many good riders in the French A team – not just good riders, too many potential winners, even. On the stage from Roubaix to Jambes, Roger Pingeon attacked on the steep, cobbled climb of the Mur de Thuin and rode away to take his first yellow jersey. Nobody knew it then, but due to Poulidor crashing and losing a packet of time a few days later, Pingeon would eventually win the Tour because the French team had, by then, no alternative but to support him if they wanted to win the race; and they did want to win the race.

It was a bad day for Tom in more ways than the others. He lost two more team mates in Bill Lawrie, who'd crashed on the Roubaix stage, and Peter Hill. This left only six Brits to contest the team time trial that afternoon in Jambes. This time trial didn't count for the individual classification, but national pride dictated that they couldn't come last. They didn't, and were quite happy to beat the Swiss and one of the French regional teams to finish the 10.5-mile event just 51 seconds behind the winners, Belgium. Tom, in fact, was quite pleased with their ride, and said, 'A few rides together and we'd improve by well over a minute at the distance.' He wasn't letting things get on top of him. It was still early days, but, although he probably wouldn't have accepted it, the odds were beginning to stack against him. At least he was still strong and full of fight.

Stage six took the race 149 miles from Jambes to Metz, and it was to be a fast day as some of the favourites tried to put Pingeon under pressure. The French team countered magnificently, and so nothing was gained. Tom sat tight and watched it all. He was sticking to his plan and was only going to move when Pingeon had fewer of his team around to help him.

Despite their setbacks (on top of the retirements, Metcalfe now had a cold, and Barry Hoban had only been back on his bike for the two weeks before the race after a six-week layoff, including a period of hospitalisation, due to an abscess), the British team now felt that things were really starting to go their way, especially when Michael Wright won the next stage. Morale was high, and Tom was fired up and ready for the first mountain stage – Strasbourg to the top of the Ballon d'Alsace.

This was going to be another day of decision and anyone who felt himself a potential winner would have to be on the pace. It turned out to be a very hard day indeed. Attacks came throughout the day, but the serious move was made on the penultimate climb. Tom, Jiménez, Poulidor, Janssens and Gimondi all made it into the lead group. Then, on the descent, Gimondi started to pile on the pressure, so much so that Poulidor took one risk too many in an effort to keep up and crashed, losing all chance of winning this Tour.

On the last climb, the Ballon d'Alsace, Lucien Aimar, seeing that his leader had fallen, set off in pursuit of the lead group. Pingeon wasn't having a good day, but he still had a reasonable cushion of time to preserve his lead, so it was up to Aimar to take up the challenge for France. He quickly caught the front group which immediately started to split under the powerful attacks which eventually won him the stage.

The heat was on and the favourites were being spread across the mountainside. Tom battled and coped well, finishing the stage in fifth place, just a few seconds behind Aimar, and moved up to ninth overall. The big losers on the day had been Gimondi and Poulidor: Gimondi had punctured, dropped back to Pingeon's group, then worked so hard to limit his losses that the Frenchman was brought back into contention, then had blown up completely and lost four minutes; poor Raymond Poulidor limped in, covered in blood from his fall, eleven minutes behind the winner.

If Tom was good that day then on the next he played a blinder. Stage nine, from Belfort to Divonnes les Bains, was a fairly flat run, designed to take the race to the foot of the Alps and, though no one realised it at the time, it was probably the day which clinched the race overall for Pingeon.

Tom and Pingeon saw the tactical possibilities of a breakaway group made up mainly of Belgian opportunists. The Belgians hadn't really got a potential overall winner of the race in their team, so any opportunities for glory would be taken with open hands. Tom threw his lot in with the group and worked hard to ensure that they gained serious time over the others, while Pingeon, who gained the most, did nothing, just sat on the back, and virtually won the Tour there and then. He already had a good lead; now, with little effort, he'd added to it. Not spectacular, but the kind of tactics that had won this race before.

Tom, of course, was spectacular. He put in big efforts and even got up there in the sprint for the stage victory, taking fourth to the very fast Guido Reybroeck. He had moved up to sixth place overall, 5 minutes 15 seconds behind Pingeon, but first by a good margin of all the favourites. The plan was still working: he was in front of the eventual second- and third-placed riders in Paris – Jiménez, and double Tour of Italy winner, Balmamion. He now had to execute the second part of it and move up on the Ventoux, but first he had to stay up there in the Alps. It was looking good, very good indeed, but everything would have to go right for him to close the gap on Pingeon. He couldn't, for example, afford a single bad day.

It came. It came on the next day, and it came on the worst day possible, the day the race went over the Galibier. Whether his physique was just too frail to win a three-week race, or whether he'd just been pushing too hard, or whether he was just unlucky and simply succumbed to a bug that was going round, we'll never know, but on this stage Tom had a terrible time.

Right from the start he had stomach problems. He couldn't keep anything down, so had to ride all day on his reserves, unable to take in any energy. He suffered terribly, fighting along every inch of the road, while Gimondi, the stage winner, was ripping the race apart. Still, he managed to finish alongside Jan Janssen in sixteenth place, losing six minutes to the Italian winner, but he'd fallen to seventh overall and the gap of five minutes on Pingeon had gone up to over eight. Plus, Jiménez, Balmamion, Gimondi, and Aimar had all climbed over him on the general classification.

At the end of the stage he was exhausted, still feeling unwell, dehydrated and desperate. Was the dream slipping through his fingers? It looked like it ... to everyone but Tom. The bad day he couldn't afford had happened, and it wasn't going to go away. He was ill, now: the stomach problems had weakened him; he had just raced one of the hardest days of the Tour on his reserves; also, I have been told, he was developing bronchitis. The cards had been dealt and he'd got nothing in his hand.

He was pushing too hard now, going too far. What was his state of mind? Did he still think he could win the Tour? Maybe he did, or perhaps thought he could at least get on the podium, but I also think that he felt backed into a corner by his ambition and by circumstances he'd been unable to control. What is certain is that he was sticking to his plan on the Ventoux, come what may. On the eve of the big stage, he seemed to have put the Galibier behind him, and was second in the bunch sprint for sixth place on the Marseilles track, beating speed merchants of the calibre of Reybroeck and Godefroot in the process.

Marseilles is a long way from home for a lad from Harworth, even today – just about as foreign a place as you can get in Europe, with its proximity to the continent of Africa. And in a little photograph taken of Tom just before the thirteenth stage of the Tour de France, on the thirteenth of July, he looks a very long way from home, indeed.

There's something I just can't put my finger on that's different about Tom in that picture. He doesn't look like the man in all the other photos I've seen of him, the man I can just remember as a glimpse of glamour in my ordinary pit-village childhood; not the man who was so sure of himself, and of what he was doing, though I know now that he wasn't always; not the man who took on the whole of Europe and beat them at their own game. It's not a publicity shot, not posed, not larking around on a boat like some of the others taken before the start that day. It's just a shot taken a few minutes before the start, a few minutes he was having on his own, perhaps thinking of the enormity of the task in front of him, the enormity of that white mountain already shimmering in record temperatures, and perhaps the enormity of what he would have to do to conquer it. On a day that would be filled with many sad pictures, for me, this is the saddest.

The whole of the Tour that year had been run off in a heatwave. Never would the heat be more of a problem than on this trek through the parched landscape of Provence, on a road that was nothing more than a ribbon of hot tar, climbing all the time towards the town of Carpentras.

From there, the riders would undertake a 70-kilometre loop over the Ventoux via Bedouin and the mountain's southern side, to finish back in Carpentras. The mountain itself is both a beautiful and sinister place. Not the steepest or longest climb in the Tour de France repertoire, but there is something about it, something about the atmosphere on it that makes it probably the most feared. Riders had collapsed there before, simply unable to suck enough oxygen from the air to keep going. They have tried to quantify it: they say that if there is a head wind then it cools you and there is plenty of air to breathe, but if the wind comes from the south, from the hot valley floor, then it takes all the oxygen away, and with it your breath.

On the day, the wind was blowing from the south, and it was incredibly hot. Legend has it that the thermometer outside the Chalet Reynard, the famous café just at the edge of the tree line, cracked after recording 54 degrees Celsius.

In these conditions the riders approached the mountain in one group, and almost with a reluctance to get there. Their main preoccupation was getting extra drinks from roadside cafés. That is the work of the *domestiques*, the helpers, those just there to serve and survive, not the preoccupation of the leaders. In accordance with the prevailing lore of the times, they would not allow themselves to drink too much, believing that they would become bloated and unable to function properly once battle commenced on the mountain. There was almost a bravado among riders in those days as to how little they could drink during a race. They were misinformed, and it was a dangerous practice.

Vin Denson was there to survive, get over the mountain as best he could, then help Tom in the coming days. In the early part of the day, and even on the preliminary slopes up to the real start of the climb in the village of Bedouin, he rode alongside his team leader. Vin is not a man who readily talks about his own victories, though they include the Tour of Luxembourg, and he is still one of only two Britons ever to win a stage in the Tour of Italy, but he talks about 13th July 1967 as though it was yesterday. It is as though talking about the friend he misses so much helps, somehow:

On the Ventoux, Tom was very nervous. This was a big day. At the start of the climb I was in a big group with Tom and Poulidor, who I viewed as the strong man for the stage. Then Poulidor punctured and some Italians attacked. Tom went after them and I rode after him. I told him it was too soon, to wait for Poulidor who would tow him up to them, but he didn't listen, so with my last strength I gave him a big push and fell back to the groups behind, leaving Tom to chase after them.

Vin had done everything he could for his friend. Now all he could do, as he watched his skinny figure disappearing up the mountain was worry, not for himself, but for Tom:

I got in a group of other big guys who looked after each other in the mountains, then, sure enough, Poulidor caught us and went steadily past, just as I had predicted. It was so hot and my thoughts were with Tom as we broke the cover of the trees on the Ventoux, out on to the glaring expanse of white rock that is the top of the mountain.

Poulidor was strong that day: he soon got himself to the front of the race from where he launched a searing attack with Julio Jiménez. This was it – two of the best climbers in the race making their move on the Ventoux – and if he was going to do damage to the others, Tom just had to go with them. He was in no condition to do so, but somehow he would have to find the strength to follow. If he couldn't, then it really would all be over and he wouldn't win the Tour de France.

He countered and got up to them, but the effort he was making in the stifling atmosphere was huge. Harry Hall, one of the British mechanics who was travelling in the team car remembers going up the climb and looking for Tom, passing rider after rider so spread out had the race become. Then he saw him, in the distance, at the head of the race, with the Frenchman and the Spanish climber.

It was a great feeling for a moment, but, as they got closer, Tom was starting to struggle. Harry remembers: 'By the time we got up to him, he had fallen back to a group containing Janssen and Aimar, but he was still sixth or seventh on the road.'

It wasn't where he wanted to be; he just wouldn't accept what was happening, and Aimar said after the stage: 'Tom kept trying to break up the group.' He was pushing like he had done so many times before; you can feel him thinking, 'It must be hurting them; they'll crack soon.' It was what he always thought. This time, though, it wasn't going to work.

As they broke from under the tree cover into the full heat of the Provençal sun, Tom began to falter. He lost contact with the Aimar group and now his efforts were even more desperate ones to limit his losses. He had suffocated himself trying to break the others and was gasping for breath.

Harry started to realise, then, that Tom might be in trouble. Suddenly, he began to weave and veer across the road:

I was worried that he might go into the side or over the edge. Eventually, he ran into the side and fell against the bank. I got to him and said, 'It's finished for you, Tom,' and I undid his straps. He said, 'No, put me back on my bike. I must go on.' So I started to push him.

They were to be Tom's last words and they are his epitaph. He just wouldn't give in, he couldn't give in, he never did give in. He went about 200 metres further; then, just one kilometre from the summit, he fell in the road. He was unconscious now.

Harry was first to him again. The race medical team were quickly on the scene and worked on him there for 40 minutes. Then he was taken by helicopter to the hospital in Avignon, but was pronounced dead there at 5.40 p.m. that day. In truth, though, he died where he fell, where a granite monument provided by British cyclists stands. It has the best view in the whole of Provence and, now, more than 30 years later, he is never alone: a constant stream of visitors of all ages and nationalities stop there to pay their respects to 'Mr Tom'.

Appendix

Tom Simpson's Palmarès

Born: 30th November 1937, Haswell (County Durham)
Height: 1.81 m. Racing weight: 69 kg.
Professional debut: 1959 (second half of season)

Amateur
1954 (age 16)

First win in club 25-mile time trial, followed by other time-trial events

Title
BLRC North Midlands Division Junior Hill-Climb Champion

1955 (age 17)
Sixteen wins as Junior in road races, plus many other wins in time trials and track races, including winning most of his races on cinder and grass tracks

Titles
National Junior Hill-Climb Champion (BLRC)
North Midlands 4,000-metre Senior Pursuit Champion

1956 (age 18)
Various wins in all disciplines. He won his first road event of the season – the Sheffield Atlas

Criterium, and his next – the Circuit of Swannick
First sub-58-minute '25' recorded when winning the Scala Wheelers '25'

International career takes off after winning a top-class pursuit at Fallowfield, then taking second place in the National Pursuit Championship, only failing in the final because of a puncture. Other performances included the bronze medal in the Olympic Games 4,000-metre team pursuit. Tom was also a member of the team that twice beat the Italian and Russian teams in a two-day international match in the then USSR; their winning time of 4.53.6 was easily the fastest of the event series.

1957
Many wins in 25-mile time trials, including the Westwood '25', where he beat two of the fastest riders in the country, Norman Sheil and John Geddes (both medallists in the World Pursuit Championship), in a time of 58.24 on a difficult course

Another '25' victory was in the Sheffield Phoenix event when he beat top roadman Billy Holmes in a time of 58.40

Track (selected performances)
International match (v France',
Italy', Denmark) at Fallowfield:
4,000-metre Team Pursuit   1st
International Omnium   2nd

Coventry Easter meeting:
4,000-metre Individual Pursuit 2nd'

Manchester International Bank
Holiday Meeting:
Four-mile Scratch Race   2nd
Team Omnium   2nd

Ordrup Int. Team Pursuit   2nd
Odense Int. Omnium   3rd

Also many other minor track wins
on U.K. and European tracks

Title
BLRC Hill-Climb Champion

1958
Numerous road and track victories,
including the National 4,000metre
Pursuit Championship where, in
the final, he beat Mike Gambrill
(previous year's champion) in a
time of 5.08.9
In the Commonwealth Games
4,000-metre Pursuit final he was
beaten by 0.3 second by Norman
Sheil (who won the World Pursuit
Championship that year, having
previously won it in 1955)

Track
National Track Championships:
4,000-metre Pursuit   1st
Grand Prix Union [Bulgaria]:
Individual Scratch Race   1st
4,000-metre Pursuit   1st

Herne Hill Good Friday
International Omnium   1st
Manchester Easter International
Omnium   1st
Cardiff Grand Prix: *Daily Herald*
Gold Cup (10-mile scratch)   1st
Manchester Bank Holiday:
4,000-metre Pursuit   1st

Grand Prix Manchester
(10-kms, motor-paced)   2nd

Titles and Medals
National 4,000-metre Individual
Pursuit Champion
BLRC National Hill-Climb
Championship   2nd

1959
Amateur/Independent (selected)

Fourgères-Rennes time trial 1st
Grand Prix de Marboue   1st
Circuit de L' Armel   1st
Route de France   24th (overall)
   Final stage   1st
L'Essor Breton   3rd (overall)
   Final stage   1st

Plus many wins in other French
races

Professional
(Team: Rapha-Geminiani)

Road
WORLD PROFESSIONAL ROAD
RACE CHAMPIONSHIP   4th
Tour of West France   18th (overall)
   Stage 4   1st
   Stage 5B (itt)   1st

Stage 1	3rd
Stage 3	3rd
Grand Prix Henon	1st
Grand Prix de Nantes	4th
Grand Prix de Geneva	5th
Manche-Océan Time Trial	5th
Circuit of Vienne	6th
PARIS-TOURS	15th

Track (selected)
Berlin: miscellaneous wins on
indoor track
Herne Hill: motor-paced	1st
Cardiff Grand Prix:	
Daily Herald Gold Cup	
(10-mile scratch race)	1st

1960 (Team: Rapha-Gitane)

Road
Tour du Sud-Est	1st (overall)
Stage 2	2nd
Stage 4	3rd
Stage 5	3rd
Stage 3	5th
Mont Faron (mountain tt)	1st
Poly Bretonne	1st
Prix de Ploerdut	1st
Genoa-Rome	3rd (overall)
'King of Mountains'	
Team Prize	
Stage 1	3rd
Circuit de Boussac	2nd
Prix de St Hilaire	3rd
Circuit de Tregor	6th
FLÈCHE WALLONNE*	7th
LIÈGE-BASTOGNE-LIÈGE*	11th
(* Combined result - Ardennes	
Weekend)	4th
PARIS-ROUBAIX	9th
TROPHY BARACCHI	
(with Elliott)	7th

MILAN-SAN REMO	25th
TOUR DE FRANCE	29th (overall)
Stage 1A	13th
Stage 1B (itt)	9th
Stage 3	3rd
Stage 4	11th
Stage 10	14th
Stage 15	3rd
Final stage	15th

Track (selected)
Grand Prix Gérard Saint [Paris]	
Team Omnium	1st
(with Rivière and Altig)	
Brussels Team Omnium	2nd
(with Ruby, Graczyk and Captein)	
Ghent Team Omnium	2nd
(with Darrigade and Geldermans)	

1961 (Team: Rapha-Gitane-
St Raphaël-Geminiani)

TOUR OF FLANDERS	1st
Challenge of France	
(Team event for season)	1st
Daumesnil Team Omnium	1st
Dunkirk 4-Days	14th (overall)
Stage 1B (ttt)	1st
Grand Prix de Eibar	retired
Stage 1B	1st
Prix de St Hilaire	2nd
Menton-Rome	2nd (overall)
Stage 3	2nd
Stage 4B (itt)	2nd
Stage 1	5th
Prix Millau	3rd
Paris-Nice	5th (overall)
	3rd (points)
Stage 3 (ttt)	1st
Stage 6B	5th
Challenge Laurens	7th

WORLD PROFESSIONAL ROAD
RACE CHAMPIONSHIP   9th
Prix de Decize   9th
Prix de Nantes   10th
TOUR DE FRANCE abandoned

Track (selected)
Good Friday Herne:
Invitation Pursuit   1st
Brussels Team Omnium   2nd
            (with Robinson)
Brussels Team Omnium (October)
2nd
(with Elliott, Maliepaard and De
Cabooter)
Paris Team Omnium
2nd
(with Van Looy, Daems and De
Hann)
World Pursuit Championships -
qualified (6.19.6)
Roadman's Trophy (Brussels)
3rd

1962 (Team: Gitane-Leroux)

Road
Challenge de France   1st
Paris-Nice   2nd (overall)
            Stage 2A   6th
            Stage 3A (ttt)   1st
            Stage 6   6th
            Stage 7 A (ttt)   3rd
            Stage 9B   5th
Criterium of Narbonne   2nd
Roue d'Or (with Darrigade) 2nd
Tour of Luxembourg   retired
            Stage 1   3rd
            Stage 2   2nd
            Stage 3   8th
Prix de St Brieuc   3rd
Nocturne de Maure   3rd
Prix d'Evreux   3rd

Criterium des As   3rd
Prix de Pougasnou   4th
Ronde de Valognes   4th
TOUR OF FLANDERS   5th
            'King of the Mountains'
Prix d'Aix-les-Bains   5th
GHENT -WEVELGEM   6th
Manx Trophy   6th
Prix de Ploerdut   7th

Circuit de L' Amorique   7th
PARIS-BRUSSELS   19th
Dunkirk Four-Days   20th
PARIS-ROUBAIX   37th
TOUR DE FRANCE   6th (overall)
            Stage 1   9th
            Stage 2A   11th
            Stage 2B (ttt)   2nd
            Stage 3   17th
            Stage 8A   20th
            Stage 8B (itt)   17th
            Stage 12   18th
            Stage 18   9th
            Stage 21   15th

Track (selected)
Antwerp: Pursuit   2nd
Madrid Six-Day   3rd
(with John Tressider)

1963 (Team: Peugeot-BP)

Road
BORDEAUX-PARIS   1st
Tour du Var   2nd (overall)
            Stage 1   1st
            Stage 2   4th
Manx Trophy   1st
Prix Miniac-Morvan   1st
Prix Jeumont   1st
Prix de St Gaudens   1st
Grand Prix Parisien (ttt)   1st
Classics Team World Cup   1st

PARIS–BRUSSELS 2nd
GHENT–WEVELGEM 2nd
Criterium des As 2nd
Grand Prix de St Lenaart 2nd
Flèche de Côte Ostende 2nd
Prix Rousiés 2nd
'Edmond Gentil Trophy'
(Rider of the Season) 2nd
Dunkirk Four-Days
        Stage 4 2nd
Grand Prix Heist 2nd
PARIS–TOURS 2nd
TOUR OF FLANDERS 3rd
Prix Arras 3rd
Prix Quillan 4th
Prix de Moorslede 4th
Prix de Lavall 7th
Grand Prix Lugano (tt) 8th
PARIS–ROUBAIX 8th
FLÈCHE WALLONNE* 10th
LIÈGE-BASTOGNE-LIÈGE* 33rd
(* Combined result - Ardennes
Weekend - 'King of Mountains')
TOUR OF LOMBARDY 10th
Coupe Agostini 15th
MILAN–SAN REMO 19th
Paris-Luxembourg 17th (overall)
        Stage 1 4th
Super Prestige Pemod (unofficial
world rankings) 2nd
Challenge of France (French
promoters' rankings) 3rd

Track (selected)
Roue d'Or (with Wolfshohl) 1st
Paris Omnium (with De Roo,
Daems and Altig) 1st
Valenciennes Derny Series 1st
Valenciennes Omnium 2nd
Ostend Omnium 2nd
Antwerp Omnium 2nd
Antwerp 'Brassard Pursuit Trophy'
(8th Round) 2nd
Brussels Omnium 2nd

Ghent Derny Series 2nd
Heme Hill Good Friday Meeting:
Omnium 3rd

1964 (Team: Peugeot-BP)

Road
MILAN-SAN REMO 1st
Prix de Chef-Boutonne 1st
Grand Prix Corona 1st
Prix d'Issoire 1st
Prix de Nantes 1st
Zolder Kermesse 1st
Circuit du Provençal 20th (overall)
        Stage2B 6th
        Stage 4 2nd
        Final stage 1st
Kuume-Brussels-Kuume 2nd
Mont Faron (mountain tt) 2nd
Grand Prix Nederbrakel 2nd
TROPHY BARRACHI
(with Altig) 3rd
Prix de Renaix 3rd
Prix Pleaux 3rd
WORLD PROFESSIONAL ROAD
RACE CHAMPIONSHIP 4th
Paris-Nice retired
        Stage 2 3rd
        Stage 7 4th
        Stage 6B 5th
Prix de Caen 6th
Criterium des As 8th
Manx Trophy 8th
Grand Prix Lugano (itt) 8th
Prix de Bource Franc 8th
Prix de Riom 8th
Tour de la Haute-Loire 9th
PARIS-ROUBAIX 10th
Circuit de la Rance 10th
Circuit de Laval 10th
HET-VOLK 18th
TOUR OF LOMBARDY 21st

Criterium du
Dauphiné Libéré 21st (overall)
     Stage 4B 8th
     Stage 5 2nd
     Final Stage 2nd
Paris-Luxembourg 25th
PARIS–BRUSSELS 30th
TOUR DE FRANCE 14th (overall)
     Stage 1 18th
     Stage 2 17th
     Stage 3A 12th
     Stage 3B (ttt) 7th
     Stage 8 10th
     Stage 9 2nd
     Stage 10B (itt) 20th
     Stage 11 15th
     Stage 13 10th
     Stage 15 12th
     Stage 19 14th
     Stage 20 18th
     Stage 22A 8th

Track (selected)
Herne Hill Omnium 1st
Nice Omnium
(with Shay Elliott) 1st
Nice 5,000-metre Pursuit 1st
Herne Hill International
'Milk Race' meeting:
     5,000-metre Pursuit 2nd

1965 (Team: Peugeot-BP)

Road
WORLD PROFESSIONAL ROAD
RACE CHAMPIONSHIP 1st
TOUR OF LOMBARDY 1st
London-Holyhead 1st
Criterium des As 1st
Prix de Charlieu 1st

Prix de Vayrac 1st
Super Prestige Pernod 2nd
Prix de Riom 2nd
Prix de Cambrai 2nd
Prix de Gourin 2nd
FLÈCHE-WALLONNE 3rd
BORDEAUX-PARIS 3rd
G P Midi-Libre 3rd (overall)
     Stage 4 4th
Circuit de Provençal 3rd (overall)
     Final Stage 3rd
     Stage3A 8th
     Stage 3B 9th
Criterium de Castellazzo 3rd
Prix de Cavaillon 3rd
Prix de Mende 3rd
Prix d'Oostrozbeke 3rd
Coupe Agostoni 4th
GP Harlebeke (G.P. E3) 5th
Prix de Gouesnou 5th
Prix de Miniac Morvan 5th
Prix de Vailly 5th
Corona Grand Prix 6th
Circuit des Onze Villes 6th
Grand Prix Forli (itt) 6th
Prix de Merelbeke 6th
PARIS-ROUBAIX 7th
Grand Prix Dortmund 7th
Montjuich Hill Race 8th
LIÈGE-BASTOGNE-LIÈGE 10th
Criterium des As 11th
Paris-Brussels 32nd
TOUR DE FRANCE abandoned
     Stage 1B (ttt) 2nd
     Stage 4 6th
     Stage 6 14th
     Stage 8 10th
     Stage 9 10th
     Stage 10 14th
     Stage 11 14th
     Stage 14 9th
     Stage 15 16th

Track (selected)

Brussels Six-Day (with Post)	1st
Antwerp Individual Grand Prix	1st
Ghent Int. Team Omnium	2nd
Brussels Roadman Omnium	2nd
Ghent Six-Day (with Post)	2nd
Grand Prix Antwerp International Criterium	3rd
Grand Prix Antwerp (individual points)	1st
Dortmund Six-Day (with Baensch)	5th
Frankfurt Six-Day (with Boelke)	5th

Voted: BBC 'Sports Personality of the Year'
British Sportswriters 'Personality of the Year'
Daily Express 'Sportsman of the Year'

1966 (Team: Peugeot-BP)

Road

Prix d'Eu-Le Treport	1st
Prix de St Hilaire	1st
Prix de Brest	1st
Prix de Saussignac	1st
GP Martini [Felletin]	1st
Prix d'Ambert	1st
Prix Periers	1st
Prix Champs	1st
Prix Laval (team criterium)	1st
Prix de Vergt	2nd
Grand Prix Gippingen	2nd
Prix de St Alvère	3rd
Prix de Trédion	3rd
Prix d'Argenton	3rd
Prix Zolder (Demy-paced)	3rd
Prix de Bale	4th

Circuit de L' Aune	4th
Prix de Musidan	5th
Prix de St Hilaire-du-Harcouet	6th
Dunkirk 4-Days	20th (overall)
Stage 2B (ttt)	1st
Grand Prix d'Eeklo	10th
Prix de Westerloo	11th
TOUR DE FRANCE	abandoned,
Stage 1	17th
Stage 11	13th
Stage 12	2nd
Stage 13	2nd
Stage 14B (itt)	5th
Stage 15	13th
Stage 16	18th

Track (selected)

Vincennes International Omnium (with Nedelec)	1st
Roue d'Or (Derny-paced)	2nd
Brussels International Omnium (with Bracke)	3rd
Antwerp Int. Omnium	4th
Zurich 6-Days (with Baensch)	5th
Frankfurt 6-Days (with Eugen)	5th

1967 (Team: Peugeot-BP)

Road

Paris-Nice	1st (overall)
Stage 4	3rd
Stage 6	2nd
Final Stage (itt)	2nd
Tour of Sardinia:	
Stage 5	1st
Stage 2	2nd
Southport 'John Players Exhibition Criterium'	1st

TOUR OF SPAIN	33rd (overall)	Berlin Six-Days (with Post)	4th
Stage 5	1st	Ghent Six-Days (with Seeuws)	4th
Stage 16	1st		
Stage 7	2nd		
Manx Trophy	1st		
Prix Camors	2nd		
Grand Prix Salvarini	3rd	Compiled by Richard Allchin	
Prix St Claud	3rd		
Polymultipliée	4th		
Prix Mont St Amand	5th		
Prix Guéret	7th		
Ghent-Welvegem	21st		
MILAN-SAN REMO	70th		
TOUR DE FRANCE	died, stage 13		
Prologue Stage	13th		
Stage 4	7th		
Stage 8	5th		
Stage 9	4th		
Stage 10	16th		
Stage 12	7th		

Track (selected)

G.P. Karel Van Wijnendaele 1st
(Ghent)
Omnium Lorient   1st
(with Merckx, Altig and Alf
Howling)
Munster Six-Days   2nd
(with Bugdahl)
Antwerp 5,000-metre
Pursuit Series: 2nd
    beat Anquetil   6.08.2
    beat Post   6.06.6
    lost to Merckx   6.07.4
Grand Prix Europe Omnium   3rd
4,000-metre pursuit   1st
   (beat Post in 4.46.3)

Antwerp Six-Days   3rd
(with Severeyns/Proost)
Vincennes Omnium   3rd
Grand Prix Stan Ockers   3rd
(Derny Championships)